Social Change in America:
The Historical Handbook
2004

Social Change in America:
The Historical Handbook
2004

Edited by Patricia C. Becker

BERNAN PRESS

Lanham, MD

ISBN: 0-89059-897-5

Cover photos: www.comstock.com; www.punchstock.com

Composed and printed by Automated Graphic Systems, Inc., White Plains, MD, on acid-free paper that meets the American National Standards Institute Z39-48 standard.

2004 2003   4 3 2 1

BERNAN PRESS
4611-F Assembly Drive
Lanham, MD 20706
800-274-4447
email: info@bernan.com
www.bernanpress.com

Contents

Chapter 1: Population

Chapter 2: Households and Families

Marital Status

Chapter 3: Social Conditions

Chapter 4: Labor Force and Job Characteristics

Chapter 5: Housing

Chapter 6: Income, Wealth, and Poverty

Chapter 7: Education

Chapter 8: Crime and Criminal Justice

Chapter 9: Health

Figures and Tables

Chapter 1: Population

Chapter 2: Households and Families

Chapter 3: Social Conditions

Chapter 4: Labor Force and Job Characteristics

Chapter 5: Housing

Chapter 6: Income, Wealth, and Poverty

Chapter 7: Education

Chapter 8: Crime and Criminal Justice

Chapter 9: Health

Chapter 10: Leisure, Volunteerism, and Religiosity

Chapter 11: Voting

Chapter 12: Government

About The Editors

Patricia C. Becker is a demographer with over 40 years of experience using federal statistics. A veteran census data user, she has served on several Bureau of the Census advisory committees. She is an active member of the Council of Professional Associations on Federal Statistics (COPAFS), and participates in most of the group's meetings. She is president of APB Associates, a Michigan-based consulting firm, and executive director of the Southeast Michigan Census Council, and uses federal statistics in her everyday work. She has written many papers and offered presentations at professional meetings dealing with a wide variety of issues regarding the census and other federal statistical agencies. Ms. Becker is a founding member of the Association of Public Data Users.

Katherine A. DeBrandt is a senior data analyst with Bernan Press. She received her B.A. in political science from Colgate University. She is a co-editor of several Bernan Press titles, including *The Who, What, and Where of America: Understanding the Census Results; The Almanac of American Education;* and *State Profiles: The Population and Economy of Each U.S. State.*

Acknowledgments

Social Change in America is truly a cooperative effort and could not have been completed without the assistance of various individuals.

First, special thanks to Katherine A. DeBrandt of Bernan Press. Katherine assisted tremendously with data research as well as with designing the tables and charts.

Second, thanks to the editorial and production departments of Bernan Press, who under the direction of Tamera Wells-Lee did the copyediting, layout, and graphics preparation. Jacalyn Houston edited the manuscript; Kara Gottschlich prepared the layout and graphics; and Christopher Jorgenson provided Kara with production support. Jacalyn, Kara, and Christopher capably handled all editorial and production aspects of this edition.

Finally, our friends and colleagues in the federal statistical agencies willingly and with enthusiasm answered my questions about the data published on their Web sites and about the availability of unpublished data and analyses.

The publication of *Social Change in America* would not have been possible without the dedication and assistance of the above-listed individuals.

Patricia C. Becker

The Internet: The Latest Harbinger of Social Change

RECENT HISTORY OF SOCIAL CHANGE

Social change is incremental. Sometimes it happens very slowly, so that decades pass before people are truly aware of the difference. Sometimes it happens very quickly, seemingly turning the world of American society "upside down" before anyone is aware that it is happening.

For the past half-century or so, it is possible to characterize each decade by the major forces which shaped its politics and culture. For example:

- **The 1950s:** the decade of the baby boom (peaking in 1957, as discussed in Chapter 1), growth of suburbia, tract housing, fathers going to work, and mothers staying home with the children. Another very important change in the 1950s was the introduction of television, thus drastically changing the ways in which information is communicated into American homes.

Following creation of the National Aeronautics and Space Administration (NASA) in 1958, the first space flights took place in the early 1960s, leading to the Apollo mission and the moon landing in 1969. The technology developed in these programs lead to commercial applications in satellite transmissions, so that television and other communication options brought the entire world much closer to Americans.

- **The 1960s:** the decade of real attitudinal and behavioral changes in Americans' attitudes toward racial minorities. At the beginning of the decade, the South was still largely segregated as communities sought ways around implementation of the landmark 1954 *Brown v. Board of Education* decision mandating integrated schools. In the North, government and private employers were struggling to provide equal opportunity in the workplace. By 1970, the majority of Americans had accepted the concept of equal opportunity, even if their attitudes did not change along with their behavior. Schools across the nation were becoming integrated in the South as a result of the Brown decision, and in the North as courts increasingly looked for ways to integrate school systems with schools that were segregated because of limited housing choices.

- **The 1970s:** the decade in which women entered the workforce in droves. The baby boom was over. Women graduating from college, or even high school, expected to work until they married, after they married until they had children, and even after they had children when family economics necessitated it or when they wanted to use their education and training. By 1980, workplaces were fast becoming integrated by gender as well as by race, although "glass ceilings" at high corporate levels still created barriers to both women and minorities.

- **The 1980s:** the decade of the networked mainframe computer. While the social changes of the 1960s and 1970s were still being absorbed, commerce was being dramatically altered by the innovation of real time access to central computers and, therefore, central decision-making. For example, instead of two airfare categories, coach and first class, all of a sudden there were dozens, with availability in any specific category being managed centrally through information placed on the home computer. Travel agents and airlines reservations agents (reached only by telephone) never knew exactly what fares they would see on their screens, and could therefore offer their customers what they could see at any given time. Similar changes in retail outlets, with new cash registers networked to the central computers instead of being stand-alone machines, permitted one-day sales and the like.

The 1980s also brought bad news: Acquired Immune Deficiency Syndrome, or AIDS. According to the Centers for Disease Control (CDC), the virus has existed in the United States, Haiti and Africa since at least 1977–1978. In 1979, rare types of pneumonia, cancer, and other illnesses were being reported by doctors in Los Angeles and New York. The common thread was that these conditions were not usually found in persons with healthy immune systems. In 1982, the CDC officially named the condition AIDS (Acquired Immune Deficiency Syndrome). In 1984, the virus responsible for weakening the immune system was identified as HIV (Human Immunodeficiency Virus). AIDS brought about important changes in adult sexual behavior.

- **The 1990s**: the decade of the personal computer and the real beginning of the Internet. The networked machines were not personal computers (PCs); they were simply terminals connected by telephone lines to the central or home computer. They had no memory and little internal computing power of their own. When the system went down, so did they. PCs, on the other hand, were miniature, free-standing, fully-powered computers. They could be programmed and they had memory, or storage.

A very early PC, in about 1987, might have had 10 or 20 mg (megabytes) of hard drive memory—a mg is slightly more than 1 million bytes, and a byte is roughly equivalent to a single letter or number. Since this memory capacity was very limited, the early PCs had little power. In the commercial world, they were first acquired by the accountants, who used the early VisiCalc and Lotus spreadsheet software. Somewhat later, they began to be used by secretaries for word processing. Meanwhile, the mainframe computers continued to be accessed using dumb terminals—dumb because they had no capacity other than to connect to the central machine. The programmers and analysts who managed the mainframe capacity looked down on PCs.

Throughout the 1990s, PC speeds and hard drive (memory, storage) capacities were increasing exponentially. By the end of the decade, it was routine to have 20 gigabytes on board a PC, a gigabyte being the equivalent of 1,024 megabytes or almost 1.1 billion bytes.

- **The 2000s:** We're not sure yet what the main social change of the current decade will be. We do know that all the trends of the past several decades, beginning with the 1960s, continue in force, and that technological innovation continues as well. The Internet, with its capacity to store and make retrievable an almost infinite amount of information, and its worldwide connections, will surely be a major part of the change that is underway.

WHAT IS THE INTERNET?

The Internet is, at base, a system for allowing computers to connect, communicate, talk to each other. Thus, in order to have the Internet, first we had to have computers. Then we had to have a means of communication, through hardware devices called *modems* and a protocol, or language, called *TCP/IP*, which stands for "Transmission Control Protocol and Internet Protocol." The Internet is not a single computer network, such as one might find in a business or university. It is a "vast, globe-spanning network of networks," which communicate with one another based on these protocols. "No single person, group, or organization runs the Internet. Instead, it's the purest form of electronic democracy."[1]

The number of interconnected networks is uncounted, and grows continually. Even when you access the Internet using your own, non-networked PC, you become an extension of that network. One of the most important things to understand about the Internet is that there is no central management, central control, or central funder. There are, however, cooperative organizations which exist to assist in developing standards and to provide education. One of these is the Internet Society, whose Internet Activities Board (IAB) handles much of the backbone issues that end users never see but which are critical to making the system work. The World Wide Web Consortium (known as W3C), develops standards for the World Wide Web. Private companies, including InterNIC and others, are Internet Registrars who assume responsibility for registering and keeping track of

---

[1] Preston Gralla, *How the Internet Works* (Indianapolis: Que Publishers, 1999). This book is the source for much of the information presented in this section.

Internet domains—those Uniform Resource Locators (URLs) that identify each individual Web site—and Internet addresses composed of a series of numbers users rarely see.

Information travels across the Internet in complex ways. The user begins, at an individual PC or as part of a local area network (LAN), with a modem/router. The modem/router connects to a service—the Internet Service Provider or ISP—by dialing a telephone number, or through another type of device such as a cable modem or a Digital Subscriber Line (DSL) modem; a large organization may have an even faster connection such as a T1 or T3 telephone line. From there, the data are broken into "packets" that the system can handle and are sent to routers, which do most of the work to direct Internet traffic. The data packets go from one router to another and then up to a Regional Network which serves a geographic area. The Regional Networks are connected by very high speed lines. When the data packets reach the regional network of their destination address, the process reverses itself until the data arrive at the intended address.

Electronic mail, or email, is older than the Internet. Back in the early 1980s, large mainframe computers were connected in ways that were a predecessor to the Internet. Users on these mainframe systems, using terminals, had access to email systems.[2]   However, it wasn't until the mid-1990s that the system evolved to the point where *attachments* could be sent along with email. By that time, standard email software packages such as Internet Explorer and Eudora were available; before that, email software was "home-grown" and circulated in university and corporate settings. Attachments have made it possible to transmit information electronically which formerly could be sent only by postal mail or, perhaps, using a facsimile (fax) machine. Computer files and documents can be shared and jointly edited in a way that was never before possible.

Another critical innovation was the development of Portable Document Format, or pdf, software which is distributed freely by Adobe Systems. This made it possible to distribute any document through the Internet. Even if the document had not originally been created on a computer, it could be scanned (using scanning hardware) into a computer file, published as a pdf, and distributed.

Two of the most powerful features of the Internet are the search function and hyperlinks. The power of modern computers make it possible to conduct electronic searches, based on key words, in seconds. Finding one document, the user may discover hyperlinks which, when clicked with a mouse, takes one to an entirely different document which is related in a key way to the first. This innovation is less than 10 years old.

HOW HAS THE INTERNET CHANGED AMERICAN LIVES?

The impact of the Internet is immeasurable and expansive, with new applications being created every year.

Example 1: the Internet has revolutionized shopping. Prior to the 1980s, most shopping, outside of going to the store itself, was done using catalogs and orders sent through the mail. By 1980, however, the cost of wide ranging telephone lines had come down greatly, leading to the availability and affordability of toll-free 800 numbers (now 888, 877, and 866 as well). Thus, the consumer could call the company and place an order from a catalog, providing faster service and turn-around than was possible by mail. With the advent of the Internet, companies began to create World Wide Web sites, or virtual stores. Some of these are online versions of "bricks and mortar" stores or those which had marketed their wares via catalogs, while others are a creation of the Internet itself. Amazon.com is the most well-known example of the latter phenomenon. The growth of Internet shopping has had a strong impact on traditional stores, which have had to adapt to the new environment.

Example 2: the Internet has revolutionized travel purchases. As recently as 1980, people purchased airfare or rail tickets via telephone, in person, or through travel agents. As previously discussed, there were only two categories of airfares: first class and coach. Travel agents were paid commissions by the travel vendors, so that their services were generally free to the customer. Hotel and motel reservations were made in a

---

[2] The author first gained access to email in 1982, using an account at Wayne State University in Detroit. At that point, most of her correspondents also had university addresses. In those pre-Internet days, the universities were connected through a system called "Bitnet," which later became the ".edu" domain on the Internet. Governement agency staff did not have email accounts until several years later.

similar fashion. Before there were toll-free numbers, the long distance call required to make a reservation was another reason for use of the travel agent.

In the 1980s, networked computer systems such as Sabre (running off of mainframe computers) became the way that travel agents made reservations. They were forced to acquire the necessary hardware and to subscribe to the system. As the use of toll-free numbers became more prevalent, airlines began to reduce the commissions paid to the travel agencies, preferring to have travelers deal directly with their own reservations systems. As the Web grew in the 1990s, both airlines and hotel chains developed their own Web sites through which travelers could make reservations online. Their commission payments to travel agents were reduced to zero, forcing many agents out of business or to charging customers for their services. By the late 1990s, Web sites such as Travelocity.com had emerged, providing consumers with the opportunity to search across vendors for the best prices on airfares and hotels.

Example 3: access to federal statistics. Prior to 1970, there was only one way to access federal statistics: in printed publications. During the 1970s, beginning with the 1970 census, some data files began to be released on magnetic tape, accessible through those ubiquitous mainframe computers. Often, the agencies charged large user fees to create special tabulations, leading to the development of user consortia to share the data. The 1980 census was delivered in all of the traditional print formats, on magnetic tape, and in microfiche—a microfilm of report pages which could be read and printed from a special microfiche reader. Other agencies followed suit.

By 1990, the need for data which could be accessed by a PC was evident, leading to the first publication of data in CD-ROM format. Unfortunately, adequate software to access the data on the CDs did not accompany the files, once again leaving users to form consortia to develop the access mechanisms. At this point, the private sector had also seen the advantage of delivering data on CDs, and several vendors created special packages which made access easier.

In the 1990s, the advent of the Web created radical changes in the delivery of public information. Every federal statistical agency developed a Web site. The government also created a Web site called Fedstats, self-defined as "the new window on the full range of official statistical information available to the public from the Federal Government. Use the Internet's powerful linking and searching capabilities to track economic and population trends, education, health care costs, aviation safety, foreign trade, energy use, farm production, and more. Access official statistics collected and published by more than 100 Federal agencies without having to know in advance which agency produces them."[3]

The Internet, the Web, and pdf have combined to shift the burden of created printed documents from the federal agencies to the users. Documentation, or metadata, is posted on Web sites in pdf format. The data are often accessible only through the same mechanism. The path of least resistance for federal agencies has been to create an "original" of a printed document using the same software and techniques as used in earlier decades, but then to post the resulting document on the Web instead of creating and distributing the book itself. Thus the user has to print the documentation or the data report instead of obtaining a bound printed copy from the Government Printing Office.

Example 4: the Internet as an encyclopedia. Before the Internet, information was distributed in printed form. Users either purchased the printed document or used a library. As every student knows, research for school assignments is now conducted via the Internet in preference to using books. Printed encyclopedias have been converted to electronic documents. Hyperlinks connect different documents together in clever, usable ways.

---

[3] See <www.fedstats.gov>.

CONCLUSION

This book and its predecessors[4] could not have been created without the modern Internet. Almost every piece of numeric information has been retrieved from a Web site. References to these sites are provided in footnotes and at the end of chapters so that readers can access updated information in future years. The quality and accessibility of the Web sites is continually improving, as it did for many of the agencies between 2002 and 2003. Web designers, with feedback from users, are improving their understanding of how information is accessed, and how to make that access easier and more user-friendly. Mechanisms for making the Internet available to the visually impaired are under development.

It's a great new world.

---

[4] Also published by Bernan: *A Statistical Portrait of the United States: Social Conditions and Trends*, First Edition (1998) and Second Edition (2002).

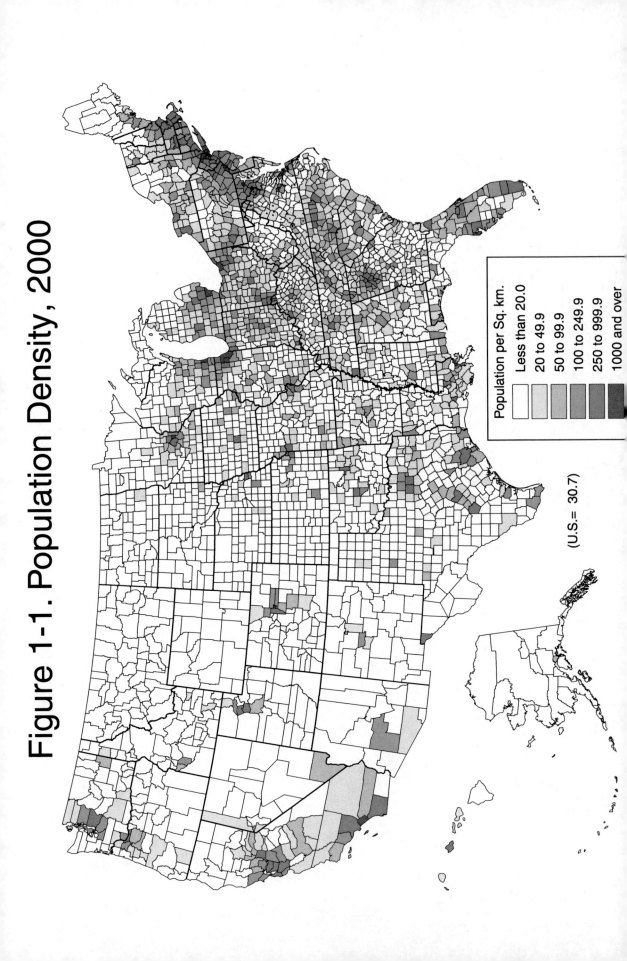

Figure 1-1. Population Density, 2000

Population per Sq. km.

Less than 20.0
20 to 49.9
50 to 99.9
100 to 249.9
250 to 999.9
1000 and over

(U.S.= 30.7)

Chapter 1
Population

This section presents basic population information in current and historical perspective, both for the United States alone and for the United States in the context of the rest of the world. The population indicators include not only the total population, but also the basic determinants of population growth (births, deaths, and migration), as well as distribution of the population by age, by race, and by a variety of geographic categories of interest.

WHAT IS THE TOTAL POPULATION OF THE UNITED STATES?

The 2000 census official count of the U.S. population was 281,421,906. By June 2003, the population had increased to 291,327,132. At this rate, the 2010 population will be about 315 million.

Internationally, the United States houses about 4.6 percent of the world's population, estimated at 6.3 billion in mid-2003. This makes the United States the world's third largest country in population, trailing China (1.29 billion) and India (1.05 billion). Most of the world's population (about 80 percent) lives in what are characterized as "developing" or "less developed" countries, according to the United Nations' scheme of development status. The "more developed" countries include the United States, most of Europe, and such countries as Japan, Australia and Canada; together they hold about 20 percent of the world's population. Because the U.S. annual growth rate is below the world's growth rate (1.4 percent per year), the share of the world's population that lives in the United States is projected to go down to about 4.2 percent by the year 2025, when the U.S. population will approach 350 million. Similarly, the share of the world's population living in developed countries is projected to decline to about 15.3 percent in 2025, provided that the characterization of the development status of countries will not change in the next 25 years. In reality, some countries that are now characterized as "developing" will become "developed" by that time.

The U.S. growth rate in the 1990s—about 1 percent per year—was only slightly higher than the annual growth rate in the 1980s. This annual growth rate statistic approached 1.7 percent during the 1950s baby boom era, the highest rate for the United States since early in the twentieth century. The baby boom era birthrate in the United States was comparable to that of the world's developing countries today (about 1.7 percent per year in 1996).

Growth rates in all regions of the world, for both developed and less-developed countries, appear to have peaked. Average annual growth rates peaked in the 1950s for developed countries and in the 1960s for less-developed countries, and have been declining for both groups ever since.

Table 1-1. United States and World Population, 2000–2025

(Numbers in thousands, percent.)

Year	World population	United States		Developed countries, excluding the United States		Less developed countries	
		Total population	Percent of world population	Total population	Percent of world population	Total population	Percent of world population
2000	6 079 007	281 422	4.6	899 779	14.8	4 901 292	80.6
2010	6 812 233	309 163	4.5	897 669	13.2	5 639 070	82.8
2025	7 835 948	349 166	4.5	864 130	11.0	6 707 572	85.6

Source: U.S. Census Bureau, Report WP/98, World Population Profile: 1998, U.S. Government Printing Office, Washington, DC, 1999. <http://www.census.gov/ipc/www/world.html>.

Table 1-2. Average Annual Rates of Growth for the United States and for the World, 1950–2000

(Rate.)

Period	World	Less developed countries	More developed countries	United States
1950–1960	1.7	2.0	1.0	1.7
1960–1970	2.0	2.0	1.0	1.3
1970–1980	1.8	2.0	0.0	1.1
1980–1990	1.7	2.0	0.0	0.9
1990–2000	1.4	1.0	0.0	1.0

Source: U.S. Census Bureau, Report WP/98, World Population Profile: 1998, U.S. Government Printing Office, Washington, DC, 1999.

POPULATION BY STATE

The Bureau of the Census divides the United States geographically into four regions. The South and West regions combined will account for 80 percent of U.S. growth between 1996 and 2025. The South will remain the most populous region in the United

Table 1-3. Population Estimates and Projections of Largest and Smallest States, 2000 and 2025

(Numbers in thousands.)

Largest 10 states

State and rank	2000	State and rank	2025
1. California	33 871	1. California	49 285
2. Texas	20 851	2. Texas	27 183
3. New York	18 976	3. Florida	20 710
4. Florida	15 982	4. New York	19 830
5. Pennsylvania	12 281	5. Illinois	13 440
6. Illinois	12 419	6. Pennsylvania	12 683
7. Ohio	11 353	7. Ohio	11 744
8. Michigan	9 938	8. Michigan	10 078
9. New Jersey	8 414	9. Georgia	9 869
10. Georgia	8 186	10. New Jersey	9 558

Smallest 10 states

State and rank	2000	State and rank	2025
1. Wyoming	494	1. Vermont	678
2. Vermont	609	2. Wyoming	694
3. Alaska	627	3. North Dakota	729
4. North Dakota	642	4. Delaware	861
5. Delaware	666	5. South Dakota	866
6. South Dakota	696	6. Alaska	885
7. Montana	799	7. Montana	1 121
8. Rhode Island	1 048	8. Rhode Island	1 141
9. Hawaii	1 211	9. Maine	1 423
10. New Hampshire	1 236	10. New Hampshire	1 439

Source: U.S. Census Bureau, Population Division, Population Projections Branch. *Population Projections: States, 1995–2025* (Report P25-1131, May 1997). <http://www.census.gov/population/projections/state/stpjpop.txt>.

States, while Western states will replace the Midwest as the second most populous region in the United States by the year 2010. California, the largest state, accounted for about 12 percent of the nation's population in 2000. Texas became the nation's second most populous state during the 1990s, while New York dropped to third. (As recently as the mid-1960s, New York had the largest state population.) According to current projections, Florida will replace New York as the third largest state in the next 15 years. At the other end of the size spectrum, Vermont, Delaware, North and South Dakota, Wyoming, Alaska, and the District of Columbia are projected to remain with total populations of less than 1 million in 2025.

PEOPLE LIVING IN CITIES AND METROPOLITAN AREAS

About 83 percent of the U.S. population now lives within metropolitan areas. The general concept of a metropolitan area is that of an urban core of at least 50,000 population, together with adjacent communities commuting to jobs within the core. Metropolitan areas comprise one or more entire counties, except in New England, where cities and towns are the basic geographic units.

The Office of Management and Budget (OMB) defines metropolitan areas for purposes of collecting, tabulating, and publishing federal data.[1] In 1970 two-thirds of the U.S. population was classified as metropolitan. Part of this proportionate increase in metropolitan population, from 67 percent to 83 percent, is attributable to changes in the definition of metropolitan area. As the suburbs expand, more counties become included in the definitions of the metropolitan areas. The outward growth of suburbs, often called "urban sprawl," is caused by several factors, including population growth in the metropolitan area overall, the fact that central cities and inner suburbs are losing both population and housing, and the

fact that the average home and lot size of new housing is much larger than housing built before and soon after World War II. There are now 362 Metropolitan Statistical Areas, known as MSAs.

After the 2000 census, a new type of area was defined: the Micropolitan Area. These areas are centered by an urban core of between 10,000 and 50,000 population, are composed of whole counties except in New England, and may include adjacent counties which are closely linked to the central county. About 10 percent of the 2000 population lived in the 560 newly defined micropolitan areas.

The metropolitan and micropolitan areas, together, are labeled "core based statistical areas" and include 93 percent of the population. This leaves only 7 percent of the nation's population living in counties which are included in such an area; these counties are labeled "outside core based statistical areas."

WHAT ABOUT THE FARM, RURAL, AND NONMETROPOLITAN POPULATION

At the turn of the twentieth century, nearly two of every five Americans (40 percent) lived on a farm. Today, persons living on farms represent fewer than 2 percent of the U.S. population. Part of this shift reflects changes in the agriculture industry itself. Fewer than half of the persons living on farms are employed in farm occupations today, and only about a third of people doing farm work live on farms. Most of this shift in residence, though, has happened because Americans have moved from rural to urban settings.

The concept of "urban" is based on density, usually defined as 1,000 persons per square mile. The official definitions of "urban"

---

[1] For more information about metropolitan areas, access <http://www.census.gov/ population/www/estimates/aboutmetro.html>. For a complete list of areas defined in June 2003, access <www.whitehouse.gov/omb/bulletins/b0304.html>.

Table 1-4. States Ranked by Population, 2000

(Number, percent.)

State and rank	Census population		Change, 1990–2000	
	April 1, 2000	April 1, 1990	Numeric	Percent
United States	281 421 906	248 709 873	32 712 033	13.2
1. California	33 871 648	29 760 021	4 111 627	13.8
2. Texas	20 851 820	16 986 510	3 865 310	22.8
3. New York	18 976 457	17 990 455	986 002	5.5
4. Florida	15 982 378	12 937 926	3 044 452	23.5
5. Illinois	12 419 293	11 430 602	988 691	8.6
6. Pennsylvania	12 281 054	11 881 643	399 411	3.4
7. Ohio	11 353 140	10 847 115	506 025	4.7
8. Michigan	9 938 444	9 295 297	643 147	6.9
9. New Jersey	8 414 350	7 730 188	684 162	8.9
10. Georgia	8 186 453	6 478 216	1 708 237	26.4
11. North Carolina	8 049 313	6 628 637	1 420 676	21.4
12. Virginia	7 078 515	6 187 358	891 157	14.4
13. Massachusetts	6 349 097	6 016 425	332 672	5.5
14. Indiana	6 080 485	5 544 159	536 326	9.7
15. Washington	5 894 121	4 866 692	1 027 429	21.1
16. Tennessee	5 689 283	4 877 185	812 098	16.7
17. Missouri	5 595 211	5 117 073	478 138	9.3
18. Wisconsin	5 363 675	4 891 769	471 906	9.6
19. Maryland	5 296 486	4 781 468	515 018	10.8
20. Arizona	5 130 632	3 665 228	1 465 404	40.0
21. Minnesota	4 919 479	4 375 099	544 380	12.4
22. Louisiana	4 468 976	4 219 973	249 003	5.9
23. Alabama	4 447 100	4 040 587	406 513	10.1
24. Colorado	4 301 261	3 294 394	1 006 867	30.6
25. Kentucky	4 041 769	3 685 296	356 473	9.7
26. South Carolina	4 012 012	3 486 703	525 309	15.1
27. Oklahoma	3 450 654	3 145 585	305 069	9.7
28. Oregon	3 421 399	2 842 321	579 078	20.4
29. Connecticut	3 405 565	3 287 116	118 449	3.6
30. Iowa	2 926 324	2 776 755	149 569	5.4
31. Mississippi	2 844 658	2 573 216	271 442	10.5
32. Kansas	2 688 418	2 477 574	210 844	8.5
33. Arkansas	2 673 400	2 350 725	322 675	13.7
34. Utah	2 233 169	1 722 850	510 319	29.6
35. Nevada	1 998 257	1 201 833	796 424	66.3
36. New Mexico	1 819 046	1 515 069	303 977	20.1
37. West Virginia	1 808 344	1 793 477	14 867	0.8
38. Nebraska	1 711 263	1 578 385	132 878	8.4
39. Idaho	1 293 953	1 006 749	287 204	28.5
40. Maine	1 274 923	1 227 928	46 995	3.8
41. New Hampshire	1 235 786	1 109 252	126 534	11.4
42. Hawaii	1 211 537	1 108 229	103 308	9.3
43. Rhode Island	1 048 319	1 003 464	44 855	4.5
44. Montana	902 195	799 065	103 130	12.9
45. Delaware	783 600	666 168	117 432	17.6
46. South Dakota	754 844	696 004	58 840	8.5
47. North Dakota	642 200	638 800	3 400	0.5
48. Alaska	626 932	550 043	76 889	14.0
49. Vermont	608 827	562 758	46 069	8.2
District of Columbia	572 059	606 900	-34 841	-5.7
50. Wyoming	493 782	453 588	40 194	8.9

Source: U.S. Census Bureau, Census 2000 Redistricting Data (P.L. 94-171) Summary File and 1990 Census.

and "rural" were changed at the time of the 2000 census. Sophisticated geographic software now available can calculate density at the city block level. These blocks were aggregated to "densely settled territory" and defined as "Urbanized Areas" if they total at least 50,000 population, and as "Urban Clusters" if they total between 10,000 and 50,000 population. The population residing in "Urbanized Areas" or Urban Clusters is identified as urban, while the remaining population is identified as rural.

In 2000, using these new definitions, 68 percent of Americans lived in urbanized areas, 11 percent in urban clusters, and 21 percent in rural areas. Of the population living in urbanized areas, 22 percent lived in the areas that have 5 million or more people, including New York, Chicago, Los Angeles, and Philadelphia.

The shift away from agriculture and the tendency toward urbanization of the population is occurring worldwide, but there are still vast differences by country: in China, for example, about 70 percent of the population now live in rural areas, the vast majority of whom are involved with agriculture.[2]

U.S. REGIONAL GROWTH AND MIGRATION

Between 2000 and 2001 (the latest data available), 17 percent of the total U.S. population moved from one address to another. Over half moved a short distance, within the same county. Another quarter moved from one county to another in the same state; of course, in many cases this involves a move within the same metropolitan area. The remaining one-quarter moved from a different state or from another country.[3] Renters are more likely to move than homeowners.

One measure of the propensity to move over a lifetime is the proportion of persons in a state who were born in that state. Americans have a cosmopolitan view of the United States, but there are several states in which over three-fourths of their populations were born in the state in which they live. Pennsylvania heads the list, with 78 percent of its 2000 population having been born in that state. Most states with low proportions of their populations born there were concentrated in the West, but one Southern state, Florida (with only 30.5 percent of its population born in that state), ranked lowest for two reasons: its large retirement-age population from other states and its large numbers of immigrants (principally from Cuba).

AGE AND DEPENDENCY

As is the case worldwide, the population of the United States is slowly aging. At the turn of the century, 4 percent of the U.S. population was over age 65. This percentage increased to 12.4 percent in 2000, and will likely reach 20 percent by the year 2030. The median age (that is, the age that divides the population in half, one half being younger than that age, the other half being older) in the United States has increased from about 22.9 years at the turn of the century to 35.3 years in 2000, and is expected to be about 38.5 years by 2030.

The *Dependency Ratio* is the number of children and elderly persons per 100 persons 18 to 64 years of age, and was at its highest point during the early 1960s, because of the baby boom.[4] There

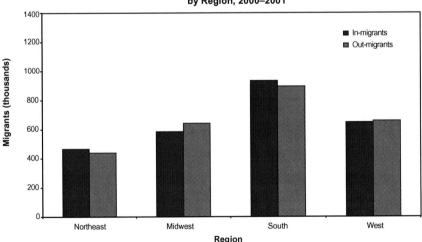

Figure 1-2. In-migrants and Out-migrants within the United States, by Region, 2000–2001

Source: U.S. Census Bureau, Current Population Survey.

---

2 See Chapter 3 for further discussion of rural America.

3 See U.S. Census Bureau, Geographical Mobility: March 1999 to March 2000, Report P20-538, issued May 2001, and the detailed tables for 2001-2002. The report is available both in hard copy and on the Internet at <www.census.gov>; the tables are only on the Internet.

4 The concept labeled the "dependency ratio" is based on the idea that persons in the "nondependent" age groups (18 to 64) provide some or all of the economic support of the "dependent" age groups. This notion is not absolute, for there are many working people in the "dependent" group, and many non-working persons in the "nondependent" group. Many teenagers work, and many persons are retiring at younger or older ages than the traditional 65.

Figure 1-3. U.S. Dependency Ratio, 1900–2030

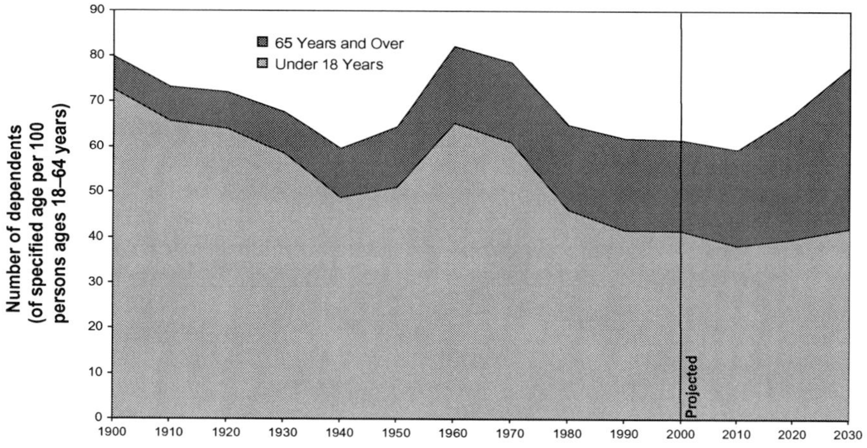

Source: U.S. Census Bureau.

Table 1-5. Ratio of Dependents to Persons Age 18 to 64 Years in the United States, 1900–2030

Year	Total dependents	Under 18 years	65 years and over
1900	79.9	72.6	7.3
1910	73.2	65.7	7.5
1920	72.0	64.0	8.0
1930	67.7	58.6	9.1
1940	59.7	48.8	10.9
1950	64.5	51.1	13.4
1960	82.2	65.3	16.9
1970	78.7	61.1	17.6
1980	64.9	46.2	18.7
1990	62.0	41.7	20.3
2000	61.6	41.5	20.1
2010	59.5	38.3	21.1
2020	67.5	39.8	27.7
2030	77.7	42.1	35.6

Source: U.S. Census Bureau, Middle Series Projections.

were 82 dependents per 100 persons aged 18 to 64 years at that time. Since the early 1960s, the dependency ratio has been declining (62 per 100 in 2000), and is forecast to continue declining until the year 2010. At that point, it will begin to rise because of the increasing aging of the population as well as the (projected) increasing number of births. In 2030 the dependency ratio is projected to be where it was in 1970, but the mix of dependents will be considerably different. In 1970, three-fourths of dependents were children, and the remainder were elderly, but by the year 2030, 53 percent of dependents will be children, with the remaining 47 percent being elderly.

HOW DO THE STATES DIFFER IN THE AGES OF THEIR POPULATIONS?

There is considerable variation by state in age distribution. Nationally, 25.7 percent of the population is under 18 years, and 12.4 percent is age 65 years and over. The national median age, the point at which half the population is older and half is younger, is 35.3 years. Florida has the highest median age (38.7), and the highest proportion of population 65 years and over (18.3). In contrast, the median age in Utah is only 27.1 years; this state leads the nation in percent under 18 years and is second lowest in the percent 65 years and

over. The median age figure is a blend of the two extremes. Utah's median age is low because it has so many children, as Florida's is high because it has so many elderly persons. Alaska's pattern is similar to Utah's, but not so extreme.

BIRTHS AND FERTILITY

The actual number of children born in the United States peaked at about 4.3 million in 1960, dropped to 3.1 million in 1975, rose again to 4.2 million in 1990, and is currently around 4 million per year. This variation describes the cycle known as the "Baby Boom-Bust-Boomlet." The baby boom is described by demographers as the years between 1946 and 1964, the year in which the fertility rate dropped below 100 per 1,000 women of childbearing age (ages 15 to 44). The boom was followed by a Baby Bust in the 1970s, when both the total number of births and the various rates which describe these phenomena dropped sharply. During this time, the number of women of childbearing age was lower (due to an earlier baby bust during the Depression of the 1930s and the World War II). In addition, women were having fewer children at a later point in life

Table 1-6. States with the Largest and Smallest Proportion of their Populations Under 18 Years and 65 Years and Over, 2000

States with largest proportion

State and rank	Percent under 18 years	State and rank	Percent 65 years and over
1. Utah	32.2	1. Florida	17.6
2. Alaska	30.4	2. Pennsylvania	15.6
3. Idaho	28.5	3. West Virginia	15.3
4. Texas	28.2	4. Iowa	14.9
5. New Mexico	28.0	5. North Dakota	14.7

States with smallest proportion

State and rank	Percent under 18 years	State and rank	Percent 65 years and over
1. District of Columbia	20.1	1. Alaska	5.7
2. West Virginia	22.2	2. Utah	8.5
3. Florida	22.8	3. Georgia	9.6
4. Maine	23.6	4. Colorado	9.7
4. Massachusetts	23.6	5. Texas	10.0
4. Rhode Island	23.6		

Median age

State and rank	Highest Median Age	State and rank	Lowest Median Age
1. West Virginia	38.9	1. Utah	27.1
2. Florida	38.7	2. Texas	32.3
3. Maine	38.6	3. Alaska	32.4
4. Pennsylvania	38.0	4. Idaho	33.2
5. Vermont	37.7	5. California	33.3

Source: U.S. Census Bureau, Census 2000 Brief. *Age: 2000*, October 2001.

than in the past. Large numbers of women entered the labor force in the 1970s, and there were also significant changes in the levels of contraceptive practice.

By the 1980s, the early baby boomers had reached childbearing age. At this point, the number of births increased sharply, although the fertility rate increased only slightly. This boomlet was the product of having a large pool of available mothers who were, on the average, having fewer children than did their mothers. In the 1990s, as the boomlet women aged out of their childbearing years, the number of births and the birth/fertility rates began to drop. At the end of this period and continuing into the current decade, rates rose slightly. The likely cause of this is increased immigration, which consists primarily of people of childbearing age. However, the crude birthrate will remain low because the total population continues to increase.

Looking at birth figures another way, the total fertility rate (TFR) was 2.034 in 2001, down from 2.056 in 2000. Part of the reason for the drop was an increase in the denominator (the number of women of child-bearing age), which went up because the 2000 census count was 7 million higher than anticipated. The TFR is the total number of children women will bear, on average, in their lifetimes. The important point to note here is that the TFR is at its lowest point in U.S. history, and is well below the replacement rate of 2.1. This means that, without immigration or a change in childbearing patterns, the U.S. population would decrease over time. The figure of 2.034 is higher, however, than that of other industrialized countries such as those in western Europe.

NONMARITAL BIRTHS, TEEN BIRTHS

Teen births, as a percentage of all births, have dropped consistently since reaching a high of about 19 percent in 1975. However, the proportion of children born to teenaged mothers has increased steadily over this period of time. This has prompted society's concern not only for these young mothers, but also for their offspring. The United States is grappling with questions such as who will provide financial support to unwed, teenage mothers, and who will provide health insurance coverage for their children? The

Figure 1-4. Number of Births and Total Fertility Rate in the United States, 1940–2000

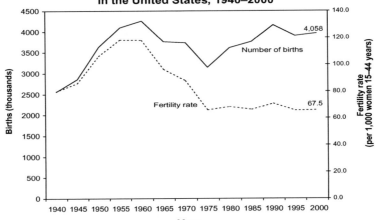

Source: National Center for Health Statistics. National Vital Statistics Reports.

birthrate for teenagers was about 51 births per 1,000 teenage women in 1998, down from about 68 in 1970 and 89 per 1,000 teenage women in 1960. At the same time, the proportion of these mothers who receive timely prenatal care increased steadily during the 1990s, to a figure of 82.8 percent in 1998.

Overall, across all age groups, the proportion of births in which the mother is unmarried was under 5 percent until 1958. Since that time, the rate has increased steadily. It was 32.8 percent, or almost one-third of all births, in 1998 (the latest year for which data have been reported). Several societal changes explain this phenomenon, including the increasing age of marriage and the increasing acceptance of single mothers giving birth to and raising their children.

MORTALITY AND LIFE EXPECTANCY: THE CHANCES OF DYING

The crude death rate in the United States has not changed much in the past 20 years, hovering between 8 and 9 deaths per 1,000 population on an annual basis

since 1975. However, when changes in age distribution are controlled by using an age-adjusted death rate, the 1995 death rate was at a record low level.

Life expectancy[5] is now 76.5 years in the United States. For women, life expectancy is over 79 years, for men about 74 years. For both sexes combined, life expectancy has increased by about 10 years since the end of World War II.

Another way to look at this question is to project, for persons of a given age now, the number of years left to live. This takes into account the fact that, at every age,

some people of that birth year have already died, and focuses only on those who are still living. So, for example, a person who was born in 1948 had an original life expectancy of 67 years. This same person, alive in 1998, had an expectation of 29 more years of life, bringing the current life expectancy to 79. Insurance companies rely on this measure of life expectancy in setting rates.

RACIAL AND ETHNIC COMPOSITION

By the time of the birth of the United States as a nation, the

Table 1-7. Selected Fertility Indicators for the United States, Selected Years, 1940–2000

(Number, rate.)

Year	Number of births (thousands)	Crude birth rate (per 1,000 population)	Fertility rate (per 1,000 women 15–44 years)	Total fertility rate (implied lifetime births per 1,000 women)
1940	2 559	19.4	79.9	2 301
1945	2 858	20.4	85.9	2 491
1950	3 632	24.1	106.2	3 091
1955	4 097	25.0	118.3	3 580
1960	4 258	23.7	118.0	3 449
1965	3 760	19.4	96.3	2 622
1970	3 731	18.4	87.9	2 480
1975	3 144	14.6	66.0	1 774
1980	3 612	15.9	68.4	1 840
1985	3 761	15.8	66.3	1 844
1990	4 158	16.7	70.9	2 081
1995	3 900	14.8	65.6	2 046
2000	4 059	14.7	67.5	2 130

Source: Martin J.A., Hamilton B.E., Ventura S.J., Menacker F., Park M.M. *Births: Final Data for 2000.* National Vital Statistics Reports; Vol. 50 No. 5. Hyattsville, Maryland: National Center for Health Statistics, 2002.

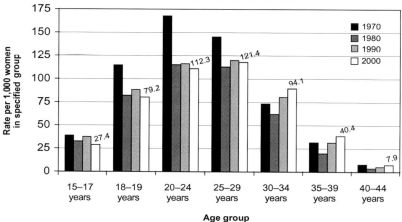

Figure 1-5. Birth Rates by Age of Mother, Selected Years, 1970–2000

Source: National Center for Health Statistics. National Vital Statistics Reports.

---

[5] Life expectancy is the average number of years that a group of infants born in a given year would live, if they were to experience the age-specific death rates prevailing during the year of their birth.

Table 1-8. Teen Birth Rates, 1970–2000

(Live births per 1,000 women.)

Year	15–44 years	15–19 years		
		Total	15–17 years	18–19 years
1970	18.4	68.3	38.8	114.7
1971	17.2	64.5	38.2	105.3
1972	15.6	61.7	39.0	96.9
1973	14.8	59.3	38.5	91.2
1974	14.8	57.5	37.3	88.7
1975	14.6	55.6	36.1	85.0
1976	14.6	52.8	34.1	80.5
1977	15.1	52.8	33.9	80.9
1978	15.0	51.5	32.2	79.8
1979	15.6	52.3	32.3	81.3
1980	15.9	53.0	32.5	82.1
1981	15.8	52.2	32.0	80.0
1982	15.9	52.4	32.3	79.4
1983	15.6	51.4	31.8	77.4
1984	15.6	50.6	31.0	77.4
1985	15.8	51.0	31.0	79.6
1986	15.6	50.2	30.5	79.6
1987	15.7	50.6	31.7	78.5
1988	16.0	53.0	33.6	79.9
1989	16.4	57.3	36.4	84.2
1990	16.7	59.9	37.5	88.6
1991	16.3	62.1	38.7	94.4
1992	15.9	60.7	37.8	94.5
1993	15.5	59.6	37.8	92.1
1994	15.2	58.9	37.6	91.5
1995	14.8	56.8	36.0	89.1
1996	14.7	54.4	33.8	86.0
1997	14.5	52.3	32.1	83.6
1998	14.6	51.1	30.4	82.0
1999	14.5	49.6	28.7	80.3
2000	14.7	48.5	27.4	79.2

Source: J.A. Martin, B.E. Hamilton, S.J. Ventura, F. Menacker, and M.M. Park *Births: Final Data for 2000*. National Vital Statistics Reports; Vol. 50 No. 5. Hyattsville, Maryland: National Center for Health Statistics, 2002.

predominant race among its approximately 4 million residents had already been transformed from Native American Indian to White. European settlers and their descendants composed about 80 percent of the U.S. population enumerated in the first U.S. Census in 1790, with Black slaves from Africa making up the bulk of the remainder. Indians were not included in the census figures until the 1890 census, because the Constitution of the United States specifically excluded "Indians not taxed" from the apportionment of representatives in Congress and, thus, Congress made no earlier attempt to enumerate Indians on reservations or in Indian Territory. In 1890, there were only about 248,000 American Indians enumerated, less than 1 percent of the population in the continental United States. They composed under 1 percent of the country's inhabitants in the 2000 census as well.

Although Blacks have remained the largest racial minority group in the United States, the proportion of the U.S. population that was of African American origin actually declined between 1790 and the turn of the twentieth century. Even in 1950, Blacks represented less than 10 percent of the U.S. population, before their proportion of the U.S. population began to increase once again. The 1990 census reported the Black population at just under 30 million, representing about 12.1 percent of the total U.S. population.

The official federal government definition of race and ethnicity is embodied in Statistical Directive 15, issued by the Office of the Chief Statistician in the Office of Management and Budget (OMB). Originally promulgated in 1977, Directive 15 called for self-identification of persons into one of five racial groups: White; Black; American Indian; Asian and Pacific Islander; and "Other." A separate question elicited identification as Hispanic or Latino, and persons identifying as such could be of any race.

During the 1990s, a substantial research project and public

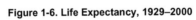

Figure 1-6. Life Expectancy, 1929–2000

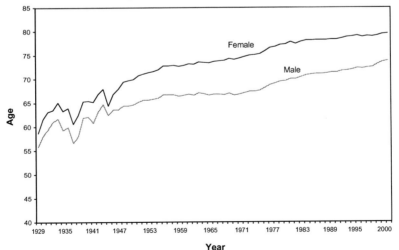

Source: National Center for Health Statistics. National Vital Statistics Reports.

hearing process was conducted to determine how, if at all, Directive 15 should be modified. Some stakeholders wanted a "mixed race" category. Hawaiians wanted to be separate from Asians. Arabs wanted a category of their own. In the end, Directive 15 was modified in two important ways. First, a sixth racial category was added for "Native Hawaiians and Other Pacific Islanders," who are now tabulated and reported separately from the aggregation of Asian groups. Second, respondents were permitted to choose "one or more races," a process generally known as "multiple-checkoff." Nationwide, about 1.4 percent of the population chose this option in the 2000 census. Finally, the separate question for Spanish/ Hispanic/Latino was maintained.

This led to tabulations on race and Hispanic origin in 2000 which are not completely compatible with those published for 1990 or earlier. (See Table 1-9.) Blacks reporting only one race are now 12.7 percent of the population, a small increase from 1990, but some of the 1.9 percent of the population reporting two or more races were included as Blacks in 1990. If we add in all of the people who reported that they were Black and were part of one or more other race categories as well, the percentage rises to about 13 percent.

Despite the rising numbers and percentages of Black population in the nation, the Hispanic population has grown to be even larger. As tabulated in the census, Hispanics may be of any race. As shown in Table 1-9, the 2000 Hispanic or Latino count was over 35.3 million, more than the Black or African American single race count, but less than the count of people who reported that they are Black along with one or more other races.

Population estimates for July 2002, issued in June 2003, show that the Hispanic population is now larger than the Black population (38.8 million to 36.7 million). The reason for this change is that Hispanics are still immigrating into the United States. Most immigrants are young, and are likely to have (more) children after arriving. The Black population is growing at a much smaller rate. Another group with significant increase is the Asian population. Again, the primary reason is immigration and the characteristics of the families coming in. These trends are expected to continue over the next several decades, with Whites continuing to decline as a proportion of the total population.

Table 1-9. Race and Ethnicity, July 2002

(Number, percent.)

Year	Number	Percent
One race	284 188 130	98.6
White	232 646 619	80.7
Black or African American	36 746 012	12.7
American Indian and Alaska Native	2 752 158	1.0
Asian	11 559 027	4.0
Native Hawaiian and Other Pacific Islander	484 314	0.2
Two or more races	4 180 568	1.4
Hispanic or Latino [1]	38 761 370	13.4

Source: U.S. Census Bureau. Census, 2000.
[1] May be of any race.

Table 1-10. Urban and Rural Population, 2000

(Number, percent.)

Year	Number	Percent distribution
Urban	222 360 539	79.0
Urbanized area	192 323 824	68.3
Urban cluster	30 036 715	10.7
Rural	59 061 367	21.0

Source: U.S. Census Bureau. Census, 2000. Summary File 1. Table P2.

FOR FURTHER INFORMATION SEE:

Forstall, Richard, and James Fitzsimmons. *Metropolitan Growth and Expansion in the 1980s.* Technical working paper No. 6. Washington, DC: U.S. Census Bureau, Population Division, April 1993.

McFalls, Joseph A. Jr. "Population: A Lively Introduction." *Population Bulletin* 46, No. 2. Population Reference Bureau (October 1991).

Monthly Vital Statistics Reports (various). Department of Health and Human Services, Centers for Disease Control and Prevention, National Center for Health Statistics.

Swanson, Linda L., ed. *Racial and Cultural Minorities in Rural Areas, Progress and Stagnation: 1980–1990.* Washington, DC: U.S. Department of Agriculture, Economic Research Service, 1997.

WEB SITES:

International Database, U.S. Census Bureau, available on the Internet: <http://www.census.gov>.

National Center for Health Statistics Web site: <http://www.cdc.gov/nchswww>.

Population Reference Bureau: <www.prb.org>.

U.S. Census Bureau Web site: <http://www.census.gov>.

U.S. Department of Agriculture, Economic Research Service Web site: <www.econ.ag.gov>.

Urban Institute: <www.urban.org/socwelfare.htm#immigration>.

Chapter 2
Households and Families

MARITAL STATUS

AGE AT MARRIAGE

Age at marriage, demographically speaking, makes a difference beyond the ceremony itself. It influences the number and timing of births, household formation, and consumer purchases, and it can influence such life events as educational attainment, career goals, and the likelihood of divorce, as well as the eventual total population of a nation.

Age at first marriage has been increasing in the United States since the mid-1960s. It is now at the highest level ever recorded; for men, the median age at first marriage approached 27 years in 2000, for women it was 25 years. During the baby boom era, in the 1950s, median age at first marriage was about 3 years younger than the current figure for men and nearly 5 years younger for women. Some demographers feel that the baby boom era, rather than the current era, is the exception, since at the turn of the twentieth century, the median age at first marriage was almost as high as it is today. The delay in age of marriage can also be seen in the percentage of young adults who have

Figure 2-1. Marital Status of People 15 Years and Over, 2000

Never married 28.1%

Widowed 6.4%

Divorced 9.3%

Separated 2.1%

Married spouse present 52.9%

Married spouse absent 1.3%

Source: U.S. Census Bureau, Current Population Survey Report, March 2000.

never married; 39 percent of men and 27 percent of women aged 25 to 34 in 1995 were never married. Both figures are considerably higher than they had been in the past several decades.

WILL PEOPLE MARRY AT ALL?

Despite the tendency to delay marriage, almost all of the young adults living in the United States will eventually marry. In 2002, for example, 7 percent of people aged 45 or older had never married[1]. A 1995 survey looked at the cohabitation, marital, and divorce experience of women 15 to 44.[2] About three out of four women in the survey had been married by age 30, with the rate slightly higher for non-Hispanic Whites and considerably lower (52 percent) for Non-Hispanic Blacks.

The 1995 study also looked at the probability that cohabitation—unmarried people living together as couples—makes the transition to marriage. They found that the length of cohabitation and the race/ethnicity of the woman both make a significant difference. (See Figure 2-3.) While only 30 percent of women had married after 1 year of cohabitation, the figure rises to 58 percent after 3 years and to 89 percent after 15 years. The figures are higher for Whites and for Hispanics than for Blacks.

WILL MARRIAGES LAST?

Almost half (43 percent) of first marriages have ended in divorce by their 15th anniversary. The probability of marriage disruption is higher for those who marry as

Table 2-1. Marital Status of People 15 Years and Over, March 2002

(Numbers in thousands, percent distribution.)

Sex and age	Total (thousands)	Percent distribution			
		Married, spouse present or absent	Separated or divorced	Widowed	Never married
Both sexes					
15 to 24 years	39 433	9.7	1.5	0.1	88.7
25 to 44 years	82 904	61.1	12.4	0.7	25.9
45 to 64 years	99 120	64.9	14.8	13.6	6.7
Males					
15 to 24 years	19 905	6.9	1.0	0.0	92.1
25 to 44 years	41 022	59.1	10.3	0.3	30.3
45 to 64 years	45 892	73.8	13.2	5.5	7.5
Females					
15 to 24 years	19 529	12.6	2.0	0.1	85.3
25 to 44 years	41 881	63.1	14.5	1.0	21.5
45 to 64 years	53 229	57.1	16.2	20.6	6.0

Source: Fields, Jason. 2003. *Children's Living Arrangements and Characteristics: March 2002.* Current Population Reports, P20-547. U.S. Census Bureau, Washington, DC.

---

[1] These statistics come from surveys conducted by the United States Census Bureau.

[2] See Department of Health and Human Services, Centers for Disease Prevention and Control, National Center for Health Statistics, *Cohabitation, Marriage, Divorce, and Remarriage in the United States*, Vital and Health Statistics, Series 23, Number 22, July 2002. Due to funding cutbacks, the National Center for Health Statistics discontinued collecting detailed information on marriages and divorces in 1996. Thus, recent data are not readily available.

teenagers, who have less than a high school education, and who have low family income. People who did not grow up in an intact two-parent home also have a higher chance of becoming divorced. However, over half of the women, under age 45, whose first marriage ended in divorce, remarry within the next 5 years, and three-quarters are remarried within 10 years.

"NON-TRADITIONAL" HOUSEHOLDS

As a result of the tendency to delay marriage (or avoid it entirely, described in the previous section), as well as of the increased divorce rates, over the last few decades we have seen a proliferation of single-person households and non-family households. In 1960, at the height of an era that has come to epitomize the positive attributes of marriage and the two-parent family in America, married-couple families were 75 percent of all households, and represented 87 percent of all families. Nonfamily households were 15 percent of households. By 2000, married-couple families represented only 52 percent of all households, while fully one-third of all households were nonfamily.[3] Families maintained by women only (without benefit of spouse) have increased from about 10 percent to 18 percent of all families during this same period; those sus-

tained by a man with no spouse present have also increased and now represent 6 percent of all families. (See Figure 2-4.)

The likelihood that children will experience life in a single-parent family at some time in their childhood has increased considerably in the past several decades. In 2000, 34 percent of children under 18 years were not living in a two-parent family; in 1970, 12 percent of children lived with one parent. Life in a single-parent family is even more likely for Black children; in 2000, fully two-thirds lived with one parent or with neither parent.

A subset of nonfamily households is composed of those who are unmarried couples, defined as persons of the opposite sex sharing living quarters. Since there are no questions directly relating to

intimacy between such persons in most surveys,[4] it is generally assumed that such persons are in fact "a couple," even though they may consist of an elderly widow renting a room to a male college student, for example. The number of unmarried couples has increased from half a million in 1970 to 4.9 million in 2000. Unmarried couples now represent 8 percent of all couples (married and unmarried) in the United States, up from 1 percent 30 years ago. Children under age 15 are living in a little over a third of these households.

Nonfamily households accounted for 43 percent of the growth in the total number of households during the 1990s. Most of them consist of persons living alone (about 83 percent). Men living alone tend to be younger than women (in 1995 the median age was about 44 years for men, and about 66 for women). The largest group of women living alone were widowed, with 30 percent over age 75 years.

Both household and family size have tended to shrink since 1970. There are many reasons for the decrease. One of the most important is the increasing life

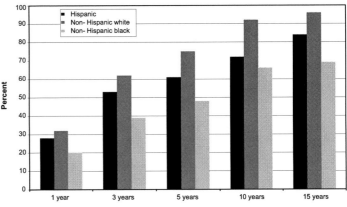

Figure 2-2. Probability that Cohabitation Transitions to Marriage, 1995

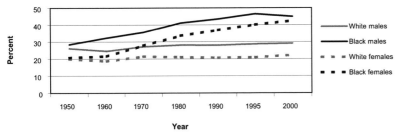

Figure 2-3. Percentage of People 15 Years and Over Who Were Never Married, by Race and Sex, 1950–2000

Source: U.S. Census Bureau. Current Population Survey Reports.

---

[3] The definitions of "household," "family," and "nonfamily household" used here are those used in U.S. Census Bureau publications. These data about households and families come from the 2000 census. A household is defined as all persons who occupy a housing unit; the term is essentially coterminous with "occupied housing unit." (Chapter 7 provides more information about housing.) A family is defined as a group of two or more persons who are related and live together in the same household. Thus, a one-person household does not contain a family. A nonfamily household is one consisting of only one person, or of two or more people all of whom are unrelated to each other.

[4] The 1995 National Center for Health Statistics survey, cited above, was a rare exception.

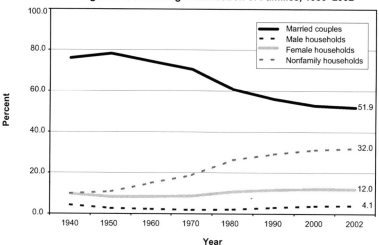

Figure 2-4. Percentage Distribution of Families, 1950–2002

lion multi-generational households in the United States. These are households which include a grandparent, a parent, a child, and perhaps a grandchild. These account for almost 4 percent of all households. In the majority of these households (2.5 million), the oldest generation is the householder, that is, the person responsible for the household. This includes the situations where young mothers live, with their children, in their own mothers' households. Another 1.4 million multi-generational households are more traditional; they include a householder, his/her parent, and one or more children of the householder. In a fraction of these cases, the household is four generational: the grandparent, parent/householder, child and grandchild.[5] These households are relatively uncommon in the Plains states. Iowa, Minnesota, Montana, Nebraska, North Dakota, South Dakota, Wisconsin, and Wyoming all show less than 2 percent of their households being multi-generational. This is also true in Maine and Vermont. On the other

span, which means that both couples and single people are living a larger proportion of their total life span in households without children. Another important factor is the fact that women are having fewer children (see discussion of fertility in Chapter 1). Divorce, and the accompanying increase in one-parent households, is another contributing factor. Overall, the average household size declined from 3.33 to 2.59 between 1960 and 2000, while average family size has declined from 3.67 to 3.14 persons. In 2000, over half of America's families had no children of their own and under age 18 living with them.

LIVING WITH GRANDMA AND GRANDPA

In 2000, there were almost 4 mil-

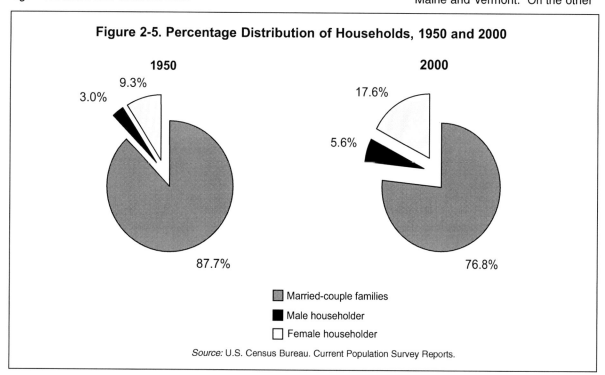

Figure 2-5. Percentage Distribution of Households, 1950 and 2000

1950

9.3%

3.0%

87.7%

2000

17.6%

5.6%

76.8%

- Married-couple families
- Male householder
- Female householder

Source: U.S. Census Bureau. Current Population Survey Reports.

5 See Census 2000 Table PHC-T-17: *Multigenerational Households for the United States, States, and for Puerto Rico,* posted at <www.census.gov> on September 7, 2001. This item was tabulated for the first time in the 2000 Census.

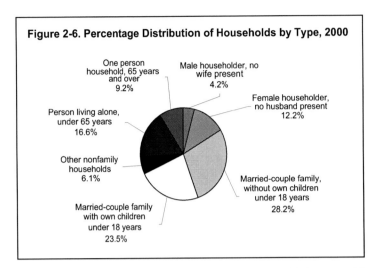

Figure 2-6. Percentage Distribution of Households by Type, 2000

One person household, 65 years and over
9.2%

Male householder, no wife present
4.2%

Female householder, no husband present
12.2%

Person living alone, under 65 years
16.6%

Other nonfamily households
6.1%

Married-couple family, without own children under 18 years
28.2%

Married-couple family with own children under 18 years
23.5%

hand, the figure for Hawaii is 8.2 percent. Other states that are at least 1 percentage point above the national figure are Mississippi, Louisiana, and New Jersey.

Nationwide, there were about 5.6 million grandparents with their own grandchildren in their households (regardless of whether or not a parent was present as well). Of these, about 42 percent (2.4 million) were responsible for the care of their grandchildren. These grandparents were 62 percent female. Over half were in the labor force (either working or unemployed), and about one in five was living below the poverty level.[6]

HOW ARE THE CHILDREN DOING?

A Census Bureau study[7] describes child well-being in terms of four types of indicators: early childhood experiences, parent-child interaction, school-age enrichment activities, and children's academic experience. With regard to the first, it found that childcare arrangements are more likely to be used by higher income and better-educated families, and that 3–5 year olds spend more hours per

week in childcare if they are children of single parents or of two-earner married couples. One-third of the children of college-educated parents had their first childcare experience before they were four months old.

CHILDCARE ARRANGEMENTS

There are no widespread government-run childcare centers in the United States. Yet, the increased incidence of mothers of young children who are in the labor force,

over the past several decades, has meant an increased need for child-care arrangements, especially for families with preschoolers. In 1997, 12.4 million children, representing 63 percent of all children under age 5, required care during the time their mothers were at work, job training, or school. Of these children, about 8 million were cared for by relatives, mostly by fathers or grandparents. About 6.9 million were in some type of non-relative care, primarily in organized facilities such as day care centers or nursery schools, or in someone else's home. Many pre-school children experience more than one type of care. Over 7 million have no regular arrangement.[8]

In spring 1997, there were 23.4 million grade-school-age children, age 5 to 14, with a working (employed) mother, or 62 percent of all children in this age group who lived with their mothers. Childcare arrangements for these children include the same options as for pre-schoolers as well as enrichment activities such as organized sports, music lessons, and the like, and self-care–the

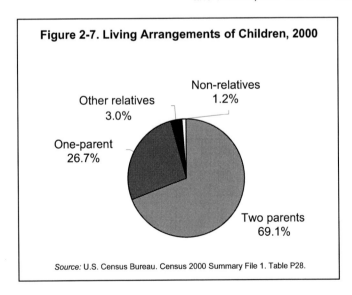

Figure 2-7. Living Arrangements of Children, 2000

Other relatives
3.0%

Non-relatives
1.2%

One-parent
26.7%

Two parents
69.1%

Source: U.S. Census Bureau. Census 2000 Summary File 1. Table P28.

---

6 These data were reported in the Census 2000 Supplementary Survey (C2SS). Similar data gathered in Census 2000 itself will be released in late 2002. See C2SS Table QT-02, available at <factfinder.census.gov>.

7 See Kristin E. Smith, Loretta E. Bass, and Jason M. Fields, *Child Well Being: Indicators From the SIPP*, Population Division Working Paper No. 24 (Washington, Bureau of the Census, April 1998). The SIPP (Survey of Income and Program Participation) is a large, national representative sample. The data in this report were collected in the Fall of 1994.

8 See Kristin Smith, *Who's Minding the Kids? Childcare Arrangements: Spring 1997*, Current Population Report P70-86 (Washington, Census Bureau, July 2002).

latchkey children. Looking at all the children age 6 to 14, about 19 percent participated in enrichment activities which served as a childcare arrangement for their parents. This type of activity was slightly more frequent in older children (9 to 14), among children who live in non-poverty or near-poverty families, and whose mothers work at least part-time. Sports were the most frequent type of enrichment activity, followed by lessons, clubs (including scouting), and before/after school programs.

About 7.3 million children were in self-care. As we would expect, the frequency of self-care is much higher for children 12–14 (42 percent of all children that age) than for those age 5 to 11 (9 percent). Most of the time, self-care is only one of the arrangements parents use for their children. The average number of hours a child was in self-care each week was about six for the younger children, and nine for the children age 12 to 14. The Census Bureau's report notes that "among older children, self-care can be an important part of the natural process of independence, allowing children structured opportunities for successful transitions to adulthood."

HOW MUCH DOES CHILDCARE COST?

The cost of childcare is an important consideration in working parents' budgets, especially if the family is low income. In 1997, the average cost of childcare for pre-schoolers with employed mothers was $2.22 per hour, or $70 per week. The cost was least when grandparents provided the care, and highest when day care centers were used. When mothers are not employed, the cost per hour rises to $3.34, but the weekly cost is only about $50. That's because most non-working mothers use day care centers, nursery schools, and in-home baby-sitters for childcare, all of which are more expensive than care by a relative or by a non-relative in the sitter's home.

For children age 5–14, the average cost and cost per week are lower, primarily because the children usually are in school for most of the hours needed for childcare. Employed mothers with children in enrichment activities reported that they spend about $4.50 per hour, and $24 per week, on this type of care. The cost per hour for children of non-employed mothers was similar, but the overall expenditures per week were lower.

All told, full-time employed mothers spent about $80 per week in childcare in 1997, with the cost averaging $60 for those with one child and about $87 for those with two or more children. If the youngest child was under 5, the average weekly cost rose to $92. Costs were highest in suburban areas and lowest outside of metropolitan areas, and generally rose with the income of the family. Very little help, from the government or from any other source, was available to help families pay the cost of childcare. When it was, it was most often offered to families receiving public assistance or to those where the mother was a student.

The data reported here were collected shortly before the implementation of welfare reform. Later data, when available, may provide a quite different picture of the way in which the nation's children are being cared for while their parents are at work or at school.

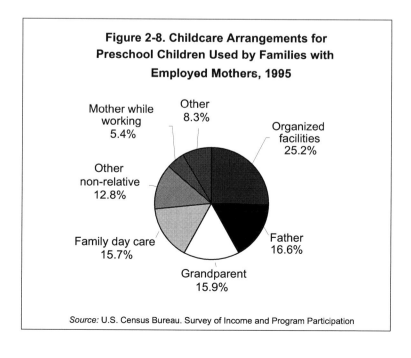

Figure 2-8. Childcare Arrangements for Preschool Children Used by Families with Employed Mothers, 1995

Mother while working 5.4%

Other 8.3%

Organized facilities 25.2%

Other non-relative 12.8%

Family day care 15.7%

Father 16.6%

Grandparent 15.9%

Source: U.S. Census Bureau. Survey of Income and Program Participation

FOR FURTHER INFORMATION SEE:

Bianchi, Suzanne, and Daphne Spain. *American Women in Transition*. New York: Russell Sage Foundation, 1986.

Bianchi, Suzanne. *America's Children: Mixed Prospects*. Population Reference Bureau, 1990.

Cherlin, Andrew. *Marriage, Divorce, and Remarriage*. (Cambridge: Harvard University Press, 1992).

Household and Family Characteristics. Current Population Reports, Series P-20 (Various years). Washington, DC: U.S. Census Bureau.

Marital Status and Living Arrangements. Current Population Reports, Series P-20 (Various years). Washington, DC: U.S. Census Bureau.

Smith, Kristin, *Who's Minding the Kids? Childcare Arrangements*, Spring 1997, Series P-70, No. 86. Washington, DC: U.S. Census Bureau. An update to this report may become available in 2004; check the Census Bureau's Web site (see below).

WEB SITES:

National Center for Health Statistics: <www.cdc.gov/nchswww>.

U.S. Census Bureau: <www.census.gov> and <factfinder.census.gov>.

Chapter 3
Social Conditions

AGING

The United States is an aging society. The number of elderly people is continually growing, both in absolute terms and as a proportion of the total population. This means that increasing societal resources must be devoted to serving this population.

In 2000, there were about 35 million people 65 years and over in the United States, comprising 12.4 percent of the total population. In contrast, 100 years earlier there were only 3 million people in this age group, and they constituted only 4 percent of the population. As shown in Figure 3-1, the proportion of elderly people is projected to rise sharply over the next 40 years, especially when the baby boomer generation begins to turn 65 in 2011.

Why this sharp increase in number and proportion? Most important, advancing medical treatments are keeping people alive

and in good health to a much more advanced age than even 50 years ago. This factor has already had great impact in many different ways. First, the health care system is increasingly serving the elderly, who constitute almost half of all hospital admissions. Second, increasing age has meant that households are composed of one or two people who have no children, as healthy senior citizens remain in their homes rather than in some form of institutional care or living with their children. Third, the booming elderly population has placed a significant strain on Social Security, which has already taken the step of increasing the standard retirement age beyond 65 for people born in 1938 or later. Medicare funding faces a similar problem. Finally, because people are living so much longer past retirement age than in the past, they face an increasing challenge of managing to have sufficient

income to live on in the style to which they are accustomed.

The Federal Forum on Aging Related Statistics, a collaboration between several federal statistics agencies, has established a set of indicators by which to measure the status of older Americans—65 years and over—across time. The following sections report on many of these indicators.[1]

CHARACTERISTICS OF THE ELDERLY

Because the White population has a longer life expectancy than do people in minority groups, the proportion of the elderly population that is White is higher than that of the total population: 84 percent in 2000. Projections for 2050, however, show that pattern changing. The White proportion will drop to 64 percent, and the percent of elderly population in each other race group and of Hispanics will increase. (See Table 3-1.)

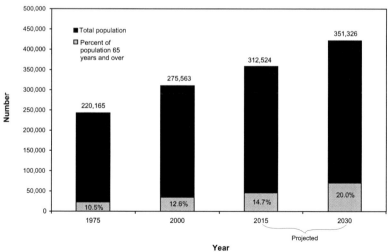

Figure 3-1. Total Population and Percent Over 65 Years, 1975–2030

Source: U.S. Census Bureau. An Aging World: 2001.

---

[1] See list of sources and Web sites at the end of this chapter for contact information.

Table 3-1. Projected Distribution of the Population 65 Years and Over, by Race and Hispanic Origin, 2000 and 2050

(Percent distribution.)

Race/ethnicity	2000	2050
Total	100.0	100.0
White, non-Hispanic	83.5	64.2
Black, non-Hispanic	8.1	12.2
American Indian and Alaska Native, non-Hispanic	0.4	0.6
Asian and Pacific Islander, non-Hispanic	2.4	6.5
Hispanic	5.6	16.4

Source: Federal Interagency Forum on Aging-Related Statistics (Forum). *Older Americans 2000: Key Indicators of Well-Being.*
Note: Data are middle-series projections of the population. Hispanics may be of any race.

Table 3-2. Marital Status of the Population 65 Years and Over, 2000

(Percent distribution.)

Marital status	65 years and over	65 to 74 years	75 to 84 years	85 years and over
Total	100.0	100.0	100.0	100.0
Married	55.3	64.4	49.5	26.7
Widowed	32.0	20.6	39.9	65.4
Divorced or separated	8.7	11.0	6.5	3.7
Never married	4.0	4.0	4.1	4.2
Men	100.0	100.0	100.0	100.0
Married	73.9	77.1	72.3	56.8
Widowed	13.9	8.7	17.9	35.9
Divorced or separated	8.3	10.2	6.1	3.9
Never married	3.9	4.0	3.7	3.4
Women	100.0	100.0	100.0	100.0
Married	41.9	53.9	34.4	12.5
Widowed	45.1	30.5	54.4	79.4
Divorced or separated	8.9	11.7	6.7	3.6
Never married	4.1	3.9	4.5	4.5

Source: U.S. Census Bureau. Census 2000 Supplementary Survey.

Table 3-3. Educational Attainment of the Population 65 Years and Over, Selected Years, 1950–1998

(Percent.)

Educational attainment level	1950	1960	1970	1980	1990	1998
High school diploma or higher	17.7	19.1	27.1	40.7	53.2	67.0
Bachelor's degree or higher	3.6	3.7	5.5	8.6	10.7	14.8

Source: Federal Interagency Forum on Aging-Related Statistics (Forum). *Older Americans 2000: Key Indicators of Well-Being.*
Note: Data for 1980 and 1998 refer to the civilian noninstitutional population. Data for other years refer to the resident population.

As we would expect, the data show that elderly people are more likely than others to be living alone, and to be widowed. The "young old," people age 65 to 74, are more likely to be married; this proportion drops with age as widowhood increases. Elderly men have a higher likelihood of being married, regardless of age, than do women. This happens because women are much more likely to be widowed than are men, and perhaps because men are more likely to remarry if their wives die. Overall, about three-quarters of men age 65 years and over are married, compared with less than half of the women. (See Table 3-2.)

Education levels among people 65 years and over have been increasing over time, much as education levels have increased across all age groups. In 2000, more than two-thirds of this population had graduated from high school, with 15 percent having completed a 4-year college degree.

ECONOMIC CIRCUMSTANCES

The economic condition of the nation's elderly has improved over time. In 1959, 35 percent of the population age 65 years and over lived below the poverty level. This rate declined sharply between 1965 and 1975, and has continued to decrease (at a slower rate), until reaching 11 percent in 2000. However, the older the person, the more likely that they live below the poverty level. People living alone show higher poverty rates as well.

In 1998, almost half (42 percent) of the elderly had annual incomes below $15,000. At the other end of the scale, one out of eight (14 percent) had incomes of $50,000 or more. The major predictors of higher income are being married and being among the "young old," under age 75. These two factors are, of course, interrelated, as the young old are more likely to be married. They are also more likely to have earned income.

Almost all elderly households receive Social Security benefits. It provides the majority of total income for more than half of its beneficiaries, and is the only source of income for 18 percent of them. A recent change permits people of full retirement age (65 years and over) to receive their Social Security benefits regardless of their level of earned income. Figure 3-2 shows that Social Security is the single largest source of income for the elderly, followed by earnings, asset income, and pensions. Social Security provides 82 percent of aggregate income for the poorest group of elderly, but only 19 percent for the highest quintile. These affluent households have significant income from assets, earnings, and pensions. The bottom line: the data clearly show that elderly who are best off in their senior years are those who are able to keep working, at least part-time, who have pensions, and who benefit from having accumulated

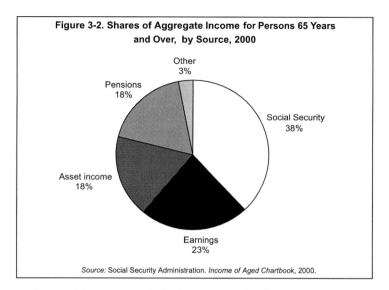

Figure 3-2. Shares of Aggregate Income for Persons 65 Years and Over, by Source, 2000

Other 3%

Pensions 18%

Social Security 38%

Asset income 18%

Earnings 23%

Source: Social Security Administration. *Income of Aged Chartbook*, 2000.

the nation's health resources at a higher rate.

Overall, elderly people rate their own health quite highly. These ratings differ significantly by race and Hispanic origin, however, and, as we would expect, younger elderly people rate their health more highly than the population 85 years and over. (See Figure 3-3.) Even so, 45 percent of the lowest rating group, Black men 85 years and over, report that they have good to excellent health, as do more than half of people in all of the other groups reported.

As we would expect, older Americans are more likely to suffer from disabilities than younger people. About 21 percent of this group reported a chronic disability in 1994, a smaller percentage than in 1982 but a growth of 600,000 in the number of disabled people, from 6.4 million to 7 million. In 1995, 29 percent of women aged 70 and over were unable to perform at least one of nine specified physical functions; these include such activities as walking a quarter of a mile, climbing 10 stairs without resting, and lifting or carrying something as heavy as 10 pounds. Men, generally, are in better condition, with only 20 percent of those 70 years and over being unable to perform one or more of these functions. However, in the 2000 census, 42 percent of people 65 years and over reported that they were "disabled," meaning that they had

savings and investments in their younger years to provide income at this point in their lives.

HEALTH

As discussed in Chapter 1, life expectancy is continually increasing. In other words, Americans are living longer than ever before. Further, the longer a person lives, the greater his or her life expectancy for the future. Thus, people who survive to age 65 can expect to live another 18 years, while those who are now 85 can expect another 6 or 7 years of life.

What are the causes of death for the elderly? Heart disease leads the list, followed by cancer and stroke. Diabetes, chronic obstructive pulmonary disease (such as emphysema), and pneumonia/influenza cause death less often, but these rates may decrease in the future as medical science finds new ways to deal with the morbid effects of heart disease and cancer. In fact, rates for diabetes and chronic obstructive pulmonary disease have risen consistently since 1980.

Chronic diseases exist over a long period of time and are rarely cured. Thus, they become a significant health and financial burden to the elderly, their families, and the nation's health system. Some of these are the conditions that

often lead to death (cancer, stroke, heart disease, and diabetes). Non-fatal conditions include arthritis and hypertension (high blood pressure); about half the elderly suffer from one, the other, or both. Another condition affecting the elderly in large numbers is memory impairment, usually called Alzheimer's Disease. The problem shows up in low numbers among the "young old," but affects more than one-third of people 85 years and over. It is somewhat more common in men than in women. Depressive symptoms also occur in 12 percent to 23 percent of the elderly, with the condition being more common among the "old old," 85 years and over. Depressed people are more likely to have physical illness as well, and to use

Table 3-4. Living Arrangements of the Population 65 Years and Over, 1998

(Percent.)

Race/ethnicity	With spouse	With other relatives	With non-relatives	Alone
Men				
Total	72.6	7.0	3.0	17.3
White	74.3	6.0	2.7	17.0
Black	53.5	14.8	6.8	24.9
Asian and Pacific Islander	72.0	20.8	0.6	6.6
Hispanic	66.8	15.0	4.3	14.0
Women				
Total	40.7	16.8	1.7	40.8
White	42.4	14.8	1.6	41.3
Black	24.3	32.2	2.7	40.8
Asian and Pacific Islander	41.3	36.7	0.8	21.2
Hispanic	36.9	33.8	1.8	27.4

Source: Federal Interagency Forum on Aging-Related Statistics (Forum). *Older Americans 2000: Key Indicators of Well-Being.*
Note: Hispanics may be of any race.

Figure 3-3. Percentage of Persons 65 Years and Over Reporting Good to Excellent Health, 1994–1996

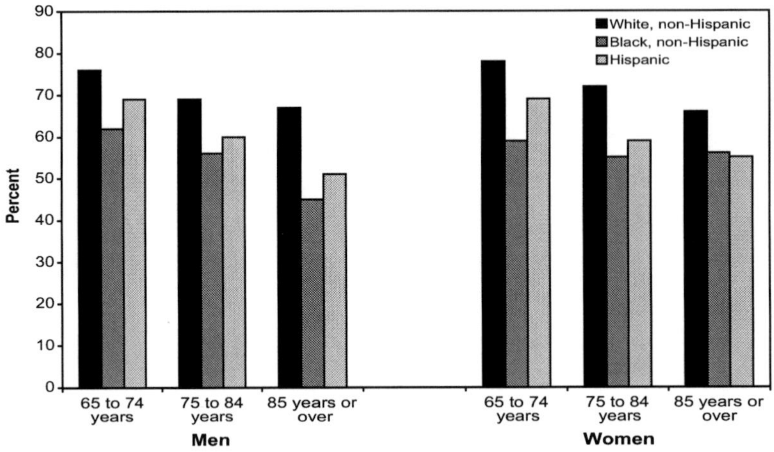

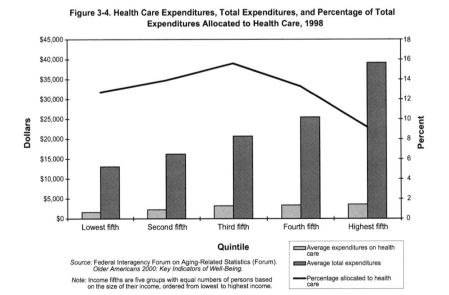

Source: Federal Interagency Forum on Aging-Related Statistics (Forum). *Older Americans 2000: Key Indicators of Well-Being.*

one or more conditions which limited what they could do and had lasted for six months or more. The figure was 32 percent for those between ages 65 and 74, and 54 percent for those 75 years and older.

Social activities and an active lifestyle benefit older Americans and tend to improve their health status and life expectancy. Most elderly people do have contact with neighbors and/or with relatives who do not live with them, on at least a bi-weekly basis. About half report engaging in other social activities such as church atten-dance, eating out at restaurants, and attending movies or group events in a two week period; a smaller percentage reported doing volunteer work over the past year. Unfortunately, there is still a sub-stantial proportion of older Americans who report having a sedentary lifestyle: about 40 per-cent for women and 30 percent for men in 1995. For those who do exercise, the most common activi-ties were walking, gardening, or stretching.

Health care issues are clearly very important for senior citizens, and more of an issue than for younger people. Medicare expen-ditures are generally rising, and go up with age, so that 1996 expendi-tures for those 85 years and over averaged more than $16,000 on an annual basis. Prescription drugs both are an increasing bene-fit and increasing financial burden for the elderly, as they are not cov-ered by Medicare. Overall, middle-income elderly households spend the greatest proportion (16 percent in 1996) of their incomes on health care; low-income families are more likely to receive assistance from Medicaid, while upper income fam-ilies can better afford the health

Figure 3-4. Health Care Expenditures, Total Expenditures, and Percentage of Total Expenditures Allocated to Health Care, 1998

Source: Federal Interagency Forum on Aging-Related Statistics (Forum). *Older Americans 2000: Key Indicators of Well-Being.*

Note: Income fifths are five groups with equal numbers of persons based on the size of their income, ordered from lowest to highest income.

care expenditures. (See Figure 3-4.)

Access to health care is, fortunately, a rare problem. In 1996, only 2 percent of elderly households reported that they had difficulty obtaining care, while another 6 percent said that they delayed obtaining care due to its cost. The delay problem actually deceases with age, perhaps because people 85 years and over are more likely to reside in a facility which provides health care as well as housing, such as a nursing home or assisted living facility. Table 3-5 (health care utilization) shows the high frequency of service usage by the elderly population, with 3 in 10 being hospitalized at least once during the year, and an average of 13 physician visits and consultations.

Almost one in five people 85 years and over resides in a nursing home. Men are less likely than women to be nursing home residents at any age, because they are more likely to have spouses at home to serve as caregivers. Older widowed women, without caregivers available, more often move into nursing homes.

IMPACT ON GOVERNMENT SPENDING

The aging of the population means, and will increasingly continue to mean, a change in government spending priorities. Children and adults 60 years and over consume the majority of net payments from government. Examples of these payment programs include Medicare, education, Social Security, and Medicaid. This demographic problem is the root of the current debate over Social Security, because the ratio between the number of wage earners paying into the system and the number of retirees collecting

Table 3-5. Rates of Health Care Service Usage by Medicare Beneficiaries, 1998

(Rate per 1,000 population 65 years or over, days.)

Type of service	
Hospitalization	365
Home health visits	5 058
Skilled nursing facility admissions	69
Physician visits and consultations	13 100
Average length of hospital stay (days)	6.1
Nursing home residence (1997)	45.3

Source: Federal Interagency Forum on Aging-Related Statistics (Forum). *Older Americans 2000: Key Indicators of Well-Being*.
Note: These data refer to Medicare beneficiaries in fee-for-service only.

income from the system is changing rapidly. Current projections are that the Social Security trust fund will be exhausted sometime between 2038 and 2050. It is even more difficult to project future costs for Medicare than for Social Security because of the uncertainty over health care expenses. Medicaid costs, which are the largest source of payment for long-term care of disabled and older people, are also projected to rise.

Overall, the Congressional Budget Office (CBO) projected in 2000 that Social Security, Medicare, and the federal portion of Medicaid would account for 16 percent of the Gross Domestic Product (GDP) by 2040, in contrast with 7.5 percent in 2000. If health care costs continue to grow at the pace of the 1990s, the figure could be as high as 20 percent. This would, inevitably, lead to increased taxes, whether in the form of income taxes or payroll taxes. One projection suggests that the payroll tax for Social Security would have to rise from its current 12.4 percent to over 21 percent in 2070, just to keep the trust funds in balance.[2]

SOCIAL SERVICES

As noted by authors at the Urban Institute,[3] social services for the elderly are now fragmented and not sufficiently available relative to need. The purpose of these serv-

ices is to facilitate continued independent residence in the community, so as to prevent, or at least delay, the need for institutional care. As the number of elderly people increases, so do the needs for these services. At present, the supply is far short of the demand. For example, for several years Michigan had a "Medicaid waiver" program in place, where funding was provided to the Area Agencies on Aging so that they could provide services which would help people to avoid nursing homes. In the recent economic downturn, this program was eliminated, even though it costs more in Medicaid funds to keep an elderly person in a nursing home than it does to provide these services.

CHILDREN

Children, defined as people under 18 years of age, are our nation's future. They are also our collective responsibility, as they generally are unable to manage all of the activities of life by themselves. The opportunities and challenges faced by children are determined primarily by the life status of their parents. It is very difficult for low-income families to rise out of poverty, and "to build the savings and assets that are critical for all families to achieve genuine economic security."[4] There is a high cost simply to being poor, especially for families with children.

[2] Population Reference Bureau, "Government Spending in an Older America," *Reports on America*, Vol. 3, No. 1, May 2002.

[3] Sheila R. Zedlewski, et al., *The Needs of the Elderly in the 21st Century*, Washington: Urban Institute Report 90-5, 1990.

[4] Annie E. Casey Foundation, *2003 Kids Count Data Book*, Baltimore, MD, 2002, p. 11. This report is updated annually and can be viewed at <www.kidscount.org>; it includes state-specific data for each of the indicators. The book also lists contacts for each state; the contact agencies produce similar data by county.

Table 3-6. Poverty Rates for Children and their Families, 1990 and 2000

(Rate per 100 population.)

Characteristic	1990	2000
All Children [1]	17.9	16.1
0–4 years	21.2	17.8
5–17 years	17.0	15.4
All Families With Children	14.9	13.6
With children under 5 years	18.3	17.0
All Families With Female Householder, No Husband Present, And		
With Children	42.3	34.3
With children under 5 years	57.4	46.4

Source: U.S. Census Bureau. 1990 and 2000 Census Reports.
[1]Poverty rates are calculated only for children who are related to the householder. Children living in group quarters are not
   included in this table. Some foster children are also excluded.

Table 3-7. National Indicators of Children's Well-Being, 1975 and 2000

(Rate per 100,000, except where noted. Percent.)

Educational attainment level	1975	2000
Percent low-birthweight babies	7.4	7.6
Infant mortality rate (age under 1 year)	16.1	6.9
Child death rates (age 1 to 14 years)	44	22
Rate of teen deaths by accident, homicide, or suicide (age 5 to 19 years)	73	51
Teen birth rate (per 1,000 females 5 to 19 years)	36	27
Percent of teens who are high school dropouts (age 16 to 19 years)	12	9
Percent of teens who are not attending school and not working (age 16 to 19 years)	12	8
Percent of children living in families where no parents has full-time, year-round employment	33	24
Percent of children in poverty	17	17
Percent of families with children headed by a single parent	17	28

Source: Annie E. Casey Foundation, *Kids Count Databook, 2003.*

CHARACTERISTICS

The 2000 census enumerated more than 72 million children, an increase of 14 percent over 1990. The growth rate was highest for the children age 12 to 17, which happened because the "baby boomlet" of the 1980s is a much larger cohort than the "baby bust" generation before it. By the mid-1990s, the baby boomlet was over, and thus the number of preschool children (age 0 to 4), increased by only 5 percent over the number for this group in 1990.

The 2000 census measured the poverty rate for children at 16 percent, 4 percentage points higher than for all people. Among families with children, the rate was 14 percent, but rose to 34 percent in families with a female householder and no husband present. The poverty rates for families with children under age 5 were even higher, at 17 percent for all families and 46 percent for those headed

by a female householder with no husband present. (See Table 3-6.) These rates are all somewhat lower than the corresponding figures for 1990. The impact of welfare reform on the children's poverty rates will be measured by further research with the 2000 census data.

INDICATORS OF CHILDREN'S WELL-BEING

The Casey Foundation and the Population Reference Bureau have developed a set of national indicators which help us to evaluate the overall status of children's well-being. Many of these indicators have shown improvement over the past 25 years, but some have not. (See Table 3-7.) The percentage of babies who weight less than 5.5 pounds at birth, the standard definition of "low-birthweight babies," is higher now than it was in 1975, although the measure dropped to

about 6.8 percent in the mid-1980s. The increase is attributed to a greater frequency of multiple births, which in turn has two causes: more older (35+) mothers and greater use of fertility drugs. The infant mortality rate, however, has dropped by more than half since 1975. Nonetheless, it remains higher than that of most other industrialized nations. The infant mortality rate for children born into poor families is more than 50 percent higher than that for children born into families with incomes above the poverty level.[5]

Other measures which have shown significant improvement over the past quarter-century include teen deaths, the teen birth rate—the rate at which women under 18 are having children, and the proportion of children who live in families in which no parents have full-time, year-round employment. The latter indicator has shown its most significant drop (from over 30 percent in the early 1990s to 24 percent in 2000) since the implementation of welfare reform. This makes sense, since most former welfare mothers are now required to work.

Despite these improvements, the percentage of children in poverty has declined only slightly over the 25-year period. However, it was much higher (about 22 percent) in the early 1990s, and has been in decline for several years. The percentage of families with children which are headed by a single parent has risen consistently since 1975. In 2000, 34 percent of these families had income below the poverty level.

These indicators are combined into a composite rank, enabling us to compare one state with another. (See Figure 3-5.) The leading state, in terms of children's well-being as measured by this set of indicators, is Minnesota, followed by New Hampshire and Utah. At the other end of the scale, Mississippi ranks last of the

---

[5] Centers for Disease Control and Prevention, "Poverty and Infant Mortality–United States, 1988," by John L. Kiely, *Morbidity and Mortality Weekly Report*, Vol. 44, No. 49, 1995 (December 15), pp. 922–927.

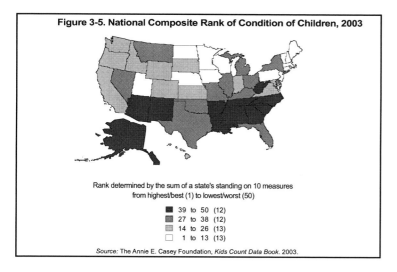

Figure 3-5. National Composite Rank of Condition of Children, 2003

Rank determined by the sum of a state's standing on 10 measures
from highest/best (1) to lowest/worst (50)

■ 39 to 50 (12)
▨ 27 to 38 (12)
▒ 14 to 26 (13)
☐ 1 to 13 (13)

Source: The Annie E. Casey Foundation, *Kids Count Data Book.* 2003.

the definition of "urban" is considered "rural."[8]

POPULATION AND MIGRATION

At the time of the first census in 1790, the nation was about 95 percent rural. The figure declined slowly but steadily until 1970, when it reached 26 percent. The percent rural number remained fairly steady for the next two decades, at about one-quarter of the nation's population. What was behind these trends? First, the nation's economy was transformed from being based on farming to being based on manufacturing throughout the nineteenth and early twentieth centuries. Many people moved from rural to urban areas in order to find jobs. In addition, most of the huge waves of immigration, especially in the early twentieth century, headed for city residence, again because that was where it was easiest to find work.

Why did the trend slow down, and even stabilize, in the late twentieth century? One reason is that the number of jobs in rural areas increased as the economy decentralized. Companies thought that they could find cheaper labor in rural areas, and perhaps with less inclination to unionize. As the primary mode of transportation

50 states, with its neighbors Alabama and Louisiana preceding it.

Another set of key indicators has been published by the Federal Interagency Forum on Child and Family Statistics.[6] It includes information on hunger, health indicators, behavior, and the social environment. Children living in homes with incomes below the poverty level are three times more likely to experience food insecurity (concern over having enough to eat) and hunger than are children in more affluent homes. On the behavior front, cigarette use among adolescents has declined, as have the violent crime victimization and offending rates. However, only a little over half of pre-schoolers are read to by a family member on a daily basis.

RURAL AMERICA

Rural America comprises over 2,000 counties, contains 75 percent of the nation's land, and is home to 17 percent of the U.S. population, or 49 million. This represents a decrease of 253 counties and 7.3 million people when compared with the same criterion applied after the 1990 census.

How do we define "rural?" A general definition, used by ERS, classifies counties as rural if they are not part of a Metropolitan Area—micropolitan areas and their counties are included in the rural definition.[7] While most counties within a Metropolitan Area are urban in character, some more rural counties are included if a significant number of residents commute to the urban area for work. As used by the Census Bureau, the official definition of "urban" includes all territory in urbanized areas or "urban clusters," a new term for small built-up communities usually centered by a city or village. All territory which is outside

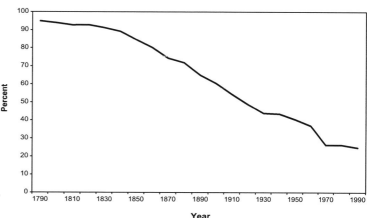

Figure 3-6. Percentage of Population Living in Rural Areas, 1790–1990

Percent

Year

Source: U.S. Census Bureau. Population Division.

---

[6] Federal Interagency Forum on Child and Family Statistics, "America's Children: Key Indicators of Well-Being 2002, Washington, DC, July 2002.
[7] See Chapter 1 for more extensive discussion of Metropolitan and Micropolitan Areas.
[8] Glenn V. Fugitt, John A. Fulton, and Calvin L. Beale, "The Shifting Patterns of Black Migration From and Into the Nonmetropolitan South, 1965-1995," Economic Research Service, U.S. Department of Agriculture, Rural Development Research Report No. 93, December 2001.

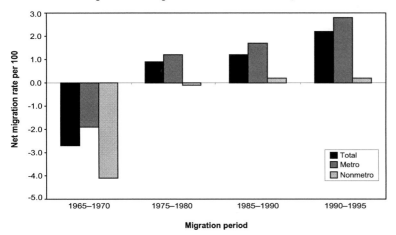

Figure 3-7. Net Migration for Blacks in the South, 1965–1995

Source: Glenn V. Fugitt, John A. Fulton, and Calvin L. Beale, "The Shifting Patterns of Black Migration From and Into the Nonmetropolitan South, 1965–1995," Economic Research Service, U.S. Department of Agriculture, Rural Development Research Report No. 93, December 2001.

switched from railroads to trucks, coupled with construction of the interstate highway system beginning in 1957, it became ever easier to transport finished products from areas which were formerly considered remote. As the number of jobs in these areas increased, so did the population. Rural areas actually gained nearly 6 million people between 1970 and 1980, and another 1.2 million in the 1980s. The rural in-migration had not been as high since the 1880–1910 period, when many immigrants headed directly to rural areas to be farmers.

Another factor driving rural growth in the latter twentieth century was the decrease in Black out-migration. In mid-decade, Blacks followed Whites to the metropolitan areas, mostly in the Northeast and Midwest. After 1965, Black migration shifted to metropolitan areas in the South, but was offset by the migration of Blacks into, or returning to, rural areas. This pattern was driven by job growth and, to some extent, by changing racial attitudes in the South. Family ties have played a role as well.[9]

However, the rate of gain in non-metropolitan population

slowed down in the 1997–1999 period. The annual average growth for those 2 years was 281,000, significantly less than the 415,000 annual gain reported for 1995–1997. Most of this gain came from natural increases (more births than deaths), as net migration was only 0.3 percent during this period. Young adults are the most likely to move, with a net loss to metro areas of 1.6 percent of the 18-to 24-year-olds, but a net gain of 1.0 percent of the 25-to 29-year-olds. This pattern shows that young people are likely to move away for college or jobs, but many return as they marry and are ready to settle down. The elderly population, 65 years and over, is the least likely to move at all.[10]

HOUSING

Access to adequate and appropriate housing is important for all people. Rural housing is often thought to be less adequate than the housing in suburbs, just as central-city housing is perceived to be less adequate. For many years, the federal government has had programs in place to promote homeownership. While this is important, it does not address the

problem of housing—owner-or renter-occupied—which is inadequate to meet basic needs and standards for shelter.

The American Housing Survey (discussed in more depth in Chapter 5) provides data on the physical condition of housing, as well as on its costs and the attitudes of the residents toward their housing and neighborhoods. Most rural households live in owner-occupied single family homes or in mobile homes. Townhouses and other attached housing, and apartments, are much more common in metro areas. The rural homes are both smaller and less costly, on the average, than the urban homes.

An analysis of the 1997 American Housing Survey data shows that, in rural areas, housing is a bigger problem for the portion of the population that is "wage-dependent," that is, households whose income depends on wages or salaried earnings. Typically, this excludes households whose primary work is farming. Low-income wage-dependent householders are generally young, with young children. Many rural families in this category find it hard to locate affordable housing which is in reasonably good condition. About 10 percent of the owners, and 15 percent of the renters, live in physically inadequate housing; about 13 percent live in crowded conditions. Over 30 percent of these households lived in mobile homes in 1997, a housing category that combines less adequate and spacious facilities with lower housing costs.[11]

CHARACTERISTICS OF FARMS AND FARM OWNERS

The Census of Agriculture provides us with a look, once every 5 years, at the situation of the nation's farms. Much of the data collected

9 John B. Cromartie, "Nonmetro Migration Drops in the West and Among College Graduates," Rural Conditions and Trends, Vol. 11, No. 2, p. 32.

10 James Mikesell and George Wallace, "Unique Housing Challenges Face Rural America and Its Low-Income Workers," Rural Conditions and Trends, Vol. 11, No. 2, pp. 75–79.

11 U.S. Department of Agriculture, Structural and Financial Characteristics of Family Farms, Report AIB-768, May 2001.

Table 3-8. Selected Characteristics of Farms, by Farm Typology Group, 1998

Farm type	Number	Percent of all farms	Average acres	Average age of operator	Percent of operators with some college
TOTAL	2 064 709	100.0	453	54	43.6
Small Family Farms (Under $250K Sales/Yr)					
Limited resource (very poor)	150 268	7.3	111	58	20.2
Retirement (operator is retired)	290 938	14.1	180	70	34.0
Residential/lifestyle (owner has another occupation)	834 321	40.4	148	49	50.9
Farming occupation, under $100K sales/yr	422 205	20.4	453	58	45.2
Farming occupation, $100K-$249K sales/yr	171 469	8.3	1 167	50	47.6
Large family farms ($250–$500K Sales/Yr)	91 939	4.5	1 747	50	59.1
Very large family farms (Over $500K Sales/Yr)	61 273	3.0	1 971	49	59.8
Non-family farms	42 296	2.0	1 670	53	60.4

Source: U.S. Department of Agriculture, Economic Research Service, *Structural and Financial Characteristics of U.S. Farms*, Agriculture Information Bulletin #768, May 2001.

refer to crop and other farm production. A farm is defined as any place from which $1,000 or more of agricultural products (crops and livestock) are sold or normally would be sold during the year under consideration. As of the late 1990s, there were about 2.1 million farms in the United States. About 40 percent of these are classified as "residential/lifestyle," where the operators of the farm report a non-farm occupation as well, and the farm brings less than $250,000 per year. (See Table 3-8.) Family farms, where farming in the primary occupation in the household, comprise another 36 percent of all farms; the majority of these have sales of less than $100,000 annually.

Limited resource farms, 7 percent of the total, have household incomes under $20,000, farm assets less than $150,000, and sales of under $100,000. These farms are located primarily in the eastern half of the nation, with a concentration in Appalachia and in the southern states. Operators of these farms have less education, overall, than those in any other farm category; almost half have not completed high school and only 11 percent have attended college. Almost half are 65 years and over. They are a significant portion of the rural poor.[12]

THE ECONOMICS OF AGRICULTURE

Farm operators and residents had a total net cash income, in 1999, of over $155 billion. Over three-quarters of this income (77 percent) came from off-farm sources, such as earnings, social security, public assistance, and investments. Government payments accounted for another 11 percent, leaving only about 12 percent of farm income attributable to agricultural sales and other farm-related sources. Most farms with off-farm income are also small, less than 500 acres.

Debt is a significant factor for farm operators. Overall, 46 percent of them owe money for the equipment needed to operate the farm. The amount of debt varies by the value of agricultural sales. The largest total is held by operators of smaller farms with sales between $100,000 and $500,000; collectively, they owe about $55 billion. Young farmers hold the largest percent of the total debt. Geographically, the highest proportions of indebted farmers are located in the Northern Plains states (Kansas, Nebraska, North Dakota and South Dakota), and in the neighboring Lake states (Michigan, Wisconsin, and Minnesota).

A farm is not likely to show a profit until it achieves sales of at least $100,000 annually. It takes

sales of $500,000 or more before the net cash income from farming exceeds that coming from off-farm sources. These data imply that small farmers take off-farm jobs out of necessity, that the farm cannot produce enough income to sustain the household.[13]

IMMIGRATION AND IMMIGRANTS

LEGAL IMMIGRATION

The number of births minus the number of deaths (labeled "natural increase" by demographers) and net migration are the determinants of growth for a country. One or both of these components can be the driving force of population change, depending on the country and the point-in-time of interest. In the United States, net immigration is projected to be a predominant factor in our future population growth. At levels presumed by the Census Bureau's middle projection series (which assume net immigration at current levels), immigrants and the offspring of immigrants who come to the United States between 1994 and the middle of the next century will be responsible for 60 percent of our total population growth during that period.

Recent concern about immigration to the United States has been fueled not only by the

---

[12] USDA, National Agricultural Statistics Services (NASS), *Agricultural Economics and Land Ownership Survey*, 1999, accessed at <www.nass.usda.gov/census/census97/aelos/>.

[13] See Philip Martin and Elizabeth Midgley, "Immigration: Shaping and Reshaping America," Population Bulletin 58, No. 2 (Washington, DC: Population Reference Bureau, 2003).

number of immigrants, but by their perceived and actual influence on the lives of non-immigrants. Historically, immigrants have borne the brunt of public scorn when economic conditions worsen. However, economic conditions in general were generally good during the 1990s, yet immigration remained a hotly contested issue in the media and at various levels of government. Part of the reason for this discussion is the differential effect of recent immigration on the resident population. Much of the negative impact is on minorities, according to some research, because the jobs recent immigrants are taking are concentrated at the bottom of the occupational ladder, where minorities are disproportionately represented.[14]

While the level of immigration is high by recent standards, the proportion of foreign-born population is not at record levels for the United States. In 2000, about 10 percent of the population was foreign born, double the percentage of foreign born in 1970 (about 5 percent) but considerably less than the figure at the turn of the century (about 15 percent).

The number of immigrants admitted to the United States has varied considerably throughout the past decade, increasing from about 600,000 in the mid-1980s to almost 2 million in 1991. After that, the number began decreasing, reaching 660,000 in 1998. One major reason for the increase, statistically, was the Immigration Reform and Control Act (IRCA) of 1996, which permitted immigration of former illegal aliens.[15] In 1995, a change in the law permitted such people to apply directly for naturalization, thus removing them from the count of immigrants. Almost 2.7 immigrants were recorded under IRCA provisions between 1989 and 1994, of whom about 75 percent "immigrated" in 1989 and 1990. Another reason for the decline was the Immigration Act of 1990, which placed a "flexible" cap on immigration of 700,000 in 1992–1994, and 675,000 thereafter.

In 2001, 63 percent of more than 1 million immigrants were admitted based on their family relationship to a U.S. citizen, while 17 percent were admitted based on job skills. Beginning in the early 1990s, Congress mandated a new "diversity" program that guaranteed about 55,000 visas to countries that had been "adversely affected" by the 1965 Immigration Act; another 4 percent of 2001 immigrants were admitted under this provision. About 10 percent were refugees or people seeking asylum, while 6 percent fell into other miscellaneous categories. These immigrants were balanced by an estimated 220,000 "emigrants."[16] who left the United States.

During this century, there has been a fairly dramatic shift in the countries of origin of immigrants, away from Europe and toward Central America and Asia. (See Figure 3-8.) As was the case throughout the 1990s, Mexico remains the source country for the largest group of immigrants (even excluding IRCA legalizations, which were predominantly from Mexico as well), representing about 20 percent of all immigrants in 1998. The other countries in the top five in 1995 include the Philippines, Vietnam, the Dominican Republic, China, and India.

Immigrants tend to cluster in a relatively small number of states, with two-thirds of the 1998 group concentrating in only six states: California, home to 26 percent of immigrants in 1998, New York (15 percent), Florida (9 percent), Texas (7 percent), New Jersey (5 percent), and Illinois (5 percent).

Figure 3-8. Immigrants by Region of Birth, 1960–1999
(Immigrants in millions.)

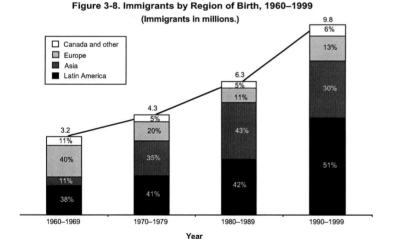

Source: © 2003 Population Reference Bureau. "Immigration: Shaping and Reshaping America," *Population Bulletin* 58, No. 2. Reprinted with permission.

---

[14] See George J. Borjas, "The New Economics of Immigration," Atlantic Monthly, November 1996.

[15] IRCA is an acronym for Immigration Reform and Control Act of 1986. This legislation legalized the immigration of approximately 3 million persons (roughly 1 percent of the U.S. population) who had entered the United States illegally or as temporary visitors after January 1, 1982. The size of the illegal population likely peaked in the mid-1980s, prior to the IRCA legalization program, declined for a few years, and now appears to be increasing again. One indication is the number of apprehensions of aliens. The number of apprehensions (arrests of aliens who are in violation of immigration law), which had peaked in the 1980s prior to IRCA and which then declined sharply after IRCA, began to increase again in the 1990s. Apprehensions totaled about 1.3 million in 1993, the country of origin of 96 percent of whom was Mexico. The law also created sanctions against employers for hiring illegal aliens not authorized to work in the United States. For further discussion, see Michael Fix and Jeffrey S. Passel, *Immigration and Immigrants* (Washington, DC: The Urban Institute, 1994) and Immigration and Naturalization Service, *1994 Statistical Yearbook*, as well as the yearbook for various other years.

[16] See Philip Martin and Elizabeth Miidgley, "Immigration: Shaping and Reshaping America," *Population Bulletin* 58, No. 2 (Washington, DC: Population Reference Bureau, 2003).

It is important to note that many persons legally enter the United States each year who are not immediately enumerated as "immigrants" in official statistics, despite the fact that many end up staying in the United States permanently. Some "classes" of persons can "adjust" to permanent status (and are thus counted as immigrants) after being in the United States for 1 year (e.g., people granted asylum or refugee status). Such persons are counted as "immigrants" only after they take this adjustment step even though they may have been in the United States for several years. During the 1990s, a major category of non-immigrant entry was the H-1B visas, permitting employers to bring in workers (or to keep workers already here) to meet employment needs which cannot be met by American citizens. Most of these jobs are technical in nature and require at least a bachelor's degree. Almost 1 million people entered the United States as temporary foreign workers in 2001.

ILLEGAL IMMIGRATION

The term "illegals" conjures up notions of undocumented (that is, without visa or other permit to enter the United States) people sneaking across the Rio Grande at night, carrying their belongings in a sack over their heads. In fact, the majority of illegal immigrants enter the United States legally and simply overstay their visit when their visas expire. Immigrants most often enter the United States as students, visitors, or temporary workers: in 1994, over 20 million people were admitted to the U.S. on a temporary basis, 17 million as visitors and, about 3 million on business. Such people represent about 60 percent of undocumented immigrants. Nevertheless, the size of the illegal immigrant population,

estimated to be somewhere in the 7 million to 9 million range in 2000 by the Census Bureau, is a significant figure (around 3 percent of the resident population) not only because of its size and the geographic concentration of undocumented people in a few states, with something on the order of half concentrated in California, but also because of the concentration of source countries, the majority coming from Mexico and Central America (over 60 percent).

EMIGRATION

Not all immigrants stay in the United States. In fact, at some times in our history (for example, during the 1930s depression era), more persons left the United States to live in another country than entered the United States. Since World War II, however, the ratio of emigrants (people leaving the country) to immigrants (people entering the country to live) has been about one to four; that is, one person left for every four who entered the United States. During the 1980s, for example, about 7.3 million people immigrated to the United States, while 1.6 million left for another country, leaving a net immigration figure of 5.7 million people. The countries receiving the largest numbers of emigrants from the United States were Mexico, the country to which nearly one of four émigrés returned during the 1980s, followed by the United Kingdom and Germany.

NATURALIZATION

Between 1907 and 2001, almost 22 million Americans achieved citizenship status through the naturalization system. Surprisingly, the greatest numbers were not in the early part of the twentieth century, when hundreds of thousands of Europeans immigrated to the United States before federal law

curtailed immigration in 1924. The greatest numeric number of naturalizations in a decade was in 1991–2000, when 7.4 million people became citizens.

In 2002, with 573,708 naturalizations, over 40 percent of new citizens came originally from Asia; the leading country was Vietnam, followed closely by China, India, and the Philippines. However, the single largest sending country was Mexico, representing 13 percent of all naturalizations. The new citizens' leading state of residence was California (26 percent of 2002s naturalizations), followed by New York, Florida, Texas, and Illinois.[17]

FOREIGN BORN

The net result of the events described above was that 11 percent of the U.S. population enumerated in the 2000 census was foreign born. Of these 31,107,889 people, about 42 percent entered the country during the 1990s. About 40 percent of them were naturalized citizens, while 60 percent were not (including all of the people who immigrated in the second half of the decade). The majority, 52 percent, of the foreign born came from Latin America; most of this population is Mexican in origin. Another 26 percent came from Asia and 16 percent from Europe. The remainder immigrated from Africa, Oceania, or North America (primarily Canada).

LANGUAGE SPOKEN IN HOME AND ANCESTRY

Among the total population age 5 years and over, 18 percent speak a language other than English in the home. Note that this figure is higher than the number of foreign born, because children who are born in the U.S. to immigrants are likely to speak their parent's native

[17] Immigration and Naturalization Services, *Statistical Yearbook*. These naturalization data are included in the 1999 edition, available at <http://www.ins.usdoj.gov/graphics/aboutins/statistics/ybpage.htm>.

tongue. However, more than half of the 47 million people who speak a language other than English in their homes also speak English "very well." This leaves 21 million, or about 8 percent of the population, unable to speak English very well. Some of these people live in households where someone speaks English well, others are linguistically isolated. The leading language spoken, as we would expect, is Spanish, accounting for over half of the people in this group. Other Indo-European languages (including Russian), and Asian languages account for most of the rest.

The ancestry question on the census is designed to determine the respondent's national origin, regardless of how long the person and his or her ancestors have been in the United States. The leading countries of origin are the traditional European sending countries of the nineteenth and early twentieth century: Germany, England, and Ireland. Seven percent of respondents indicated an ancestry of "United States" or "American;" many African-Americans respond this way. Russian is the largest Eastern European category at about 2.6 million. About 1.2 million responses indicated one or more of the predominantly Muslim Middle-Eastern, or "Arab," countries.

FOR FURTHER INFORMATION SEE:

2002 Statistical Yearbook of the Immigration and Naturalization Service. Washington, DC: Office of Immigration Statistics, Bureau of Citizenship and Immigration Services, Department of Homeland Security, available on the Internet at <www.immigration.gov/graphics/shared/aboutus/statistics/ybpage.htm>.

Annie E. Casey Foundation, *2002 Kids Count Data Book*, Baltimore, 2002.

————, *2002 Kids Count Pocket Guide*, Baltimore, 2002.

————, *Children At Risk: State Trends 1990–2000, A First Look at Census 2000 Supplementary Survey Data*, a PRB//KIDS COUNT Special Report, Baltimore, 2002.

Dacquel, Laarni T., and Donald C. Dahmann. *Residents of Farms and Rural Areas: 1991*. Current Population Reports, Series P-20, No. 472. Washington, DC: U.S. Department of Agriculture, Economic Research Service, and U.S. Census Bureau joint report.

Fix, Michael, and Jeffrey S. Passel. *Immigration and Immigrants*. Washington, DC: The Urban Institute, 1994.

Fix, Michael, and Jeffrey S. Passel. "U.S. Immigration at the Beginning of the 21st Century," testimony prepared for the Subcommittee on Immigration and Claims, Committee on the Judiciary, U.S. House of Representatives, August 2, 2001.

Fast Facts and Figures About Social Security, Social Security Administration, Office of Policy, Office of Research, Evaluation and Statistics, August 2000.

Income of the Aged Chartbook: 2000, Social Security Administration, Office of Policy, Office of Research, Evaluation and Statistics, April 2002.

Income of the Population 55 and Older, Social Security Administration, Office of Policy, Office of Research, Evaluation and Statistics, February 2002.

Martin, Philip, and Elizabeth Midgley, "Immigration: Shaping and Reshaping America," *Population Bulletin* 58, No. 2. Washington, DC: Population Reference Bureau, 2003.

Older Americans 2000: Key Indicators of Well-Being, Federal Interagency Forum on Aging Related Statistics. Contact: Kristen Robinson, Ph.D., Staff Director, 6525 Belcrest Rd, Rm 790, Hyattsville, MD 20782.

U.S. Census Bureau, Census *2000 Supplementary Survey*, Public Use Microdata Sample file.

Zedlewski, Sheila R., and Roberta O. Barnes, *et al.*, *The Needs of the Elderly in the 21st Century*, Washington, Urban Institute Press, 1990.

WEB SITES:

Economic Research Service: <www.ers.usda.gov>.

Federal Interagency Forum on Aging Related Statistics: <www.agingstats.gov>.

National Agricultural Statistics Service: <www.nass.usda.gov>.

Office of Immigration Statistics: <www.immigration.gov>.

Population Reference Bureau: <www.prb.org>.

Social Security Administration: <www.ssa.gov/policy>.

U.S. Census Bureau: <www.census.gov> or <factfinder.census.gov>.

Chapter 4
Labor Force and Job Characteristics

INTRODUCTION

Statistics about people working and looking for work are critical indicators of the nation's economic standing and the socio-economic conditions of its population. Employment is essential in providing the means through which most persons satisfy their and their families' material requirements as well as, at least in many cases, their own psychic needs.

The first statistic in this category is the *Labor Force*, defined as the number of people who are employed plus the number who are looking for work. The second statistic, the *Unemployment Rate*, is defined as the percentage of the labor force that is not employed and is looking for work. The lower the unemployment rate, the more healthy the economy.

LABOR FORCE GROWTH

The United States' labor force has expanded at a remarkable pace in recent decades. In 2002, about 145 million Americans were in the labor force, 62 million more than in 1970. This impressive expansion is mainly explained by two factors: the growth of the population of working age (16 and over), and women's sustained increase in labor force participation. While men have slightly reduced their participation in the labor force in recent decades, by retiring earlier in their lives than in the past as well as by living longer after retirement, women have continued to increase their job market roles. (See Table 4-1 and Figure 4-1.)

The increase in the population of working age is explained by all of the factors affecting population growth: the baby boom following World War II, lengthening life span, and immigration. People are also more likely to remain in the labor force (even for part time work) after the "normal" retirement age of 65, partly to supplement retirement

incomes and partly because better health permits more activity. The number of people age 65 and over who are part of the civilian labor force increased from 2.8 million in 1985 to 4.5 million in 2002. Even among people 75 and over, about 800,000, or 5 percent of this age group, is still in the labor force.

The proportion of the female population 16 years and over that was either working or actively looking for work increased from 39.3 percent in 1965 to 59.2 percent in 2002. This sharp rise in work activity, combined with the increase in the female population, has more than doubled the number of American women in the labor force in the last third of the century, taking

Table 4-1. Population and Labor Force Growth, Selected Years, 1950–2002

(Number in thousands, percent.)

Year	Civilian non-institutional population [1]	Civilian labor force	Labor force participation rate
Both Sexes			
1950	104 995	62 208	59.2
1960	117 245	69 628	59.4
1970	137 085	82 771	60.4
1980	167 745	106 940	63.8
1990	189 164	125 840	66.5
2000	212 577	142 583	67.1
2002	217 570	144 863	66.6
Men			
1950	50 725	43 819	86.4
1960	55 662	46 388	83.3
1970	64 304	51 228	79.7
1980	79 398	61 453	77.4
1990	90 377	69 011	76.4
2000	101 964	76 280	74.8
2002	104 585	77 500	74.1
Women			
1950	54 270	18 389	33.9
1960	61 582	23 240	37.7
1970	72 782	31 543	43.3
1980	88 348	45 487	51.5
1990	98 787	56 829	57.5
2000	110 613	66 303	59.9
2002	112 985	67 363	59.6

Source: U.S. Bureau of Labor Statistics.
[1] 16 years and over.

Figure 4-1. Labor Force Participation Rate in the United States, 1950–2002

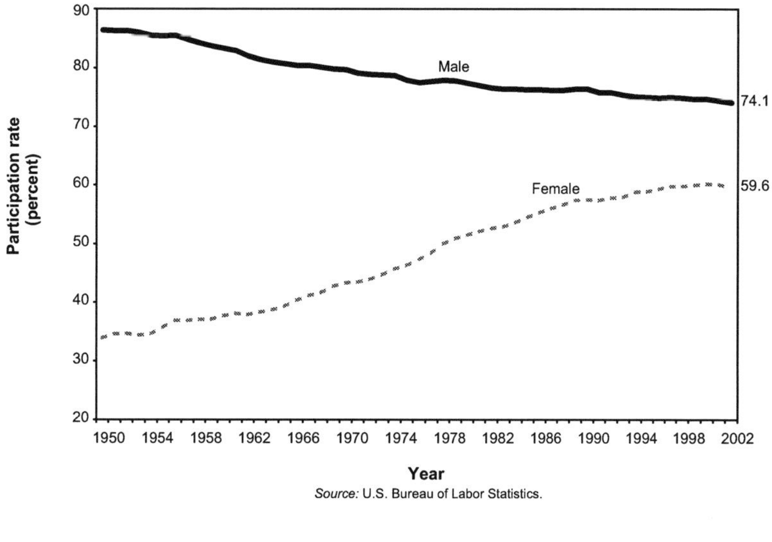

Source: U.S. Bureau of Labor Statistics.

it from 26.2 million in 1965 to 67.4 million in 2002.

Of course, owing to the rapid growth of their population, the number of men in the labor force increased as well over this period, from 48.2 million in 1965 to 77.5 million in 2002. This increase occurred despite the slow down-drift in the rate of labor force participation among men.

The sustained and very strong increase in the rate of labor force participation among women over the past third of a century has more than offset the slight decline among men, resulting in a rise in the rate of labor force participation among all persons from 61.2 percent in 1965 to 66.6 percent in 2002. All of these figures were slightly higher in the late 1990s, but declined between 2000 and 2002 because the economy was weaker. When jobs are hard to find, a larger proportion of people stop looking for them.

Why People Aren't Working

Most of the 73 million people who aren't working or looking for work do not want a job. This group includes retirees—including older women who were never in the labor force, people staying home to raise children, and students. Only 18 million people in this group are age 25 to 54, the prime working age years. Almost two-thirds are women.

There were, however, about 4.7 million people in 2002 who wanted a job but did not have one and were not actively seeking work. Of these, 1.3 million are available to work. One-quarter of them are discouraged—they believe that no work is available, that they lack the necessary skills or training, or that they are the wrong age. The remainder cite family responsibilities, being in school or training, being in ill health, having a disability, or some other reason for not looking for work even though they would accept a job if one were offered.

Table 4-2. Number of Children Under 6 Years by Type of Family and Labor Force Status of Mother, 2000

(Number in thousands, percent.)

Characteristic	Number (thousands)	Percent distribution
All children under 6 years	21 834	100.0
Mother in labor force	12 148	55.6
Children in married-couple families	15 772	100.0
Mother in labor force	8 931	56.6
Children in families maintained by women	4 608	100.0
Mother in labor force	3 217	69.8
Children in families maintained by men	1 453	100.0
Mother in labor force	0	0.0

Source: U.S. Census Bureau.

Table 4-3. Families by Presence and Relationship of Employed Members and Family Type, 1993 and 2002

(Number in thousands, percent distribution.)

Characteristic	1993		2002	
	Number (thousands)	Percent distribution	Number (thousands)	Percent distribution
Married-Couple Family	53 248	100.0	56 280	100.0
No earners	7 281	13.7	9 303	16.5
Husband, not wife	10 832	20.3	11 174	19.9
Wife, not husband	3 184	6.0	3 613	6.4
Husband and wife	31 266	58.7	28 873	51.3
Other earners only	685	1.3	3 317	5.9
Family Maintained By Woman [1]	11 087	100.0	13 215	100.0
No earners	2 607	23.5	3 047	23.1
Householder is earner	7 080	63.9	8 503	64.4
Other earners only	1 399	12.6	1 666	12.6
Family Maintained By Man [1]	2 859	100.0	4 674	100.0
No earners	312	10.9	698	14.9
Householder is earner	2 227	77.9	3 379	72.3
Other earners only	319	11.2	598	12.8

Source: U.S. Bureau of Labor Statistics. Division of Labor Force Statistics.
Note: Detail may not sum to totals due to rounding.
[1]No spouse present.

Table 4-4. Employed Persons 16 Years and Over, by Sex, Selected Years, 1950–2002

(Number in thousands, percent.)

Year	Employed (thousands)	Employed as percent of population
Both Sexes		
1950	58 918	56.1
1960	65 778	56.1
1970	78 678	57.4
1980	99 303	59.2
1990	118 793	62.8
2000	136 891	64.4
2002	136 485	62.7
Men		
1950	41 578	82.0
1960	43 904	78.9
1970	48 990	76.2
1980	57 186	72.0
1990	65 104	72.0
2000	73 305	71.9
2002	72 903	69.7
Women		
1950	17 340	32.0
1960	21 874	35.5
1970	29 688	40.8
1980	42 117	47.7
1990	53 689	54.3
2000	63 586	57.5
2002	63 582	56.3

Source: U.S. Bureau of Labor Statistics.

MOTHERS IN THE LABOR FORCE

One factor in the increasing labor force participation rate for women is their attachment to jobs. Relative to the past, women are marrying at later ages, and, on average, they are postponing having children to later ages. In addition, mothers of young children no longer tend to leave the job market. As shown in Table 4-2, about 56 percent of all children under 6 years of age had a mother who was either employed or looking for work in 2000. The figure for families maintained by women, without a spouse, was even higher at nearly 70 percent.

As shown in Table 4-3, there have been some significant changes in these patterns over the past few years. Between 1993 and 2002, the proportion of married-couple families where only the husband worked dropped slightly, while the proportion of married couples where both husband and wife worked increased. The patterns for families maintained by men or by women, without spouses, show little change.

The fact that women have developed ever stronger attachment to their jobs, with many having also attained relatively high-paying positions, may be one of the driving forces leading to the slight but persistent decline in the labor force participation among men of prime working age. For men 35 to 44, for example, the participation rate has declined from 80.7 percent in 1965 to 74.7 percent in 2000. While the slow downdrift in the labor force participation among these men may be largely attributable to other factors (such as an easing of the rules allowing those with some disability to cease working), some men have, no doubt, assumed the role

of homemakers, while their wives have assumed the role of the primary family earner.

TRENDS IN UNEMPLOYMENT

Throughout the 1990s, with the American economy continuing to expand vigorously, the ranks of the unemployed—persons without a job who were actively looking for work—continued to shrink. The proportion of the labor force that was unemployed had dropped to only 4.0 percent in 2000. By contrast, the unemployment rate had generally been much higher during most of the preceding quarter of a century, having approached 10 percent in the early 1980s.

The official government definition of "employed" and "unemployed" tends to measure the low range of an unemployment rate. A person age 16 or older is considered employed if he or she did any work at all for pay or profit during the week for which the data are collected. This includes part-time and occasional work such as lawn care, snow-shoveling, and baby-sitting. People are also considered employed when they are on vaca-

tion, out of work because of illness, on leave, involved in a labor strike, or prevented from working because of bad weather. To be counted as unemployed, a person 16 or older has to not have a job, have actively looked for work during the past four weeks, and be available for work, or be on layoff from a job to which they expect to be called back. People who only look at want-ads are considered out of the labor force rather than unemployed.[1]

Of course, unemployment is a highly cyclical phenomenon, rising sharply when economic growth slackens and dropping quickly as the economy recovers its productive rhythm. This largely explains the fluctuations in the unemployment rate as shown in Figure 4-2. In 2001, a new recession emerged. The unemployment rate rose all year, reaching 5.7 percent in November, and the annual average rate for 2002 was 5.8 percent.

Some population groups are much more likely to encounter unemployment than are other groups. Teenagers, who may be looking for their first regular jobs, or who may merely look for

Figure 4-2. Unemployment Rate, 1950–2002

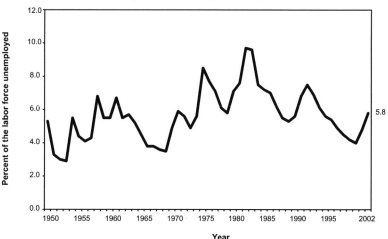

Source: U.S. Bureau of Labor Statistics.

[1] Bureau of Labor Statistics, "How the Government Measures Unemployment," at <www.bls.gov/cps/cps_htgm.htm>. Note that the Current Population Survey (CPS) provides monthly estimates for all states, the District of Columbia, and the New York and Los Angeles metropolitan areas. The survey provides annual average estimates for some large cities and metropolitan areas; the data are published in the "Geographic Profile of Employment and Unemployment." All other local unemployment estimates are derived from the Local Area Unemployment Statistics (LAUS) program.

temporary jobs while studying and preparing for a career, have by far the highest rate of unemployment among the major population groups. In 2002, the teenage (16-19) unemployment rate averaged 16.5 percent. For adults, unemployment is still a serious problem but not as bad as for teenagers. As shown in Table 4-5, in 2002 the jobless rate averaged 5.3 percent for men 20 years of age and 5.8 percent for women in this age bracket.

The fact that jobless rates for adult men and women have recently been nearly equal is another reflection of the progress made by women in becoming a very large and relatively permanent portion of the nation's labor force. Only a few decades ago, by contrast, women were more likely to be considered as a "secondary" source of workers. Indeed, women were then much more likely than men to leave and reenter the labor force many times in response to changes in demand or in their family situations. Because women often alternate between being in the labor force and leaving, historically adult women had a generally higher unemployment rate than men. In 1970, for example, when unemployment averaged only 3.5 percent for men 20 years and over,

the rate for women in the same age group was 4.8 percent.

EMPLOYMENT STATUS OF BLACKS AND HISPANICS

Although the general labor market indicators for the United States performed particularly well in the 1990s, there are some groups of workers that continue to lag far behind the national averages. This is particularly the case for Black workers and, to a lesser extent, for those of Hispanic origin. The unemployment rates for these two groups, as well as for Whites, are shown in Table 4.6.

The substantial differential between the unemployment rates of White workers and those of Blacks and Hispanics has changed little over the past several decades. The percentage of Black workers trying to find a job has consistently run two to two-and-one-half times the comparable statistic for White workers. Persons of Hispanic origin, a group that has been growing rapidly in the United States, have generally experienced unemployment rates that are lower than those for Blacks but still much higher than those for Whites.

EXTENT OF WORK DURING THE YEAR

The statistics examined thus far relate to the employment and unemployment during a given year. These numbers, while very important, do not fully reflect the dynamics of labor force activity. Since many people work or look for work for only a part of the year, the total number with some labor force activity during a given year is usually much greater than is shown in

the averages for that year. For example, students may work or look for work only in the summer. Some people operate seasonal businesses. Some work only during busy retail seasons, such as December.

In 2001, while the average number of employed people was 136 million, the total number with at least some employment during the year was over 152 million. And while the average number of people looking for work during the year was 6.8 million and the year's average unemployment rate was 4.7 percent, the total number of people encountering some unemployment during the course of the year was 15.8 million, equaling 10.4 percent of all those with some labor force activity during the year. (See Table 4-7.) These significant differences show the impact of the labor market on individuals.

Of all the persons with a job during 2001, about 66 percent worked full time for the entire year. Another 14 percent also worked predominantly on a full-time basis, but not for the entire year. The remainder, about 20 percent, worked predominantly on a part-time basis for periods that varied from a few weeks to the entire year. As shown in Table 4-7, the numbers for 2000 and 2001 are almost the same. We expect that the 2002 numbers, when available, will show some changes as the economy worsened.

PERSONS WITH MORE THAN ONE JOB

Many American workers hold more than one job. In fact, nearly 8 million managed to hold two or more jobs simultaneously during 2000. These "multiple jobholders" accounted for 5.7 percent of the average number of employed persons for the year.

The reasons that workers cite for holding more than one job vary considerably. Financial necessity is usually cited by about two-fifths of such workers—specifically 37 percent in a special 1979 survey and

Table 4-5. Unemployment Rate, 2002

(Annual average rate.)

Characteristic	Unemployment rate
Total, all workers	5.8
Men, 20 years and over	5.3
Women, 20 years and over	5.1
Teenagers (both sexes), 16–19 years	16.5

Source: U.S. Bureau of Labor Statistics.

Table 4-6. Unemployment Rates, Selected Years, 1970–2002

(Annual average rate.)

Year	Total, all races	White	Black	Hispanic [1]
1970	4.9	4.5	. . .	. . .
1980	7.1	6.3	14.3	10.1
1990	5.6	4.8	11.4	8.2
2002	5.8	5.1	10.2	7.5

Source: U.S. Bureau of Labor Statistics.
[1] May be of any race.
. . . = Not available.

Table 4-7. Extent of Labor Force Activity, 2000 and 2001

(Number in thousands, percent.)

Characteristic	2000	2001
Extent Of Labor Force Activity		
Civilian noninstitutional population, 16 years and over	214 292	216 788
Total who worked or looked for work	152 417	152 300
Percent of the population	71.1	70.3
Total who worked during the year [1]	150 787	150 286
Percent of the population	70.4	69.3
Total with unemployment	13 401	15 834
Percent with unemployment	8.6	10
Percent Distribution By Extent Of Employment		
Total who worked during the year [1]	100.0	100.0
Full-time [2]	80.5	80.6
All year	66.7	66.3
Part of year [3]	13.7	14.3
Part-time [4]	19.5	19.4
All year	9.3	9.3
Part of year [3]	10.2	10.1

Source: U.S. Bureau of Labor Statistics.
[1] Time worked includes paid vacation and sick leave.
[2] Usually worked 35 hours or more per week.
[3] Worked less than 50 weeks.
[4] Usually worked 1 to 34 hours per week.

44 percent in a similar survey conducted in 1989. Other multiple job-holders cited a variety of nonfinancial motivators, such as getting experience in a new field or building up a "side business."

OCCUPATION, INDUSTRY, AND EDUCATION OF WORKERS

One of the most important changes that's taken place over time in the American economy is the shift from goods-producing jobs (manufacturing) to services-producing jobs. Over time, manufacturing has become much more efficient and "productive"—meaning that it takes fewer workers to create the same amount of goods to sell. At the same time, the "service sector" of the economy has grown tremendously. All of the jobs which support the technology we've become accustomed to having are service jobs. The health industry—doctors, hospitals, clinics, laboratories—has grown explosively.

These changes have, in turn, led to a re-ordering of the occupational landscape, with a rapid increase in white-collar and services occupations and a relative decline in the traditional blue-collar occupations. Most notable has been the increase in white-collar employment, particularly in managerial and professional occupa-

tions. At the same time, there has been a steady erosion in the proportion of workers in lower-skill jobs, particularly in the blue-collar sector.

Table 4-8 shows the distribution of workers among the various occupation and industry groups into which the economy is classified. In the occupation section, the first five categories (through administrative support) constitute what has been traditionally called the "White Collar" jobs. Service occupations are sometimes called

"Pink Collar," and the next two groups comprise the "Blue Collar" segment of the economy. High white collar occupations constituted about 30 percent of all jobs in 2000, as compared with 16 percent in 1989. These are the jobs that, generally, require at least some college and which are primarily located in the "service sector." Blue collar jobs, on the other hand, declined from 27 percent in 1989 to 24.5 percent in 2000. Administrative support jobs have also declined as a proportion of all jobs over this 11-year period.

Looking at industry, the manufacturing sector declined from 16.4 percent of all jobs in 1989 to 14.7 percent in 2000. This represents the continuation of a long trend; the comparable figure in 1980 was 22.5 percent, and 26.2 percent in 1970. The service sector, on the other hand, increased from 41.6 percent in 1989 to 42.8 percent in 2000. All other industry groups remained about the same for the 2 years.

Table 4-9 shows the relationship between education and occupation. Over three-quarters of the people holding professional specialty jobs report having 4 years of college. Many have more,

Table 4-8. Employment by Occupation and Industry, 1989 and 2000

(Number in thousands, percent.)

Group type	1989		2000	
	Number	Percent diotribution	Number	Percent distribution
Total	117 342	100.0	135 207	100.0
Occupation Group				
Executive, administrative and managerial	14 848	12.6	19 774	14.7
Professional specialty	15 550	13.3	21 113	15.7
Technicians and related support	3 645	3.1	4 385	3.2
Sales occupations	14 065	12.0	16 340	12.1
Administrative support, including clerical	18 416	15.6	18 717	13.8
Service occupations	15 556	13.3	18 278	13.5
Precision production, craft and repair (skilled workers)	13 818	11.8	14 882	11.0
Operators, fabricators and laborers	18 022	15.4	18 319	13.5
Farming, forestry and fishing	3 421	2.9	3 399	2.5
Industry Group				
Agriculture and mining	3 787	3.1	3 826	2.8
Construction	7 276	6.1	9 433	7.0
Durable goods manufacturing	11 385	9.5	12 168	9.0
Non-durable goods manufacturing	8 326	6.9	7 772	5.7
Transportation and public utilities	8 526	7.1	9 740	7.2
Wholesale trade	4 622	3.8	5 421	4.0
Retail trade	20 521	17.1	22 411	16.6
Finance, insurance and real estate	7 975	6.6	8 727	6.5
Professional services	28 365	23.6	32 784	24.3
Other services	13 694	11.4	16 911	12.5
Public administration	5 782	4.8	6 015	4.4

Source: U.S. Bureau of Labor Statistics.

Table 4-9. Education and Occupation, 1999

(Percent distribution.)

Occupation	Not a high school graduate	High school graduate only	Some college	College graduate or more
Total	100.0	100.0	100.0	100.0
Executive, administrative, and managerial	5.0	12.3	23.4	47.9
Professional specialty	1.1	2.6	8.4	29.8
Technicians and related support	0.5	2.3	5.5	2.4
Sales occupations	6.0	10.6	10.8	8.1
Administrative support, including clerical	5.0	16.9	18.2	4.9
Service occupations	24.7	16.1	11.4	2.5
Precision production, craft, and repair (skilled workers)	19.3	16.0	10.8	1.9
Operators, fabricators, and laborers	31.0	20.3	9.5	1.5
Farming, forestry, and fishing	7.4	2.6	1.6	0.6
Armed forces	0.0	0.3	0.7	0.4

Source: U.S. Bureau of Labor Statistics.

including physicians, dentists, attorneys, and judges. About half of the people in executive, administrative, and managerial positions completed 4 years of college, while another 29 percent have at least some college. The people in this category who do not have college educations are generally small business owners. In contrast, people without a high school diploma are a significant portion only of the service and blue collar occupation groups, but are a minority of those as well. Completion of high school and, increasingly, college education are becoming essential for jobs at all skill levels.

YEARS WITH CURRENT EMPLOYER

The average number of years that the typical worker has been with the same employer has changed little over the past two decades. For all workers 25 years of age and over—men and women combined—the median years with the current employer was 4.7, as reported in a 2000 survey, slightly lower than reported in previous "job tenure" surveys in 1983 and 1991. However, the stability of these "average" numbers masks important changes in tenure for some groups of workers, namely a general increase for women and a rather sharp and disturbing decline for men in the middle age groups and pre-retirement years.

When the job tenure numbers are broken down by sex, they show clearly that women are staying in their jobs longer and longer, whereas men have seen a rather sharp decline in the average number of years spent with the same employer. For men in the advanced age groups, this may be largely a reflection of the voluntary trend toward earlier retirement. The same cannot be said for the men in the middle age groups, who have also exhibited large declines in job tenure. For these men, there has been an obvious decline in job security, probably as the inevitable result of the "downsizing" of many American firms, which has forced many of them to restart their careers with new employers.

As the result of these developments, the traditional gap in average job tenure between men and women has shrunk significantly. Whereas in 1983 the median years of tenure in one's job were 5.9 for men 25 and over, but only 4.2 for women of the same age, the numbers for the two groups are much closer together. The February 2000 survey yielded a median job tenure of 5.0 years for men 25 and over and 4.4 years for women in the same age bracket.

Naturally, the job tenure numbers tend to increase with age. But they dip again for persons 65 and over, many of whom are evidently in post-retirement jobs of relatively short duration. It is interesting to note in this context that for workers 55 and over, the tenure numbers are now virtually the same for women as for men.

HOW AMERICANS TRAVEL TO THEIR JOBS

Most American workers drive alone to and from their jobs, and their tendency to do so has been increasing. Nearly three-fourths used this mode of transportation in 1990, up considerably from 1980; 2000 is only slightly higher than 1990. (See Table 4-11.) In contrast, the proportion riding with others or using public transportation has continued to shrink despite public and private efforts to

Table 4-10. Median Years with Current Employer, Selected Years, 1983–2000

(Years.)

Sex and age	January 1983	January 1991	February 1996	February 2000
Total				
25 years and over	5.0	4.8	4.7	4.7
25 to 34 years	3.0	2.9	2.7	2.6
35 to 44 years	5.2	5.4	5.0	4.8
45 to 54 years	9.5	8.9	8.1	8.2
55 to 64 years	12.2	11.1	10.1	10.0
65 years and over	9.6	8.1	7.8	9.5
Men				
25 years and over	5.9	5.4	4.9	5.0
25 to 34 years	3.2	3.1	2.8	2.7
35 to 44 years	7.3	6.5	5.5	5.4
45 to 54 years	12.8	11.2	9.4	9.5
55 to 64 years	15.3	13.4	11.2	10.2
65 years and over	8.3	7.0	7.1	9.1
Women				
25 years and over	4.2	4.3	4.4	4.4
25 to 34 years	2.8	2.7	2.5	2.5
35 to 44 years	4.1	4.5	4.5	4.3
45 to 54 years	6.3	6.7	7.2	7.3
55 to 64 years	9.8	9.9	9.6	9.9
65 years and over	10.1	9.5	8.7	9.7

Source: U.S. Bureau of Labor Statistics.

Table 4-11. Means of Transportation to Work, 1980, 1990, and 2000

(Percent.)

Means of travel to work	1980	1990	2000
Total	100.0	100.0	100.0
Car, truck, or van	84.1	86.5	87.5
Drove alone	64.4	73.2	76.3
Carpooled	19.7	13.4	11.2
Public transportation (including taxicab)	6.4	5.3	5.2
Walked	5.6	3.9	2.7
Other means	1.6	1.3	1.4
Worked at home	2.3	3.0	3.2

Source: 1980 Census, 1990 Census, and 2000 Census. U.S. Census Bureau.

Table 4-12. Travel Time to Work, 1990 and 2000

(Percent.)

Travel time to work (minutes)	1990	2000
Total, Working Away From Home	100.0	100.0
Less than 5 minutes	3.9	3.4
5–9 minutes	12.5	11.0
10–14 minutes	16.1	15.0
15–19 minutes	17.0	15.8
20–24 minutes	14.5	14.5
25–34 minutes	18.3	19.0
35–44 minutes	5.2	5.9
45–59 minutes	6.4	7.4
60–89 minutes	4.5	5.2
90 minutes or more	1.6	2.8

Source: 1990 Census and 2000 Census. U.S. Census Bureau.

reverse this trend (through the subsidizing fares, institution of special traffic lanes, and prioritized parking for car pools). Only 12 percent of the American workers carpooled in 2000, down from 20 percent in 1980, and there was also a further decline—to less than 5 percent—in the proportion of workers using public transportation. The small proportion of workers who walked to their jobs has declined consistently since 1980, while the proportion using other means (such as bicycles, motorcycles, etc.) also shrank between 1980 and 2000. The category of "worked at home," however, has grown over the past 20 years.

Average commuting time did not change much between 1980 and 2000. Census data show that the average (mean) travel time was about 24.3 minutes compared with 21.7 minutes in 1980. However, as Table 4-12 shows, there was a wide variation in

reported travel time: about 3 percent of the workers (excluding those working at home) reported it took them less than 5 minutes to reach their jobs. At the other extreme, about 8 percent of the workers surveyed had to travel in excess of 1 hour to reach their jobs.

UNION REPRESENTATION

American workers are less likely to belong to a union than they were in the past. While the extent of union membership differs significantly across the industrial spectrum, the proportion of all wage and salary workers[2] belonging to unions or employee associations similar to labor unions has declined from nearly a fourth in the late 1970s to only 13.2 percent in 2002. (see Table 4-13.) The proportional decline is related both to the rapid increase in employment in services-providing industries, where participation in the union movement has traditionally been very low, and to the decline or relative stagnation in employment in those goods-producing industries where union membership has historically been more prevalent.

The actual number of workers belonging to unions remained fairly stable, in absolute terms, during the 1990s, after declining rapidly in the 1980s. However, because total wage and salary employment has continued to increase rapidly, the proportion of workers belonging to unions has continued to shrink as a percentage of the total.

Table 4-13. Union or Association Members, Selected Years, 1977–2002

(Number in thousands, percent.)

Year	Total wage and salary employment (thousands)	Wage and salary employees who were union or employee association members (thousands)	Union or association members as a percent of wage and salary employment
1977	81 334	19 335	23.8
1980	87 480	20 095	23.0
1985	94 521	16 996	18.0
1990	109 905	16 740	16.1
1995	110 038	16 360	14.9
2001	122 482	16 837	13.4
2002	122 009	16 108	13.2

Source: Data from the Current Population Survey: May 1977–1980, U.S. Bureau of Labor Statistics, Annual Averages, 1983–2001. U.S. Census Bureau
Note: Data for 1985 may not be directly comparable with the data for 1977 and 1980 because of some survey changes. Furthermore, data beginning with 1995 also may not be strictly comparable with those for prior years.

---

[2] A "wage" worker is one who is usually paid by the hour, such as factory and service employees. A "salary" worker is usually paid a set annual or monthly amount. This category excludes workers who are self-employed or who work in a family-owned business.

Table 4-14. Nonfatal Occupational Injury and Illness Incidence Rate, 2001

(Rate per 100 full-time workers.)

Industry	Incidence rate
Private Industry	5.7
Agriculture, forestry, and fishing	7.3
Mining	4.0
Construction	7.9
Manufacturing	8.1
Durable goods	8.8
Nondurable goods	6.8
Transportation and public utilities	6.9
Wholesale and retail trade	5.6
Wholesale trade	5.3
Retail trade	5.7
Finance, insurance, and real estate	1.8
Services	4.6

Source: U.S. Bureau of Labor Statistics.

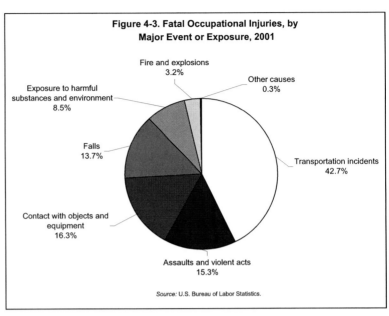

Figure 4-3. Fatal Occupational Injuries, by Major Event or Exposure, 2001

Fire and explosions 3.2%
Other causes 0.3%
Exposure to harmful substances and environment 8.5%
Falls 13.7%
Transportation incidents 42.7%
Contact with objects and equipment 16.3%
Assaults and violent acts 15.3%

Source: U.S. Bureau of Labor Statistics.

Occupation-Related Injuries, Illnesses, and Fatalities

Although, with advances in education, an increasing share of the American work force has moved to the white-collar field where the risk of injuries and work-related illnesses has traditionally been very low, millions of Americans still occupy jobs where such risk is relatively high. And, although relatively rare, fatalities stemming from work-related injuries are still a problem in certain fields of work.

Concern about the safety and health of American workers has increased significantly in recent decades, and employers in the United States are now responsible for reporting any injury or job-related illnesses among their employ-

ees. According to such reports, in 2001 there were 1.5 million nonfatal injuries and work-related illnesses among American workers which required either recuperation away from work or restriction of duties.

The major occupational group with the highest relative risk of injury is that which includes operators, fabricators, and laborers. These blue-collar workers are more than twice as likely as the average worker to sustain an injury or illness resulting in lost work days. Over half of the injuries occurred to workers aged 25 to 44. The relative risk of work-related injuries or illnesses is higher for

men than for women, particularly in the younger age groups (16 to 34). In the upper age groups, the risk is only slightly higher for men than for women.

There were 5,900 fatal work injuries during 2001, averaging about 16 for each day of the year.[3] Transportation incidents accounted for 41 percent of the total, but were responsible for most of the deaths in the transportation and material moving occupations, including truck drivers. Violent acts and assaults accounted for 15 percent. Farmers and other agricultural workers were especially at risk of dying from being struck by an object, while falls occurred disproportionately in the construction trades. Homicides were largely a white-collar phenomenon, except among taxi-drivers and chauffeurs.

The Retirement Years

Americans are spending more and more years in retirement. This is because their life span has increased considerably over the past century, while, at the same time, there has been a tendency to retire from their jobs at ever earlier ages. (Changes in Social Security law, designed to counteract this trend, begin to take effect in 2003).

Table 4-15. Employer Sponsorship and Coverage Rates of Pension Plans, 1999

(Percent.)

Type of employment	Employer sponsors a plan	Workers covered by plan
All Wage And Salary Workers	64	50
Full-time	69	57
Part-time	42	16
Private Workers	58	44
Full-time	64	51
Part-time	37	14
Public Sector Workers	90	77
Full-time	92	85
Part-time	78	32

Source: U.S. Bureau of Labor Statistics.

---

[3] These figures account only partly for the deaths that took place on September 11, 2001. In many cases, the Bureau of Labor Statistics could not obtain the information through its survey questionnaires because the businesses of the World Trade Center no longer existed there.

Table 4-16. Full-Time Employees Participating in Employee-Provided Benefit Programs, Selected Years, 1991–1998

(Percent, days.)

Benefit program	Medium and large private establishments				Small private establishments				State and local government			
	1991	1993	1995	1997	1990	1992	1994	1998	1990	1992	1994	1998
Paid holidays	99	96	91	89	84	82	82	80	74	75	73	73
Average days per year	9.8	9.4	9.4	9.3	9.5	9.2	7.5	7.6	13.6	14.2	11.5	11.4
Paid vacation	99	98	97	95	88	88	88	86	67	67	66	67
Paid sick leave	67	69	65	56	47	53	50	50	67	67	66	67
Medical care plans	97	90	82	76	69	71	66	64	93	90	87	86
Employee contribution required for:												
Health insurance for self	36	44	61	69	42	47	52	52	38	43	47	51
Health insurance for family	58	64	76	80	67	73	76	75	65	72	71	75
Life insurance	96	92	91	87	64	64	61	62	88	89	87	89

Source: U.S. Bureau of Labor Statistics.
Note: Small private establishments employ fewer than 100 workers. Medium and large private establishment employ 100 workers or more.

The result of these two crosscurrents has been a large increase in the number of years that the average worker expects to spend in retirement. For this reason, the eventual availability of retirement benefits—and the amount of those benefits—has become of importance to American workers.

Social Security benefits, under a government-sponsored program, have been available to most retired workers since about 1940, and the coverage of this program has been expanded significantly over the years, becoming gradually almost universal. For many retirees, however, the benefits available under this program have not been sufficient to maintain the desired living standards. To relieve this problem, additional retirement benefits pro-

vided through employer-specific or union-sponsored pension plans have become increasingly popular and their coverage has expanded significantly in recent decades.

For government workers—be it at the federal, state, or local level—employer-sponsored pension plans have long been prevalent. By 1999, 92 percent of full-time government workers had coverage. In the private sector, however, the proportion of workers covered by employer-specific or union-sponsored pension plans has been much lower. That proportion averaged about 50 percent from the 1970s to the early 1990s, but increased to 58 percent in 1999 among all workers and 64 percent for full-time workers. (See Table 4-15.) Pension sponsorship

is much more prevalent for workers covered by union contracts than for those without such protection.

However, working for an employer with a pension plan doesn't mean that all workers are covered. Some may opt out, while other workers may be too new to qualify for coverage or fail to meet other criteria. Private sector coverage rates—the proportion of workers actually covered by their employers' plans—were about 44 percent in 1999, rising to 51 percent for full-time workers but dropping to only 14 percent for part-time workers. As employers have shifted jobs from full-time status to part-time, overall coverage rates are dropping as well. Again, public sector workers fare better than

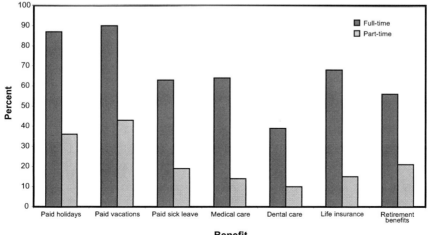

Figure 4-4. Percentage of Employees Participating in Selected Benefit, 1999

Source: U.S. Bureau of Labor Statistics.

those in the private sector.

There are essentially two broad categories of private-sector retirement plans: defined-benefit and defined-contribution. A defined-benefit plan obligates the employer (or union) to pay retirees an annuity at retirement age, with the amount based on a formula specified in the plan. Defined-contribution plans generally specify the amount of the employer contributions as well as what the employees may contribute, but not the actual benefits to be paid upon retirement, which will depend on the amount of funds available at the time. The amount of funds available will hinge largely on the success with which these funds are invested.

CURRENT EMPLOYEE BENEFITS

There is a range of benefits that full-time employees have come to expect, at least from larger employers. Table 4-16 shows the trends since 1991 for a variety of commonly offered items. Some benefits, such as paid holidays, paid vacation, medical insurance, and life insurance were nearly universal in 1991. Over the years, there has been attrition in the number of full-time employees receiving these "standard" benefits. Further, in the case of medical insurance, employees have increasingly been required to share the cost. In companies where cost-sharing was required—over two-thirds of employees were working in such companies—the

average monthly contribution was $39 for employee coverage only, and $130 for family coverage, in 1997. These figures have roughly quadrupled since data collection on cost-sharing began in 1983.

There is no reason to expect that this trend will not continue. The decrease in union membership, as a percentage of all workers, and the increasing pressures on employers to contain costs contribute to the problem. Data for the late 1990s, when available, may show a reversal due to tight labor markets, but as the economy weakens benefits are likely to decrease.

FOR FURTHER INFORMATION SEE:

Data on the labor force are produced by two federal agencies, the Bureau of Labor Statistics (BLS) and the Census Bureau. Decennial census data are generally published, or made available electronically, by the Census Bureau. Labor force data from the Current Population Survey (CPS) are more often published by BLS. Information on commuting is drawn from the decennial census. Data on pensions are produced by the Pension and Welfare Benefits Administration, another Department of Labor agency.

HARD COPY:

Jacobs, Eva E., ed. *Handbook of U.S. Labor Statistics*. Lanham, MD: Bernan Press, Fifth Edition, 2001.

Reich, Robert B. *The Work of Nations: Preparing Ourselves for 21st Century Capitalism*. New York: Vintage Books, 1992.

Spain, Daphne, and Suzanne M. Bianchi. *Balancing Act: Motherhood, Marriage, and Employment Among American Women*. New York: Russell Sage, 1996.

U.S. Department of Labor, Bureau of Labor Statistics. Employee Benefits Survey.

WEB SITES:

Pension and Welfare Benefits Administration: <www.dol.gov/pwba>.

U.S. Bureau of Labor Statistics: <www.bls.gov>.

U.S. Bureau of Transportation Statistics: <www.bts.gov>.

U.S. Census Bureau: <www.census.gov>.

Chapter 5
Housing

INTRODUCTION

Perhaps the earliest example of housing as a social indicator was the work of social reformer Jacob Riis, whose graphic descriptions (in 1890) of slum conditions in the United States led to passage of legislation to cure tenement ills. Since that time, there has been a considerable amount of study and legislation on all aspects of housing.[1] For the majority of householders, slum conditions are unknown today. The family's home is likely to be the largest expenditure they will make in a lifetime. Housing is the largest component of family budgets; for most owners, it is the best vehicle for accumulating wealth.

In 2000, the nation's housing inventory included almost 116 million homes, apartments, and mobile homes, more than double the number just 40 years earlier. Like population, the greatest increase in housing units is in the Sunbelt regions of the South and West. (See Table 5-1.) These two regions continue to increase their share of the housing stock at the expense of the Northeast and Midwest. These latter areas are growing as well, but at a slower rate.

The nation's 116 million housing units, enumerated in the 2000 census, included 105.5 million occupied units and about 10.4 million vacant units, of which about 4.5 million were part of the active housing market. The remaining units were held off the market for various reasons. Some are for seasonal, recreational or other occasional use or house migrant farm workers. Others are not marketable because of their condition or because their owner chooses not to place them on the market. (See Table 5-2.)

Americans like single-family homes. In 2000, about 94 percent of homeowners lived in single-family or mobile homes, while 34 percent of renters were in one-family units. There are substantial size differences in single-family owner and renter units. The typical single detached owner home is about 1,800 square feet, and the smaller renter unit is about 1,300 square feet. The typical owner-occupied unit has a lot size of about a third of an acre, while rental units are closer to a quarter of an acre.

HOMEOWNERSHIP

Since early in the twentieth century, public policy at various levels of government has encouraged both construction and ownership of the single-family home.

Homeownership has often been cited as a major part of the American Dream. However, that dream has been realized for the majority of Americans only in the past three decades, and significant gaps exist among household groups.

Measurement of homeownership in the United States began in the last decade of the nineteenth century, when a little under half of all households were occupied by their owners. As vast numbers of immigrants moved into mostly rented quarters in American cities, the homeowner rates slipped downward, to a low point of 46 percent in 1920. The boom times of the 1920s reversed that trend, but the

Table 5-1. Regional Distribution of Housing Units, 1990 and 2000

(Number in thousands, percent distribution.)

Region	1990		2000		Percent change, 1990 to 2000
	Housing units	Percent distribution	Housing units	Percent distribution	
United States, total	102 764	100.0	115 905	100.0	12.8
Northeast	20 811	20.3	22 180	19.1	6.6
Midwest	24 993	24.3	26 964	23.3	10.1
South	36 065	35.1	42 383	36.6	17.5
West	20 895	20.3	24 378	21.0	16.7

Source: U.S. Census Bureau. *Housing Characteristics: 2000.*

Table 5-2. Distribution of Housing Units by Occupancy/Vacancy Status, 2000

(Number in thousands, percent distribution.)

Unit type	Number (in thousands)	Percent distribution
All Housing Units	115 905	100.0
Occupied	105 480	91.0
Vacant	10 425	9.0
All Occupied Units	105 480	100.0
Owner-occupied	69 816	66.2
Renter-occupied	35 664	33.8
All Vacant Units	10 425	100.0
In the market:	4 521	43.4
For rent	2 615	25.1
For sale	1 204	11.6
Rented or sold, not occupied	702	6.7
Not in the market:	5 903	56.6
For seasonal, recreational, or occasional use	3 579	34.3
For migrant workers	25	0.2
Other vacant (boarded, not offered, etc.)	2 299	22.1

Source: U.S. Census Bureau. *Census 2000 Summary File 1 (SF 1) Tables H3 and H4.*

---

[1] See Fred Lewis, *Makers of the City* (Amherst: University of Massachusetts Press, 1990).

Figure 5-1. Percentage of Homeownership, 1900–2000

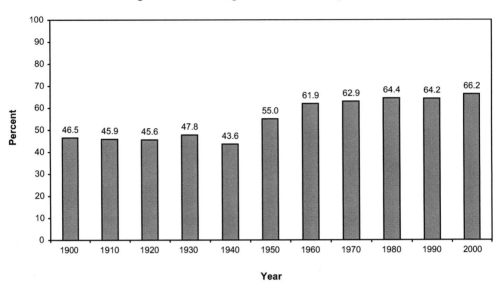

Source: U.S. Census Bureau.

disastrous effects of the Great Depression in the 1930s fell particularly hard on housing, where the 1940 census found only 44 percent of households owner-occupied.

The decades after World War II brought unprecedented growth in the homeowner rate. Between 1940 and 1950 the United States went from a nation of renters to one of homeowners. The 1950 census found 55 percent and the 1960 census found 62 percent of households owner-occupied. Rate increases in the two following decades showed slight gains: up 1 percent to 63 in 1970 and another 1 percent to 64 percent in 1980. (See Figure 5-1.) This apparently modest increase in the rate represented a net addition of 19 million new homeowners.

A small decline in the homeowner rate was recorded in the 1990 census. However, the pattern reversed itself again and increased for younger households in the 2000 census. Rates for older households declined slightly, perhaps because of the increased availability of congregate housing and assisted living facilities. This creates renter households among older persons who might otherwise be living with their children or in group housing facilities. (See Table 5-3.)

Table 5-3. Homeownership Rates by Age of Householder, Selected Years, 1980 to 2000

(Percent.)

Age	1980	1990	2000
15 to 24 years	22.1	17.1	17.9
25 to 34 years	51.6	45.3	45.6
35 to 44 years	71.2	66.2	66.2
45 to 64 years	77.3	77.3	76.9
65 years and over	70.1	75.2	78.1

Source: U.S. Census Bureau. 1980, 1990, and 2000 Censuses.

Table 5-4. Homeownership Rates by Race of Householder, Selected Years, 1980 to 2000

(Percent.)

Race/ethnicity	1980	1990	2000
White	67.8	68.2	71.3
Black	44.4	43.4	46.3
American Indian, Alaska Native	53.4	53.8	55.5
American and Pacific Islander	52.5	52.2	53.2
Other Race	36.9	36.1	40.5
Hispanic origin [1]	43.4	42.4	45.7

Source: U.S. Census Bureau. 1980, 1990, and 2000 Censuses.
[1] May be of any race.

INDICATORS OF HOUSING QUALITY

When Franklin Roosevelt stated in his second inaugural address in 1936 "I see one-third of a nation ill-housed, ill-clad, ill-nourished,"[2] little was known about the characteristics of the housing stock. Congress responded by authorizing housing questions in the 1940 census. That first comprehensive look at housing quality focused almost exclusively on physical aspects. Standard housing required complete plumbing and was required to be not in need of major repair (later termed not "dilapidated"). Thus, "substandard"

2 *Inaugural Addresses of the Presidents of the United States from George Washington 1789 to George Bush 1989*, Bicentennial Edition (Washington, DC: GPO, 1989), 277.

became lacking complete plumbing or dilapidated. However, interviewer ratings of structural conditions (sound, deteriorating, dilapidated) were dropped after the 1970 census when the census enumeration began to be done by mail, the use of complete plumbing continues. Figure 5-2 shows the dramatic drop in the incidence of lacking complete plumbing as a housing problem over the past 60 years. It is now, effectively, a non-issue.

The American Housing Survey, which is conducted through personal interviews, provides an opportunity for the enumerator to observe the characteristics of the house and the neighborhood in which it is located. The results from the 2001 survey are shown in Table 5-5. While housing structural deficiencies are relatively uncommon, occurring only about 5 percent of the time, problems with neighborhood characteristics such as streets, trash accumulation, and non-residential buildings occur much more often.

AGE OF HOUSING

In 1940, the median age of housing units in the United States was about 25 years, indicating that one-half were built before 1915. The median age dropped to 23

years in 1970 and 1980 after several decades of high residential construction rates, but in recent years has gradually moved upward until reaching nearly 30 years in 2000. Generally speaking, owner-occupied housing units are newer, by 4 years, than renter-occupied units. Elderly owner-occupied households tend to be older (with a median of 39 years), primarily because many elderly persons have lived in the same house for decades; they are also less likely to purchase a newly-built owner-occupied unit. Elderly renters, on the other hand, live in somewhat newer structures (median 28 years), probably because many apartment units designated for the elderly were built in the 1980s and 1990s.

CROWDING

Crowding, usually defined as more than one person per room, has been used as a housing quality measure at least since 1940. The 1940 census found that more than one-fifth of all households were crowded. Smaller household size and larger homes reduced the crowding rate to one-quarter that level (5.7 percent) by 2000. Renters were more likely to be living in crowded conditions than

owners (3.1 percent for owners; 11.0 for renters). These numbers represent an increase over 1990, however, since new immigrants are often poorly housed in crowded conditions.

RECENT QUALITY TRENDS

The American Housing Survey (formerly the Annual Housing Survey) became operational in 1973. It contains a number of housing quality indicators designed, in part, to replace items no longer collected after the 1970 census as part of the old substandard measure. These items include plumbing, heating, water and sewer systems, and service breakdowns, as well as upkeep and maintenance questions. When tabulated in different combinations, they are known variously as housing that is "inadequate," "with physical problems," "needing rehabilitation" or "substandard."

American Housing Survey interviewers observe certain conditions of neighborhoods. The number one problem, cited for about one-third of all housing units, is street repair. It is followed by street noise or traffic. Owner/renter status is not a significant factor in the recitation of individual problems, but overall, there are more problems

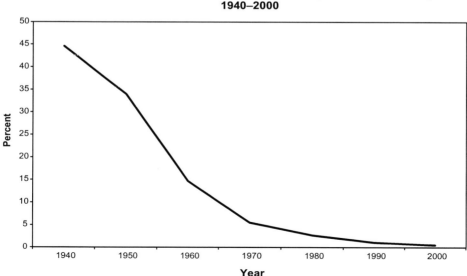

Figure 5-2. Percentage of Housing Units Lacking Complete Plumbing, 1940–2000

Source: U.S. Census Bureau.

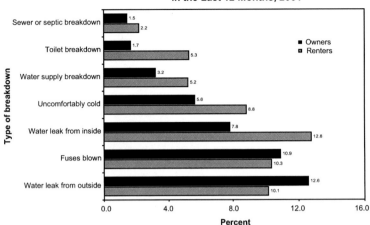

Figure 5-3. Percentage of Households with Breakdowns in the Last 12 Months, 2001

Source: U.S. Census Bureau. *American Housing Survey for the United States: 2001.*

in renters' neighborhoods than in owners'. The likely correlation is that neighborhoods occupied primarily by renters are often older and less affluent. (See Table 5-5.)

What do American families think of their homes and neighborhoods? When asked to rate their homes and neighborhoods on a scale of 1 to 10, with 1 being the worst and 10 the best, most of the persons questioned seemed satisfied with their housing conditions. In Table 5-6 for neighborhoods and Table 5-7 for housing, "worst" is a rating of 1, 2, or 3, and "best" is a rating of 8, 9, or 10. Owners rate both their homes and their neighborhoods higher than renters. It is important to note, however, that these ratings are subjective, and that people become accustomed to the character of the homes and neighborhoods in which they live. Research in Detroit in the 1970s indicated that respondents will indicate satisfaction with their homes and neighborhoods at a level far higher than that assigned by an independent observer.

Table 5-7 reports on indicators of quality in the respondent's housing. A fair number have one or more of the housing amenities listed, with porches or balconies being the most common. In terms of deficiencies, the most frequently mentioned problem is mice and/or rats. All of the negative qualities are cited more often by renters than by owners.

The American Housing Survey includes information on the frequency of breakdowns, or failures of the systems within the housing unit. Overall, about one household in 15 experienced some kind of system failure over a year's time. Figure 5-3 shows us that the most frequent problems were with water leaks, either from outside—more common with owners, or from inside—more common with renters. One household in nine experienced blown fuses or circuit breakers over a three month period, and a quarter of these experience this as a frequent, repeated problem. Renters were especially subject to heating failures, resulting in their being uncomfortably cold.[3]

HOUSEHOLD CHARACTERISTICS AND AMENITIES

The definitions of requirements and amenities have changed significantly over the past half-century. Questions about the availability of some household items (for example, electricity, lighting, and

Table 5-5. Enumerator Reported Housing and Neighborhood Quality Issues, 2001

(Percent.)

Characteristic	Total	Owner	Renter
Signs of rodents in the past three months	8.0	7.0	10.1
Holes in floors	1.1	0.8	1.8
Open holes or cracks in the interior	5.4	4.0	8.2
Broken plaster or peeling paint	2.5	1.8	4.2
Rooms without electric outlets	1.2	1.0	1.8
Streets need repairs	34.4	32.1	39.1
Accumulation of trash, litter, or junk	9.2	6.8	14.3
Commercial or institutional neighborhood	25.8	16.8	45.0
Industrial/factory neighborhood	3.5	2.4	6.0
Missing roofing material	3.9	3.4	4.9
Missing bricks, siding, outside wall material	3.0	2.3	4.3
Broken windows	4.3	3.6	6.0
Foundation crumbling or has open crack or hole	2.9	2.5	3.7

Source: U.S. Census Bureau. *American Housing Survey for the United States, 2001.*

Table 5-6. Indicators of Housing Quality, 2001

(Percent.)

Characteristic	Total	Owner	Renter
Overall Opinion of Own Building as a Place to Live			
Worst	1.6	0.7	3.5
Middle	27.0	20.9	39.9
Best	71.4	78.4	56.6
Median score (scale of 1 to 10)	8.3	8.5	7.3
Presence of Selected Amenities			
Porch, deck, balcony, or patio	83.6	90.6	68.7
Fireplace	33.0	43.0	11.8
Separate dining room	47.2	56.1	28.1
Garage or carport	60.7	74.4	31.7

Source: U.S. Census Bureau. *American Housing Survey for the United States, 2001.*

3 For a summary report on this topic, see U.S. Census Bureau, "Out of Order: 1999," Report AHB01/1, May 2001.

radios) have been dropped from the decennial census and other surveys because they are virtually universal in the United States. For example, in 1940 about 44 percent of households reported having a mechanical refrigerator. By 1995, more than 99 percent had the appliance, and there was no discernible difference among owners, renters, or various categories of household groups. Color televisions are similarly universal.

Most single family homes now have clothes washers and dryers, while only one in five multi-family units have these features. The presence of dishwashers, on the other hand, is more closely tied to the age of the structure, being found in only 30 percent of homes built before 1950, but in 77 percent of homes built since 1990. Other features, such as basements, are correlated with the section of the country. Basements are very common in the northeast and midwest, but quite rare in the south and west. The south and west have a higher proportion of mobile homes than the older portion of the country.

HEATING EQUIPMENT

The presence and type of heating equipment in the nation's homes has long been viewed as directly related to the health and safety of the occupants. In 1940, about 42 percent of occupied units did not have central heat; by 2001, this figure had been reduced to 11 percent. About 11 million households do not have central heat. Some of these, of course, are located in parts of the country where central heat really is not needed, for example Hawaii and South Florida, and, in fact, about 600,000 households have no heating equipment at all. Others, however, are in the mid-South where it often gets cold enough to need central heat, but where lower-value units occupied by poorer households do not have this amenity. In many cases,

unvented room heaters are used at substantial risk to the occupants.[4]

HOUSEHOLD ENERGY USE AND EXPENDITURES

Over the past 60 years, there have been enormous changes in the way families in the United States heat their homes. In 1940, three out of four households used the solid fuels, coal, and wood. By 2001, coal had virtually disappeared and the use of wood was down to 2 percent. Piped utility gas ("natural" gas), the use of which increased substantially after World War II with the extension of gas pipelines to suburban areas, was used by 50 percent of all households, while bottled gas is used by another 6 percent. (See Table 5-7.)

The development of more efficient reverse-cycle heating and cooling equipment, together with high population and housing growth in warmer areas of the country where the equipment is most effective, has resulted in a rapid increase in the number of households using electricity as the main house-heating fuel. In 2001, there were more than 30 million homes using electricity, nearly two-thirds of which were located in the South.

According to the Residential Energy Consumption Survey, conducted by the Energy Information Administration, the average U.S. household spent $1,488 on energy

in 2001. Almost half of this cost was for electricity to provide lighting and run appliances, while heating accounted for 30 percent. The remainder of the costs were for water heating and air conditioning.

There are differences in the type of space heating fuel used in different parts of the country, along with varying costs. Natural gas is used more heavily in the Midwest, while fuel oil remains an important heating source in the Northeast. Electric heating is most common in the South, but is also used by one-third of the households in the West. Of course, the southern portions of the west region (southern California, Arizona, and New Mexico) resemble the southern states in terms of their heating needs. The cost of heating is higher in the Northeast, than in the Midwest, apparently because natural gas is a less costly heating fuel than fuel oil.

HOUSING COSTS AND AFFORDABILITY

In recent years, the issue of affordability has begun to overshadow physical condition in discussions of housing quality. "Affordability," in this context, generally means the relationship of gross rent or homeowner cost to household income. The traditional view of household budget experts in the United States was that more than 25 percent of income spent for housing was

Table 5-7. Type of Household Heating Fuel, Selected Years, 1940–2001

(Percent.)

Heating fuel	1940	1960	1980	2001
All Households	100	100	100	100
Utility gas	11	43	53	50
LP gas	0	5	6	6
Electricity	0	2	18	32
Fuel oil, kerosene	10	32	18	9
Coal	55	12	1	2
Wood	23	4	3	7
Other, none	1	2	1	0

Source: U.S. Census Bureau. *1940, 1950, 1960, 1980 Census of Housing*, variously titled, and *American Housing Survey for the United States, 2001*.

4 American Housing Survey, 2001, Report H150/01.

Table 5-8. Energy Relevant Characteristics of Households by Census Region and Structure Type, 1997

(Number in millions, percent.)

Characteristic	Total	Census region				Type of housing unit		
		Northeast	Midwest	South	West	Single-family	Multi-family	Mobile homes
Number of households (millions)	107.0	20.3	24.5	38.9	23.3	73.7	26.5	6.8
Percent owner-occupied	67.9	64.0	71.4	72.2	60.5	85.8	14.7	83.8
Structure Type (Percent Distribution)								
Single-family	68.9	59.3	74.7	73.5	63.5			
Multi-family	24.8	37.5	20.4	18.1	29.3			
Mobile homes	6.4	3.2	5.0	10.0	7.2			
Homes With (Percent):								
Basement	36.6	61.5	61.0	20.3	16.4	48.0	NA	NA
Garage or carport	54.6	44.6	64.7	51.5	57.6	76.6	NA	28.4
Clothes washer	78.6	72.6	80.8	84.0	72.7	94.9	31.7	84.5
Clothes dryer	73.7	65.5	78.5	77.7	68.8	90.1	27.2	76.1
Personal computer	56.1	54.1	57.5	53.1	61.5	63.0	84.1	40.0

Source: Department of Energy. Energy Information Administration. *A Look at Residential Energy Consumption in 1997.*
NA = Not applicable.

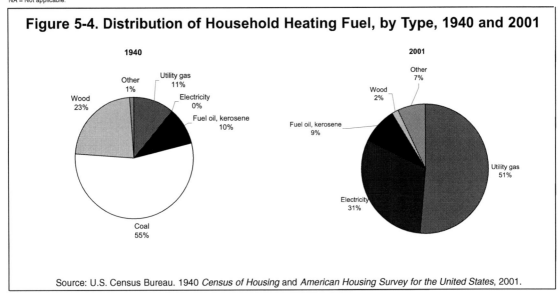

Figure 5-4. Distribution of Household Heating Fuel, by Type, 1940 and 2001

Source: U.S. Census Bureau. 1940 *Census of Housing* and *American Housing Survey for the United States*, 2001.

excessive and evidence of housing or affordability problems. That somewhat arbitrary standard has edged upward to the currently used 30 percent level. Most federal and local housing assistance programs require households to contribute 30 percent of their income toward rent. (Prior to 1981, the standard was 25 percent.) Eligible-income households that spend more than 50 percent of income for rent are considered to have "worst case needs" and have top priority for federal aid.

Data in earlier sections have suggested that there has been substantial improvement in the quality of the nation's housing stock. Despite the good economy of the 1990s, almost half of all households were paying more than 30 percent of their income for housing, while almost one-fourth were paying more than 50 percent. Part of the problem may be, however, that households have overextended themselves by contracting for more housing costs than they can really afford.

Discussions of shelter cost and relation to income for owners are couched in slightly different terms than for renters. A distinction must be made between mortgaged and non-mortgaged homes, because their cost structure is very different. For owners, the largest single component of shelter cost is principal and interest for mortgaged units. Moreover, there is the presumption of a greater range of housing choices for homeowners because of their substantially higher incomes. The median household income in 2001 for renters was $26,800, while the owner level was almost double at $50,500.

As shown in Figure 5-6, lower income households must purchase homes at prices five times their income, which in turn may produce mortgage payments (including taxes) that are much more than 30 percent of income. High income families, with median housing values at only 1.6 times their income, do not have this problem. It should be noted, however, that some subsidies may be available for the very low income families, which may make their houses more affordable. Figure 5-7 shows the same trend with a different statistic: median monthly housing costs. The less income the household has, the greater a proportion of it is spent on housing, even with the availability of subsidies.

Generally, renters have higher housing costs than owners, for nearly every house size. (See Figure 5-5.) Note that, except for the category with incomes under $5,000 annually, housing costs are very high for lower income households and decrease steadily as income increases. People with incomes under $5,000 are likely to live either in paid off homes or in subsidized facilities where the rent is tied to income.

Affordability can also be measured by taking into account home prices, incomes, interest rates, and other factors. For example, the National Association of Realtors calculates a composite Housing Affordability Index. (See Table 5-9.) When the index measures 100, a family earning the median income has the amount needed to purchase a median-priced home. In the spring of 2003, the index was 140.3, more than enough to purchase a home. The primary reason for the recent improvement in the Index is the historically low mortgage rates available in 2003.

The Census Bureau also issues estimates of affordability by including factors such as assets, cash on hand, and debt, in addition to price and interest rates.

However, the last report was for 1995 data, when about 56 percent of all families could afford a modestly priced house. Only 10 percent of renter families could afford the same house. A modestly priced house is priced at the 25th percentile of all owner-occupied homes in the geographic area. The ability to purchase a modestly priced house differs significantly by race and ethnicity and by whether a family currently owns or rents. Owner families are far more likely to be able to afford to relocate than renter families, and more White renter families can afford to purchase than minority renter families. (See Figure 5-8.)

HOME PURCHASE LENDING TRENDS

About 25 years ago, Congress passed a law known as the Home Mortgage Disclosure Act (HMDA). Its purpose is to monitor the home-related lending activities of financial institutions, so that the data can tell us whether or not individual banks and other institutions engage in discriminatory lending, or "red-lining." Originally applicable just to banks, the law was expanded several times to include

other forms of financial institutions such as credit unions and mortgage companies, and to cover applications for home improvement loans as well as primary mortgages. The Federal Financial Institutions Examination Council (FFIEC) was formed several years later for the purpose of aggregating and reporting the information which is reported under HMDA by the variety of financial institutions, each to their own oversight agency.

Overall, in 2002, the nearly 8,000 lenders covered by HMDA reported a total of 31 million loans and applications. Table 5-11 shows the results of these loan applications by income and the race or ethnicity of the applicant. As we would expect, all approval rates increase with income. However, the approval rates for Black applicants were consistently lower than for any other group listed, regardless of income. American Indians and Hispanics had the next lowest rates. Asians, on the other hand, have very high approval rates; the numbers are higher than those for Whites. These numbers show that the problem of discriminatory lending is still with us. The FFIEC data set permits analysis of the data at the

Figure 5-5. Median Monthly Housing Costs by Number of Rooms, 2001

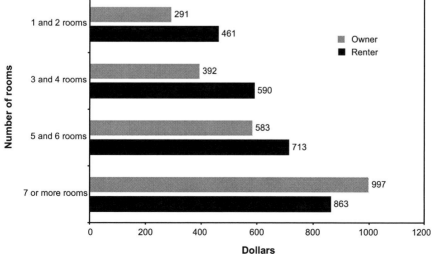

Source: U.S. Census Bureau. American Housing Survey for the United States: 2001.

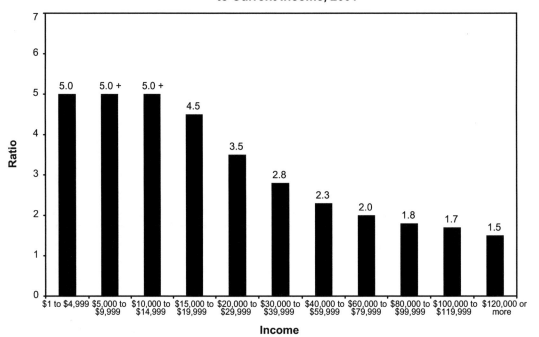

Figure 5-6. Median Ratio of Value of Owner-Occupied Units to Current Income, 2001

Source: U.S. Census Bureau. *American Housing Survey for the United States: 2001.*

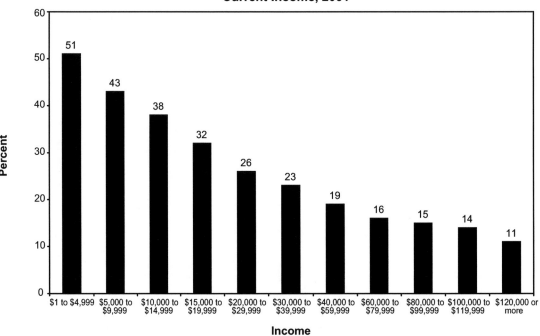

Figure 5-7. Median Monthly Housing Costs as Percent of Current Income, 2001

Source: U.S. Census Bureau. *American Housing Survey for the United States: 2001.*

Table 5-9. Composite Housing Affordability Index, 1991, 2000 and 2002

(Dollars, rate, index.)

Year	Median price existing single-family home	Mortgage interest rate	Median family income	Qualifying income	Composite affordability index
1991	$100 300	9.30	$35 939	$31 825	112.9
2000	139 000	8.03	50 732	39 264	129.2
2002	158 100	6.55	52 692	38 592	136.5

Source: National Association of Realtors.

Table 5-10. Home Loan Applications Approved, 2002

(Percent.)

Race/ethnicity	Income				
	Approved	Denied	Withdrawn	Other	Total
Race/ ethnic identity					
American Indian/ Alaskan Native	66.2	23.3	7.5	2.9	100.0
Asian/ Pacific Islander	80.1	9.8	7.7	2.0	100.0
Black	61.9	26.3	8.4	3.0	100.0
Hispanic	70.5	18.2	8.1	3.0	100.0
White	80.7	11.6	6.1	1.0	100.0
Other	76.3	11.8	8.6	3.0	100.0
Joint (white/ minority)	78.8	11.4	7.8	2.0	100.0
Income (percentage of metropolitan area median) [1]					
Less than 50,000	61.7	28.8	6.7	2.0	100.0
50,000–$79,000	74.2	16.5	6.7	2.0	100.0
$80,000–$99,000	78.5	12.3	6.8	2.0	100.0
$100,000–$119,000	80.4	10.3	7.0	2.0	100.0
$120,000 or more	82.6	8.0	7.2	2.0	100.0

Source: Federal Financial Institutions Examination Council (FFIEC), Nationwide Summary Statistcs for 2002 HMDS Data, Fact Sheet.
[1]Metropolitan area median is median family income of the metropolitan area in which the property related to the loan is located.

census tract level and for individual lending institutions.

NON-TRADITIONAL HOUSING

Not every U.S. resident lives in a household or a housing unit. In 2000, about 7.8 million people, or almost 3 percent of the U.S. population, lived in a group quarters facility. Group quarters are places where unrelated people live and eat together. Because they are not housing units, the decennial census collects no housing data for them, and they are not included in the American Housing Survey. Group quarters are classified in two main categories: institutional and non-institutional. Generally speaking, the difference is that institutionalized people are not free to come and go at will, whereas persons living in non-institutionalized group quarters have the same freedom as people living in housing units.

Table 5-12 shows the overall distribution of the group quarters by type of place. The largest single category is college dormitories, housing over 2 million in 2000; this includes everyone living in housing managed by the college or university. The other large specific categories are correctional institutions (almost 2 million) and nursing homes (1.7 million). Figure 5-9 shows the distribution by age and sex. Children under 18 account for a small proportion (about 4 percent) of the total group quarters population; most of them are in the "other" categories which include children's group homes, shelters for teenaged runaways, and the like. Among adults 18-64, college dormitories and correctional institutions account for most of the group quarters population; almost all of the adults in correctional institutions are men, while college dormitories are almost evenly split.

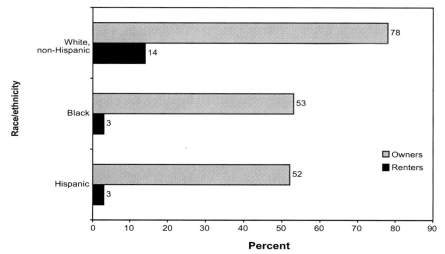

Figure 5-8. Percentage of Families Who Can Afford Modestly Priced Houses in Their Area, by Race, 1995

Source: U.S. Census Bureau. *Who Can Afford to Buy a House in 1995?* Current Housing Repots, Series H121991.

Military quarters account for a small proportion of this group quarters population, and again is primarily male. Among the elderly, over three-fourths of the group quarters population lives in nursing homes, with most of the remainder in a variety of non-institutionalized situations.

EMERGENCY AND TRANSITIONAL SHELTER POPULATION

This group, often called the Homeless, is composed of the population which does not live in conventional housing, whether housing units or group quarters. It is essentially impossible to enumerate everyone in this situation, because they have no addresses at which they can be definitively located. The 2000 census employed a variety of enumeration techniques intended to reach as much of this population as possible. On a single night, March 27, 2000, enumeration was conducted in facilities including emergency shelters, shelters with temporary lodging for children, shelters for abused women and their children, transitional shelters, and

Table 5-11. Group Quarters Population, 2000

(Number, percent.)

Characteristic	Population	Percent distribution
Total group quarters	7 778 633	
Under 18 years	322 911	100.0
Institutionalized population	158 118	49.0
Correctional institutions	21 130	6.5
Nursing homes	48	0.0
Other institutions	136 940	42.4
Non-institutionalized population	164 793	51.0
College dormitories (includes college quarters off campus)	10 528	3.3
Military quarters	2 260	0.7
Other non-institutional group quarters	152 005	47.1
18 to 64 years	5 462 101	100.0
Institutionalized population	2 259 845	41.4
Correctional institutions	1 939 007	35.5
Nursing homes	162 652	3.0
Other institutions	158 186	2.9
Non-institutionalized population	3 202 256	58.6
College dormitories (includes college quarters off campus)	2 053 495	37.6
Military quarters	352 889	6.5
Other non-institutional group quarters	795 872	14.6
65 years and over	1 993 621	100.0
Institutionalized population	1 641 076	82.3
Correctional institutions	15 882	0.8
Nursing homes	1 557 800	78.1
Other institutions	67 394	3.4
Non-institutionalized population	352 545	17.7
College dormitories (includes college quarters off campus)	105	0.0
Military quarters	6	0.0
Other non-institutional group quarters	352 434	17.7

Source: U.S. Census Bureau. Census 2000 Summary File 1 (SF 1) Table P38.

hotels/motels used to provide shelter for people without conventional housing. The next day, March 28, census enumerators counted people at soup kitchens and mobile food vans. Finally, on March 29, people in targeted non-sheltered outdoor locations were enumerated.

Nationwide, the total number of persons enumerated in emergency and transitional shelters in 2000 was 170,706. The Census Bureau is careful to note that this

tabulation "is not representative of, and should not be construed to be, the total population without conventional housing, nor is it representative of the entire population that could be defined as living in emergency and transitional shelters."[5]   However, while the total number enumerated may be too low, the demographic characteristics of the enumerated population should be considered representative of the people who do not live in conventional housing.

Blacks and Hispanics are over-represented in the Emergency and Transitional Shelter population as compared with their share of the total population in 2000. About one-quarter of this population are children. Two states, New York and California, account for more than one-third. These shelters are primarily located in cities, so that states with a larger urban population (as well as a larger total population) are likely to have more of them. Almost one in five homeless people enumerated nationwide (19 percent) was found in New York City. Other cities with large populations of this type include Los Angeles, Chicago, Boston, Cleveland, Philadelphia, and Seattle.

The National Coalition for the Homeless (NCH) says that there is

Table 5-12. Characteristics of the Population in Emergency or Transitional Shelters, 2000

(Numbers in thousands.)

Characteristic	Total	Percent distribution
United States	170 706	100.0
Race		
White alone	69 637	40.8
Black alone	69 046	40.4
American Indian and Alaska Native alone	4 092	2.4
Asian alone	3 922	2.3
Native Hawaiian and other Pacific Islander alone	489	0.3
Some other race alone	15 842	9.3
Two or more races	7 678	4.5
Hispanic or Latino (of any race)	34 013	19.9
White alone, not Hispanic or Latino	57 173	33.5
State		
New York	31 856	18.7
California	27 701	16.2
Texas	7 608	4.5
Florida	6 766	4.0
Illinois	6 378	3.7
Massachusetts	5 405	3.2
New Jersey	5 500	3.2
Pennsylvania	5 463	3.2
Washington	5 387	3.2
Ohio	5 224	3.1
All other states	63 418	37.1
Age		
Under 18 years	43 887	25.7
18 years and over	126 819	74.3

Source: U.S. Census Bureau. Smith, Annetta C. and Denise I. Smith, Census Special Reports, Series CENSR/01-2, *Emergency and Transitional Shelter Population: 2000*, U.S. Government Printing Office, Washington, DC, 2001.

5 U.S. Census Bureau, *Emergency and Transitional Shelter Population: 2000*, Report CENSR/01-2, October 2001.

no easy answer to the question, "how many homeless are there," and that the question itself is misleading. "In most cases, homelessness is a temporary circumstance—not a permanent condition. A more appropriate measure of the magnitude of homelessness is therefore the number of people who experience homelessness over time, not the number of "homeless people."[6] There is a difference between a "point-in-time" count, such as that determined by Census 2000, and an estimate of the number of people who are homeless over a given period of time (say, three months); this is referred to as a "period prevalence count." Many people are periodically homeless; they lose housing, and then find it, and then lose it again. For example, a man may live for awhile with his significant other, then be homeless, then his mother takes him in, then she tells him to leave, and so on. According to NCH, point-in-time counts overestimate the proportion of people who are chronically homeless, especially those who are mentally ill and/or substance abusers and who therefore have a much harder time finding permanent housing. In addition, any attempt to count the homeless will miss people because they can't be found or identified.

Several studies identified by NCH all estimate counts of the homeless at a much higher level than the 170,000 counted in the 2000 census. They also assert that homelessness is increasing, primarily because the number of shelter beds is growing. They emphasize, however, that the focus should be on ending homelessness rather than on knowing the precise number of homeless.

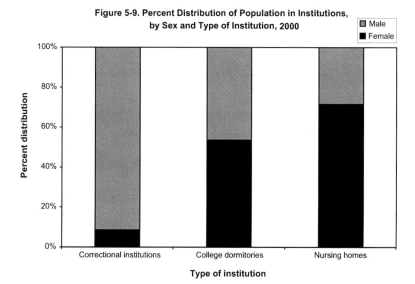

Figure 5-9. Percent Distribution of Population in Institutions, by Sex and Type of Institution, 2000

[6] National Coalition for the Homeless, "How Many People Experience Homelessness?, " NCH Fact Sheet #2, February 1999.

FOR FURTHER INFORMATION SEE:

The primary sources of housing data are the decennial census, the upcoming American Community Survey, and the American Housing Survey. All of these data sets and their reports are available at <www.census.gov> and/or <factfinder.census.gov>. Other Web sites with relevant data include:

Energy Information Administration: <www.eia.doe.gov>.

National Association of Realtors: <www.realtor.org>.

National Coalition for the Homeless: <www.nationalhomeless.org>.

U.S. Department of Housing and Urban Development: <www.hud.gov./ and <www.huduser.org>.

Chapter 6
Income, Wealth, and Poverty

INCOME

UNDERSTANDING INCOME STATISTICS

The term "income" refers to several different ways of measuring the money available to households, families, and individuals. The income of people who are working is better labeled "earnings." Earnings, or earned income, are only one of several sources of income to households and families. Others include self-employment income, social security, welfare, private pensions, income from investments, and child support.

In census terms, a household is defined as all the people who live in an occupied housing unit. A family is defined more narrowly, as two or more people related to each other and living in the same household. Thus, a one-person household (someone living alone) is not a family, nor is a household consisting entirely of unrelated individuals. A household can include two or more families, and can include both one or more families and one or more unrelated individuals.

HOUSEHOLD INCOME

As measured by the Census Bureau, the nationwide median household income in the year 2001 was $42,228. This means that half the households had income higher than this figure, and half had income that was lower. This value was slightly higher than the value for 2000, which was the highest level (in real terms, or inflation-adjusted) that had ever been recorded.

What types of households had higher incomes, and what types had lower? Demographic groups with higher median income levels, over $50,000 in 2001, included those headed by married-couple households, those with Asian and Pacific Islander householders, those with householders aged 35 to 54, and those located in suburban areas. Demographic groups with lower median income levels below $35,000 in 2001, included those where there was no family (primarily one-person households), those with a woman heading a

family, Black households, those headed by a very young person (under age 25), or by an elderly person (65 or over), and those located outside metropolitan areas. Table 6-1 shows the trends in median income for different educational attainment groups.

Comparing the 2001 data with comparable tabulations for 1993, the median income level increased for every group reported. Median income in real dollars in 1993 was at a low point, coming off of a difficult economic period in 1990–1991. The overall increase was almost 15 percent, from $36,700 in 1993 to $42,100 in 2000. These gains were especially large for Black households and for those headed by a foreign-born person.

Figure 6-1 shows the historic income pattern by race/ethnicity. The slope of increase rose sharply in the 1990s, much faster than it had in previous decades, but then dropped between 2000 and 2001. This statistic helps us to understand why the 1990s were such a prosperous decade, and how the economic downturn that began in 2001 has affected income.

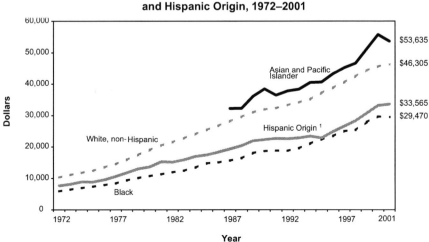

Figure 6-1. Median Household Income by Race and Hispanic Origin, 1972–2001

Asian and Pacific Islander — $53,635

White, non-Hispanic — $46,305

Hispanic Origin [1] — $33,565

Black — $29,470

Year

[1] May be of any race.

Source: U.S. Census Bureau. Income Surveys Branch.

Figure 6-2. Percent Share of Household Income and Mean Income by Quintile, Selected Years, 1970–2000

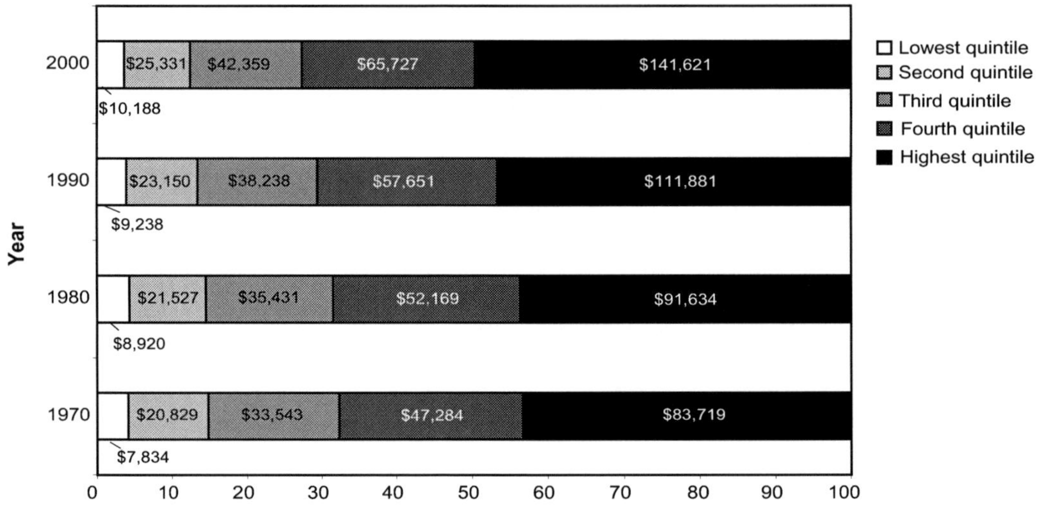

Source: U.S. Census Bureau. *Money Income in the United States: 2000.*

Note, however, that the differences by race/ethnic group remain constant even as the slope increases or decreases. Black households, as a group, still have the lowest income in the United States, with only two-thirds the income level of White households. Asian and Pacific Islander households are highest. This is partly due, however, to the average number of wage-earners in their households. When per capita income is calculated (by dividing the household income by the number of people in the household), White, and especially White non-Hispanic, households had the highest income levels.

INCOME INEQUALITY

Another trend was evident during the 1970–2000 period: that of increasing "income inequality." This tendency was not restricted to the United States; income inequality increased in the Organization for Economic Cooperation and Development (OECD) countries as well during this period. What does this often-used term mean and why is it important to persons in the United States? American society is firmly rooted in the belief in equality of opportunity. But that

does not mean that Americans believe in general that income should be equal regardless of skill, effort, and education (nor that certain segments of society—Blacks or women, for example—were not excluded from that belief). And at the same time, residents of the United States seem to hold the belief that differences in lifestyle between the poorest and the richest Americans should be diminishing over time, not increasing.

Similarly, Americans tend to believe that extremes of poverty, if not wealth, are somehow foreign to U.S. culture, despite the persistent appearance of both. Thus, for example, few would argue against the Chief Executive Officer (CEO) of a large company earning more than an assembly-line worker in one of the company plants. But, what is the appropriate ratio of their incomes? Should the CEO make 10 times that of the assembly-line worker, 50 or 100 times as much? And should that gap be increasing or diminishing, and under what conditions? A recent article indicated that the CEOs of many large corporations, including Lockheed Martin, Black and Decker, Fannie Mae, CSX, Gannett, and ExxonMobil earn

annual salary, bonus, and stock options ranging from $4 million to $24 million. Executive salaries of that magnitude range between 80 and 800 times the average income of U.S. workers in 1995. While some feel such income differences are obscene, there is no sign of revolution.

The Census Bureau uses two measures of income inequality. One is called the Gini index, also known as the index of income concentration. The index would be 0.0 if all households have equal shares of income. If one household had it all and the rest of the households had none, then the index would be 1.0. Thus, the lower the index figure, the more equal the distribution of income among households. In 2000, the Gini index was .460, a significant increase over the 1995 figure of .450. This index level did not change between 2000 and 2001.

Another way of measuring income inequality is to look at the differences between income levels at the top and at the bottom. This involves ranking households and then dividing the ranked list into quintiles—where one-fifth, or 20 percent of the households are in each. As Figure 6-2 shows, the proportion of income going to the top quintile has gradually increased over time, while the proportion going to the bottom two quintiles has gradually decreased. This signifies increasing income inequality. The lowest quintile has seen only a 30 percent increase in real income over the 30-year period (1970–2000), while the increase for the highest quintile is 69 percent. The second and third quintiles have even smaller increases than the lowest (22 percent and 26 percent, respectively). As it's often put, "the rich get richer and the poor get poorer."

There are a number of factors behind this trend. One of the most important is the increasing number of households with two earners, because both husband and wife are in the labor force. This has sharply increased the number of high income households. People subsisting only on government benefits (welfare and/or social security) have seen some increase in real income over the past 30 years. The minimum wage has increased, but not enough to pull the working poor up into what many call the middle class. The decrease in unionized manufacturing jobs and increase in hourly, part-time service sector jobs has had a severe impact on the earnings of workers with lesser amounts of education. The proportion of retiree households has increased, and these households generally have lower income than those with earners.

In fact, the lowest quintile is characterized by persons living alone (56 percent of households in the quintile), householders aged 65 and older (40 percent), and households with no earner (57 percent). In contrast, almost all of the households in the highest quintile are married-couple families (80 percent), households in the prime earning years of 35 to 54 (61 percent), and have two or more earners (75 percent).

NON-CASH INCOME

The discussion above has focused on money income alone. In recent years, the Census Bureau has conducted research on the effect of defining income in other ways. The most important factors here are government transfers. Income taxes and Social Security payroll taxes reduce income, while the earned income tax credit (EIC), employer-paid health insurance, and government subsidies increase income. The Census Bureau has created some 15 different measures of income, taking one or more of these factors into account.

The impact of using one or another of these definitions is measured by the changes in percentage difference between the official median income figure and the revised figure. For most types of households, these changes do not make a significant difference in the measurement of income, but do make a difference in their relative income as compared with other types of households. For example, using the official measure of income, elderly households have less than half the median income of households with children. When all the variations in income definition are included, the difference improves to 70 percent: $35,700 for elderly and $50,800 for families with children in 2000.

One household in five (20 percent) in the United States receives some form of non-cash benefit. Most of these households receive a means-tested benefit such as Temporary Assistance to Needy Families (TANF) and/or Supplementary Security Income (SSI). With that cash income comes access to non-cash benefits such as housing subsidies, food stamps, free or reduced school lunches, and/or Medicaid. Not surprisingly, the characteristics of households which are most likely to receive this type of income include central city residents, renters, householders under 25 years of age, households which include no earners and/or include disabled persons, and female-headed families with no husband present. About one-third of the nation's households with children receive one or more non-cash benefit.

TRENDS BY EDUCATIONAL LEVEL

Educational attainment appears to be playing an increasingly important role in determining income. (See Table 6-1.) Some education-level categories dropped between 1991 and 1995, which indicates that their income levels were not keeping up with inflation. However, the median income differences between poorly-educated households and well-educated households remained relatively constant. In all 3 years shown, those with professional degrees

Table 6-1. Trends in Household Median Income by Educational Attainment of Householder, Selected Years, 1991–2001

(Dollars.)

Educational attainment level	1991	1995	2001
Median income, householders 25 years and older	$31 032	$35 235	$43 592
Educational Attainment			
Less than 9th grade	13 221	15 043	18 120
9th to 12th grade, no diploma	17 535	18 298	23 251
High school graduate or GED	28 487	31 376	36 055
Some college, no degree	35 150	37 156	45 810
Associate degree	39 700	42 118	51 162
Bachelor's degree	48 705	52 857	67 165
Master's degree	55 173	64 960	78 902
Professional degree	77 949	82 010	100 000
Doctorate degree	70 316	80 005	92 806

Source: U.S. Census Bureau. Annual Demographic Survey.

(generally physicians, dentists, attorneys, and judges) had about six times the income than households where the householder had less than a ninth grade education.

We should note, however, that the number of households with poorly educated householders decreased during this 10-year period, from 9.3 million to 6.8 million for those with less than ninth grade education, and from 10.3 million to 9.4 million for those with some high school but no diploma; at the same time, the total number of households was increasing by about 10 percent. The losses in households at the low end of the education scale are more than balanced out by gains at the top end; households where the householder had a bachelor's degree or higher increased from 20.8 million to 28.5 million during the same period.

CHANGES IN INCOME OVER LIFETIME

Income level in the United States is not static. Thus, discussions about the poor or the rich in the 1970s versus the 1990s does not mean that those groups are composed of the same individuals at both time periods. There is considerable evidence of large annual as well as lifetime shifts in income level. Such life cycle events as leaving the parental home, graduating from college, getting one's first "real" job, marriage, divorce, disability, and retirement (not necessarily in that order) can have profound impact on income. Typically, income peaks in the ages between 45 to 54 and then begins to taper off (on average) as people begin to retire. But patterns vary by sex, for example, with women who are maintaining a family, due to divorce or death of a spouse, having reduced income compared with their previous status as a married-couple household.

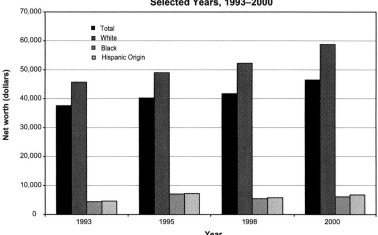

Figure 6-3. Median Net Worth of Families, by Race and Hispanic Origin, Selected Years, 1993–2000

Source: U.S. Census Bureau. *Household Wealth and Asset Ownership, 1993, 1995, 1998 and 2000.*

WEALTH

NET WORTH

Income is not the only influence on the economic well-being of an individual. Wealth is another factor. One often-used gauge of wealth is "net worth," defined as the value of assets (for example, equity in one's home, stocks, savings, and checking account balances) minus liabilities (for example, debt on credit cards). The median net worth for all U.S. households in 2000 was $55,000 a considerable increase from the 1995 level of

$40,600 (in 2000 dollars).

Households with very low income had a median net worth of about $6,650, while those in the highest income group had a median net worth of nearly $143,000. For White, non-Hispanic (also referred to as Anglo) households, median net worth in 2000 ($67,000) was about 10 times the median net worth of minority households in 2000 (about $6,200 for Blacks and $6,800 for Hispanics).

Since the passage of time offers increased opportunity to accumulate wealth, it is not surprising that net worth increases

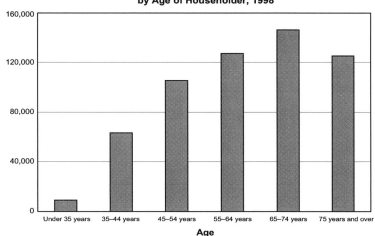

Figure 6-4. Median Net Worth of Families, by Age of Householder, 1998

Source: The Federal Reserve. *Federal Reserve Bulletin*, January 2000. Results from the *1998 Survey of Consumer Finances.*

with age of the householder, until retirement age. The median net worth of households in which the head was under 35 was only about $6,000 in 2000, but increased to $118,950 for householders in the 70 to 74 age group before beginning to taper off for older households. (See Figure 6-4.) As is the case with income, the net worth of married-couple households is typically more than either households maintained by a man or woman without benefit of a spouse in the household. Regardless of the age of householder, those maintained by a married couple typically have double the net worth of other household types. Households headed by a woman under age 35 had the lowest median net worth. Education is also strongly associated with wealth; the median net worth of households in which the householder was a college graduate ($108,900) was almost triple that for households in which the head had completed only high school ($40,000).

TYPES OF ASSETS

The nation's homeowners, who represent about 67 percent of households in the United States, had an average net worth of $231,500 in 2000, which was 10 times the net worth of households that rent (about $27,600). Among those homeowners, their home equity (its net value) was a substantial amount of their total net worth. The average equity position was about $87,600.

In the 1990s, families came to hold less of their financial assets in regular savings or checking accounts, while holding more in tax-deferred retirement accounts, publicly traded stocks, and mutual funds. (See Table 6-2.) By 1998, over three-quarters of families' financial assets were in such investments. Ownership of vehicles (including cars, trucks, and motorcycles as well as mobile

Table 6-2. Distribution of Net Worth by Asset Type, Selected Years, 1993–2000

(Percent distribution.)

Type of asset	1993 (1995 dollars)	1995 (1995 dollars)	1998 (2000 dollars)	2000 (2000 dollars)
All Assets	100.0	100.0	100.0	100.0
Interest-earning assets at financial	11.4	9.6	8.1	8.9
Other interest-earning assets	4.0	4.5	2.7	1.7
Regular checking accounts	0.5	0.6	0.4	0.3
Stocks and mutual fund shares	8.3	8.4	18.8	15.6
Own home	44.4	44.4	33.7	32.3
Rental property	6.7	6.2	4.5	3.7
Other real estate	4.6	4.3	3.2	3.6
Vehicles	6.4	8.3	4.4	3.7
Business or profession	6.4	5.6	7.3	7.7
U.S. savings bonds	0.8	0.8	0.6	0.5
IRA or Keogh accounts	6.7	8.3	7.0	8.6
401K and thrift savings plans	. . .	. . .	8.6	9.7
Other financial investments	3.0	2.8	2.6	1.6
Unsecured liabilities	. . .	-3.6	-3.4	-3.0

Source: U.S. Census Bureau. *Net Worth and Asset Ownership of Households: 1998 and 2000* and *Household Net Worth and Asset Ownership: 1995.*
Note: Because net worth is assets less liabilities, unsecured liabilities are subtracted from the distribution of net worth and are shown as negative.
. . . = not available.

Table 6-3. Families Holding Debt, by Type of Debt and Median Amount of Debt, 1998

(Percent, dollars.)

Type of debt	Percent with specified debt	Median amount (dollars)
Mortgage and home equity loans	43.1	$62 000
Other residential property	5.1	40 000
Installment loans	43.7	8 700
Other lines of credit	2.3	2 500
Credit card balances	44.1	1 700
Other debt	8.8	3 000
Any debt	74.1	33 000

Source: The Federal Reserve. *Federal Reserve Bulletin*, January 2000. Results from the *1998 Survey of Consumer Finances*.

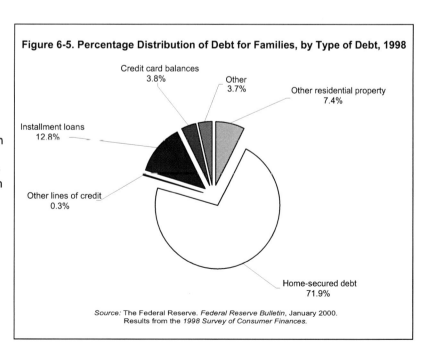

Figure 6-5. Percentage Distribution of Debt for Families, by Type of Debt, 1998

Credit card balances 3.8%
Other 3.7%
Other residential property 7.4%
Installment loans 12.8%
Other lines of credit 0.3%
Home-secured debt 71.9%

Source: The Federal Reserve. *Federal Reserve Bulletin*, January 2000. Results from the *1998 Survey of Consumer Finances*.

homes, boats, and airplanes) is one of the most commonly held non-financial assets—with 83 percent of households having one or more vehicles with a median value of $10,000. There has been a slight decrease in the tendency of families to own such assets, with an increased tendency for households to lease rather than buy their automobiles, particularly among higher-income households.

DEBT

The debt of the average household in 1998 represented about 14 percent of its assets. This fraction (known as the "leverage ratio") did not change much during the 1990s. Another gauge of debt, known as the "debt burden," is the ratio of total debt to total household income. The median debt burden decreased between 1989 and 1998, from 16.0 percent to 14.5 percent. The median debt for all households, including such debt as mortgage and home equity loans, credit card debt and installment purchases was about $33,300 in 1998. (See Table 6-3 and Figure 6-5.) The median credit card debt (that is, the outstanding balance after paying the most recent bill) was about $1,700 in 1998, up from $1,100 in 1992. The proportion of households that have credit card

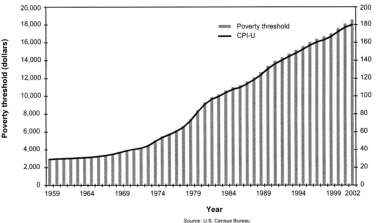

Figure 6-6. Average Poverty Threshold for a Four-Person Family, and Consumer Price Index (CPI-U), 1959–2002

Source: U.S. Census Bureau.

debt increased from about 40 percent to 48 percent between 1989 and 1995, but dropped to 44 percent in 1998. It is important to note that, while current data are not available, the burden of debt has likely increased since 1998, and especially since 2001, as the economy has worsened.

POVERTY

DEFINING POVERTY

Official measurement of poverty in America began in the mid-1960s during the presidency of Lyndon Johnson; it was the advent of his

administration's "War on Poverty" that introduced a variety of anti-poverty programs. Prior to the mid-1960s, no official government gauge of the extent and distribution of poverty in the United States existed. An often-used gauge of poverty during the early 1960s had been the number of families with annual incomes below $3,000 combined with the number of unrelated persons with annual income below $1,500. Such a fixed gauge did not take into account differences in family size (and thus the varying living expenses) or changes over time in the amount of income required to sustain a family.

In the early 1960s, Mollie Orshansky, an economist at the Social Security Administration (SSA), devised a gauge that did factor in differences in size and composition of families. She also devised a mechanism for adjusting the poverty "thresholds" for inflation. Within a few years, the Orshansky, or SSA, poverty definition was being used as a budget and planning tool by federal agencies and as the basis for eligibility for certain programs. In 1969, the SSA definition of poverty was adopted by the Budget Bureau[1] for use in the official statistical series

Table 6-4. Poverty Thresholds for Families, 2002

(Dollars.)

Size of family unit	Weighted average poverty threshold
One person	
Under 65 years	$9 359
65 years and over	8 628
Two persons	
Householder under 65 years	12 047
Householder 65 years and over	10 874
Three persons	14 072
Four persons	18 556
Five persons	22 377
Six persons	25 738
Seven persons	29 615
Eight persons	33 121
Nine persons or more	39 843

Source: U.S. Census Bureau. Current Population Reports, Series P60-219, *Poverty in the United States: 2001.*

---

[1] Budget Bureau Circular No. A-46, Transmittal Memorandum No. 9, August 29, 1969. The Budget Bureau is the predecessor of the present-day Office of Management and Budget.

for the U.S. Government to be published by the U.S. Census Bureau. The poverty definition provides a sliding scale of income thresholds by family size, age of householder, and number of related children under 18 years of age. (See Table 6-4.)

The original basis for these income thresholds was in a minimally adequate food budget devised by the Agriculture Department and in the ratio of food to total spending for a typical family around 1969 (which was about a third). Thus, minimum food requirements for various family compositions were multiplied by a factor of three to come up with the original poverty thresholds. Families or individuals with income below their appropriate threshold are classified as poor; those with income above their poverty threshold are classified as not poor.

In 2002, for example, the average poverty threshold for a family of four was $18,556; and other average thresholds varied from a low of $8,628 for a person 65 or older living alone to $39,843 for a family of nine or more members. Poverty thresholds are updated every year to reflect changes in cost of living using the Consumer Price Index (CPI–U). Thus, for example, the poverty threshold for a family of four was $2,973 in 1959, $8,414 in 1980, $10,989 in 1985, $13,359 in 1990, and $15,569 in 1995. (See Figure 6-6.)

Over the years, the SSA definition of poverty has been criticized by those who think it is too stringent as well as those who think it is too lenient. The definition has been the subject of several major studies examining what some perceive to be technical deficiencies, although most criticisms have been around since the defini-

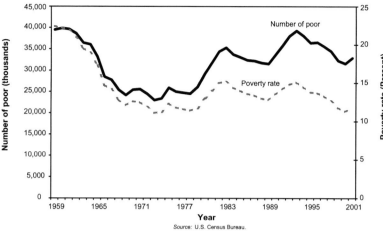

Figure 6-7. Number of Poor Persons and Poverty Rate, 1959–2001

Source: U.S. Census Bureau.

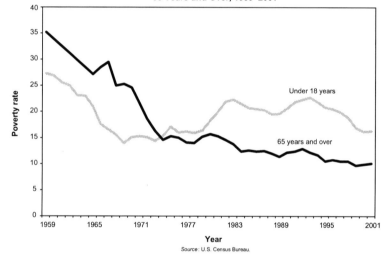

Figure 6-8. Poverty Rate for Persons Under 18 Years and Persons 65 Years and Over, 1959–2001

Source: U.S. Census Bureau.

tion was first proposed. Some of these criticisms were anticipated by Ms. Orshansky in her original research.[2] The latest study, conducted by the National Research Council in 1995, suggests important new changes to the concept and measurement of poverty.[3]

To date, there has not been a convergence of both the technical/programmatic need for a change in the definition of poverty and the political climate necessary for such a change to occur. (No

president wants an increase in poverty—a likely product of a change in definition—on his "watch," whether or not it was statistically induced.) For example, the poverty threshold for a family of four cited above was essentially the same as that already used for all families, $3,000, at the time of its adoption as the official measure. However, see below for a discussion of the experimental measure of poverty currently being developed at the Census Bureau.

[2] Mollie Orshansky, *Counting the Poor: Another Look at the Poverty Profile, Social Security Bulletin 28,* No. 1 (January 1965), and *Who's Who Among the Poor: A Demographic View of Poverty, Social Security Bulletin 28,* No. 7 (July 1965).

[3] Constance F. Citro and Robert T. Michael, ed., *Measuring Poverty: A New Approach* (Washington, DC: National Academy Press, 1995). Earlier work in this area includes: Department of Health, Education and Welfare, *The Measure of Poverty* (Washington, DC: Government Printing Office, 1976), and Bureau of the Census, *Proceedings of a Conference on the Measurement of Noncash Benefits* (Washington, DC, December 12–14, 1985).

TRENDS IN THE NUMBER OF POOR

Using the official definition of poverty, the number of poor people decreased dramatically in the 1960s and the early 1970s, down from a high of nearly 40 million people in 1960 to a low of 23 million by 1973. (See Figure 6-7.) The proportion of the U.S. population living in households with poverty-level income fell as well, from a high of 22 percent in 1960 to half that figure by 1973. The early 1970s marked a turning point in income growth in the United States—a point at which income, adjusted for inflation, began to stagnate. While there was some fluctuation (with business cycles) in the number and proportion of poor between the mid-1970s and the early 1990s, neither the number of poor nor the poverty rate returned to the lowest levels of the early 1970s.

The cycle began to improve in 1994 and continued to 2000. The official 2000 poverty rate of 11.3 percent is almost as low as it was in 1972–1973. The number of poor shows a somewhat different picture because the total population is constantly growing, but it too has declined in recent years in spite of the population increase. However, there were small

increases in 2001, and it's unlikely that the 2002 or 2003 numbers will show improvement.

Why poverty in America has not been eradicated, despite large government programs and investment, is the subject of considerable debate. Conservatives tend to assert that government intervention has perpetuated poverty and created a dependent class. Liberal arguments tend to put the blame on insufficient government assistance, along with environmental influences and economic conditions that perpetuate poverty. Data can be brought forth to support either position. An often lost detail in these arguments is that, among individual people and families, there is considerable movement up and down the income ladder; the poor in 1995 are not the same people who were poor in 1965 (or even their children). About one out of four persons who were poor in a given year were not poor the next, according to some longitudinal data for the mid-1980s and early 1990s. Welfare reform, enacted into law in 1996, will make some difference, but the fate of the former welfare recipients is often subject to the overall economic situation.

WHO IS POOR?

The demographic groups with higher than average proportions of

population in poverty include children, Blacks and Hispanics, women living alone, non-citizens, people living in central cities, and families headed by a woman with no husband present. Population groups with lower than average proportions include Whites, non-Hispanics, people aged 35 to 59, native born people, suburban residents, and people living in married-couple families. The improvements over the late 1990s were primarily among some of the worst-off groups, including Blacks, Hispanics, younger people (under age 25), and people living in female-headed families.

In 2001, the U.S. economy headed into another recession, the first since 1990–1991. Later data will show whether the gains made by some of the groups will hold in this poorer economy, or whether they will revert back toward their pre-1994 levels.

Over the long term, one of the groups that has experienced considerable reduction in poverty since 1959 is the elderly. Persons 65 years and over had a poverty rate over 35 percent in 1959, higher than any other age group. However, by 2001 the poverty rate for the elderly had declined to less than a third of its 1959 level (10.1 percent) and has been lower than the rate for all ages combined since the early 1980s. Much of this reduction has been attributed to the automatic inflation adjustment of Social Security benefits that began in the early 1970s, as well as an increasing proportion of the aged eligible for such benefits. A larger than average proportion of the elderly have incomes just above the poverty level, however, and thus are at risk of falling below that subsistence level if faced with unavoidable and unusually large expenses.

Children, on the other hand, experienced little reduction in poverty from the time government figures became available in 1959 and 2001. The poverty rate of 16.3 percent in 2001 was about the same as it was in the mid-1970s.

Figure 6-9. Poverty Rate for Families, by Type and Race/Hispanic Origin of Householder, 2001

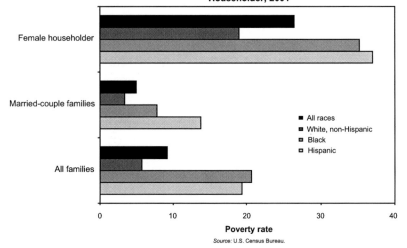

Poverty rate

Source: U.S. Census Bureau.

(See Figure 6-8.) The poverty rate for children under 18 years was lower than that of the elderly until the early 1970s, but it is currently almost twice that of older age groups. One of six American children under age 6 lived in a poor household in 2001. Because of their relatively high poverty rate, children under 18 years of age represented 36 percent of all poor persons in 2001.

Blacks are another group for whom official poverty has declined considerably in the past 30 years. Over half (55 percent) of Blacks were poor in 1959, when poverty statistics were first tabulated. The poverty rate for this group declined to 22 percent in 2000, its lowest figure ever, although there was a slight rise in 2001. This progress has been made despite the presence of several countervailing trends that tend to increase poverty in this group, particularly the incidence of single-parent families. Much of the original concern with measuring poverty, at the Social Security Administration, had been with women left alone to sustain their children without benefit of a spouse, since historically such families have had poverty rates higher than married-couple families. Originally, this concern was fostered by widowhood, but children growing up in single-parent families are now likely to have parents who are divorced or who had children outside of marriage, rather than by the death of a parent.

Among families headed by a single woman, the 2001 poverty rate was higher for Hispanics (37.0 percent) as for Blacks (35.2 percent), whereas for Whites the poverty rate for families in this group was 26.4 percent. (See Figure 6-9.) Married-couple households have much lower poverty rates at less than 5 percent overall, and 7.8 percent for Blacks. Hispanic married-couple families had a poverty rate more than three times that of Anglo families (14 percent versus 5 percent) and almost twice that of Black families.

Even though the poverty rate for Hispanic families was higher than that for Blacks within each family type, the overall poverty rate for families with an Hispanic householder was about the same as that for Black families because of the vastly different family composition of these two groups; only one-fourth of Hispanic families are maintained by women without husbands, and fewer than half of poor Hispanic families are headed by women alone.

Unrelated individuals (that is, people who live alone or with other people who are not related to them—such as a roommate, boarder, etc.) have increased both in absolute terms and as a proportion of all poor persons. About one in five of these unrelated persons was poor in 2001, less than half of their poverty rate in the early 1960s (when a larger proportion of them were elderly persons living alone). The number of poor unrelated individuals has increased from about 5 million in 1959 to 9.2 million and are about 28 percent of the poor, over twice their representation in 1959.

This fraction likely would be even larger if homeless persons, who are largely missed in survey counts of the poor, were included in official counts. Estimates of how many homeless persons there are vary considerably, from approxi-

mately 500,000 as a point-in-time estimate in 1988 to a figure of 12 million who have experienced homelessness (or had to double up with relatives or friends) at some point in their lifetime. The causes associated with increasing homelessness are as varied as the estimates of the number of homeless and include stagnating or falling wages and diminished work opportunities for the low-skilled, the lack of affordable low-rent housing, the demolition of millions of single room occupancy (SRO) housing units in flop houses and cubicle hotels, the increased tendency to de-institutionalize the mentally ill, and drug and alcohol abuse.

Other characteristics (other than membership in a minority group or living in a single-parent family) are also associated with higher than average poverty rates. (See Figure 6-10.) Foreign-born non-citizens have poverty rates nearly double those of persons born in the United States (20 percent versus 11 percent); persons living in large central cities have poverty rates twice those of persons living in suburban areas, while those living in rural areas have an intermediate rate that falls between the city and suburban rates; work effort is highly correlated with poverty status, as only 8 percent of persons in a family with

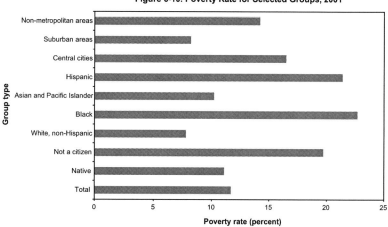

Figure 6-10. Poverty Rate for Selected Groups, 2001

Source U.S. Census Bureau.

a worker were poor, compared with 29 percent in families with no workers.

DEPTH OF POVERTY

Classifying people as either "in poverty" or "not in poverty" is a fairly simple, dichotomous, way of looking at economic position. The Census Bureau has developed two "depth of poverty" measures that more fully reflect the distribution of economic well-being.

The first measure is the ratio of income to poverty. This is a measure of the degree of poverty, both among those below the poverty threshold and those who are just above it. In 2001, 41 percent of the nation's poor were very poor, defined as having an income of less than 50 percent of their poverty threshold. As might be expected, the population groups most affected in this measure are the young (under 25), minorities (Blacks and Hispanics), children, and unrelated individuals. The latter, of course, by their definition, are limited to one person contributing to their income. Another group of people, about 12.4 million, were living just above the poverty level in 2001, up to 1.25 percent of their threshold.

The second measure of depth of poverty is called the Income Deficit. This is the difference, in dollars, between the family's income and its threshold, and averaged $6,800 in 2001. The deficit tends to be higher for families and lower for unrelated individuals (in part because the poverty threshold for single persons living alone is so low). On a per capita basis, the deficit is higher for unrelated individuals than for people living in families.

THE GEOGRAPHY OF POVERTY

Poverty is not evenly spread throughout the country. By state, Mississippi had the highest 1999 poverty rate, as measured in the 2000 census, followed by Louisiana, New Mexico, and West Virginia. In contrast, 17 states had poverty rates below 10 percent, with the lowest found in New Hampshire, Minnesota, and Connecticut. Within cities, poor people tend to live in their own neighborhoods, and the poverty rate in cities (16.1 percent) was more than twice that of suburbs (7.8 percent). Rural areas also often have concentrations of people living below the poverty level. This isolation of poor people from the more affluent segments of the population is increasing, influenced by the flight of middle-class blacks to the suburbs, housing discrimination against disadvantaged groups such as immigrants, and a growing mismatch between where low-income workers live and where their jobs are located.[4]

EXPERIMENTAL POVERTY MEASURES

The Census Bureau has, to date, developed several experimental poverty measures. The work is based on two important components: (1) how does one measure a family's (or person's) needs? and (2) what resources should be counted as income for meeting those needs? The National Research Council Panel's 1995 report is the basis for the project, with research being conducted to refine some of the measurement methods and to examine how various adaptations of the Panel's recommendations would affect the number of poor and the poverty rate.

The results for 2001 show little variation in the overall rate, although all of the experimental measures show slightly higher rates than the official figure of 11.7 percent. By demographic group, generally the senior citizen (65 years and over) poverty rate shows increases among the experimental rates, while the rate for children shows decreases.

---

[4] Daniel T. Lichter and Martha L. Crowley, *Poverty in America: Beyond Welfare Reform*, Population Reference Bureau, *Population Bulletin* Vol 47, No 2, June 2002.

FOR FURTHER INFORMATION SEE:

Burt, Martha and Barbara Cohen. *America's Homeless: Numbers, Characteristics, and Programs That Serve Them*. Washington, DC: Urban Institute Press, 1989.

DeNavas-Walt, Carmen and Robert W. Cleveland. *Poverty in the United States: 2001*, Census Bureau, Current Population Report P60-218, September 2002.

Jones Jr., Arthur E. and Daniel Weinberg. *The Changing Shape of the Nation's Income Distribution*, Census Bureau, Current Population Report P60-204, June 2000.

Kennickell, Arthur B., Martha Starr-McCluer, and Brian J. Surette. "Recent Changes in U.S. Family Finances: Results from the 1998 Survey of Consumer Finances", Board of Governors of the Federal Reserve System, *Federal Reserve Bulletin*, January 2000.

Lichter, Daniel T. and Martha L. Crowley. *Poverty in America: Beyond Welfare Reform*, Washington, DC, Population Reference Bureau, June 2002.

Link, Bruce et al. "Lifetime and Five-Year Prevalence of Homelessness in the United States," *American Journal of Public Health*, December 1994.

Orzechowski, Shawna and Peter Sepielli. *Household Net Worth and Asset Ownership: 1998 and 2000*, Census Bureau, Current Population Report P70-88, May 2003.

Proctor, Bernadette D. and Joseph Dalaker. *Money Income in the United States: 2001*, Census Bureau, Current Population Report P60-219, September 2002.

WEB SITES:

Census Bureau Web site <www.census.gov>. The sections for Income Data and Poverty Data were used for this chapter, supplementing the Income and Poverty reports cited above.

Federal Reserve System Web site <www.federalreserve.gov/rnd.htm>. This site provided the Kennickell report cited above.

Chapter 7
Education

SCHOOL ENROLLMENT

In October 2000, a total of more than 72 million people, more than one out of four persons in the United States, was currently enrolled in school. While most of these students were in elementary school, high school, or college, there were 8.2 million children enrolled in nursery school or kindergarten. The college student figures, about 15.3 million overall, include 2.5 million people who are over the age of 34, and thus beyond the traditional school enrollment age range. These groups at the enrollment age extremes have seen the largest proportional increases in school attendance in the past several decades.[1]

The proportion of children aged 3 and 4 who are enrolled in nursery school has increased continuously over the past several decades, and is now about 52 percent of all children of this age. Children of higher-income families are more likely to be enrolled, most likely because of the cost involved in paying for private education. College-graduate mothers and mothers in the labor force are also significantly more likely to enroll their young children in nursery school. The availability of full-day programs means that, for some children, the school serves as a day-care facility as well.

Pre-primary enrollment is still linked to income, despite government efforts such as Head Start and other state and locally administered pre-primary programs, to make this education available to any student (or student's parent) who desires it. Government programs are typically restricted to families with low incomes. For example, about 61 percent of 3- and 4-year olds in families with an income over $40,000 were enrolled in 2000, compared with about 46 percent of comparable children in families with incomes under $20,000. Children whose mothers have less than a high school education are half as likely to be enrolled as those whose mothers have at least a bachelor's degree. Given the disparities in parental income and educational attainment, these enrollment rate disparities are likely to be perpetuated in the next generation.

Kindergarten, elementary, and high school enrollment patterns are closely linked with the total population in these age groups. In the late 1990s, the "baby boomlet" of the 1980s had brought school enrollments back to the level of the baby boom years; in both 1970 and 1999, there were 49 million children enrolled in elementary and high school. In 2000, however, the level was back down to 44.3 million.

Figure 7-1. School Enrollment Rates by Age, 1964 and 2000

Source: U.S. Census Bureau. Current Population Survey.

Figure 7-2. Nursery School Enrollment of Children 3 and 4 Years Old, by Mothers' Level of Education, October 2000

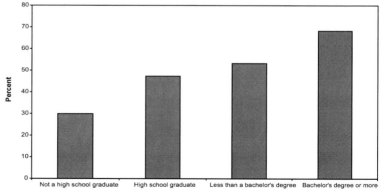

Source: U.S. Census Bureau.

---

[1] Amie Jamieson, Andrea Curry, and Gladys Martinez, *School Enrollment in the United States —Social and Economic Characteristics of Students, October 1999*, Current Population Report P20-533 (Washington: U.S. Census Bureau, March 2001). The data reported here do not include students enrolled in vocational or technical training programs unless it leads to a diploma or a degree. Although the cited report presents 1999 data, 2000 data are available at <www.census.gov> and are used in this chapter.

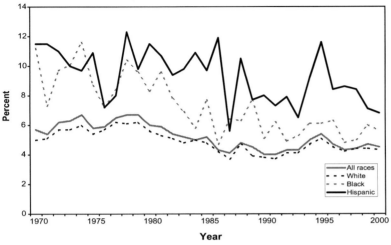

Figure 7-3. Annual High School Dropout Rate, by Race and Hispanic Origin, 1970–2000

Source: U.S. Census Bureau.

The high immigration levels of the 1990s also contribute to these high enrollment figures. In 2000, almost one student in five had a foreign born parent, including 6 percent who were themselves foreign born. These patterns, emerging in the mid-1990s, have had many school districts scrambling to provide sufficient enrollment capacity after years of dealing with a surplus of classroom space.

About 90 percent of elementary and high school students attend public schools. Children living outside of metropolitan areas are slightly less likely to attend private school. At the nursery school level, about half the children enrolled are in a public school environment, and half private, with children living in suburbs more likely to attend a private school. For kindergarten, the figure rises to 83 percent public.

In addition to the enrollment in regular schools indicated above, an additional 4 million people 15 and over in the United States were enrolled in vocational training in the fall of 2000. Such training includes enrollment in business, trade, technical, secretarial, or correspondence courses, but not on-the-job training. Most of this group is working age, between 25 and 64 years old, and has at least a high school diploma. One-third report that they have completed a bachelor's degree. Almost one-quarter are also currently enrolled in college, although there may be some overlap between the two categories. Another data set, looking at persons 18 to 44 years of age, shows that while participation in credentialed programs (leading to a college degree, diploma or certificate) decreases by age, participation in other types of adult learning activities remains high, at about 50 percent, for all age groups.[2]

HIGH SCHOOL DROPOUTS

At the other end of the enrollment spectrum, high school dropout rates have tended to decline in the past 20 years, to an annual figure of about 4.5 percent of 10th through 12th graders in 2000. For Whites, the rate has not changed much; it increased in the 1970s but came back down; for Blacks, the dropout rate is now half their 1970 rate, but remains higher than that for Whites (5.6 percent for Blacks, 4.3 percent for Whites in 2000). The annual dropout rate for Hispanics (6.8 percent) is higher than that for either Blacks or Whites. Asian and Pacific Islander dropout rates, reported for the first time in 1999, were only 3.3 percent in 2000.

Annual dropout rates do not show the cumulative effect that dropping out of school makes on the population. In 2000, 10 percent of 18-to 24-year-olds were not high school graduates and were not attending school. This figure was 26 percent for young persons living in households with a family income under $20,000. In contrast, it was only 4 percent in families with income of $50,000 or more.

COLLEGE ENROLLMENT AND COMPOSITION OF STUDENT BODY

In 2000, over half (56 percent) of the 18-to 24-year-olds in the nation were either currently or formerly enrolled in college. This represents a very substantial increase over the 31 percent figure 25 years earlier. The number of 18- and 19-year-olds enrolled in college in 2000 was only somewhat higher than the comparable figure in 1975—about 3.5 million. Yet, total college enrollment has increased from 10.9 million to 15.3 million during that period.

Older students make up the difference. The number of college students who are 35 and over has increased from 1.2 million to 2.5 million, and these older students now represent 16 percent of all enrollment. Reasons for the change include the drastic changes in the work force since 1975, including the return of women to the labor force, the large increase in the number of persons aged 35 to 55, and the availability

2 *The Condition of Education 2001*, (U.S. Department of Education, National Center for Education Statistics), 12.

Figure 7-4. Selected Characteristics of College Students, 1974 and 2000

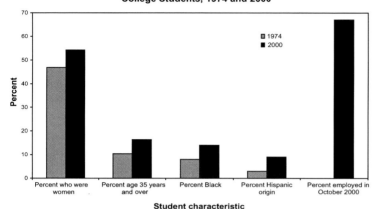

Source: U.S. Census Bureau.
Note: Employment data for college students in 1974 are not available.

of community college programs.

Both Blacks and Hispanics represented larger proportions of the total college population in 2000 than they did in the early 1970s. Blacks had increased from 8 percent to 14 percent of all college students and Hispanics had increased from 3 percent to 9 percent of all persons enrolled in college. Hispanics were still somewhat underrepresented in college compared with their proportions among the total population (about 13 percent), while Blacks had achieved parity between the two figures.

Women, who represented about one-third of all college students in 1950, became the majority of all college students in the United States during the late 1970s, and, by 2000, represented about 56 percent of total college enrollment.

GAUGING PROGRESS IN SCHOOL

One gauge of how well students are doing in school is the proportion enrolled below their modal grade. Modal grade is the year of school in which the largest proportion of students of a given age is enrolled. For example, the modal grade for 11-year-olds is the sixth grade. By the time they were 15 to 17 years old, 30 percent of students were enrolled below their modal grade in 2000. When they were 6 to 8 year olds in 1991, only 21 percent of this same cohort were enrolled below their modal grade. Since 1971, the proportion of students enrolled below their modal grade has been increasing for each age group.[3] Currently, about 1 student in 10 is held back sometime between beginning school and high school.

The National Assessment of Educational Progress (NAEP) provides comparisons over time on standardized tests. These scores are an additional gauge of progress in school and of how well our educational system is preparing students for an increasingly technical world of work. Average mathematics proficiency scores achieved by 17 year olds between 1977 and 1999 indicate an increase in proficiency, while reading proficiency scores have remained stable.

The Scholastic Assessment Test (SAT) is used as an admission criterion for college and has been taken by students who are contemplating college attendance. It is usually taken in the senior year of high school. The proportion of high school graduates who take the SAT has increased as the availability of college education has increased. The proportion of minorities who take the SAT has increased as well. Even though the average scores of minorities (with the exception of Asian-American math scores) were lower than those of Whites, the average scores in 2000 for all test-takers, regardless of race, are as high, in both mathematics and verbal areas, as they have been since the early 1970s (although not as high as they were in 1972). Average SAT scores have increased considerably for minority test-takers, while average scores for Whites have fallen a few percentage points in the past 20 years.[4]

COMPUTER USAGE

Computer literacy is likely to influence the employment opportunities available to today's students and is likely to restrict the opportunities of those without computer skills. The proportion of households with a computer has increased from about 8 percent in 1984 to 51 percent in 2000. About 65 percent of students aged 3 to 17 live in homes with computer access, with the likelihood of having a computer increasing by the age of the student. Students from higher-income families were considerably more likely to have computer access at home and to use the Internet. Home computer access was nearly universal (93 percent) for children living in families with incomes of $75,000 or more in 2000.[5]

---

[3] *School Enrollment in the United States—Social and Economic Characteristics of Students: October 1999*, Current Population Report P20-533 (Washington: U.S. Census Bureau, March 2001). Note that many factors may be involved in students being one year behind the modal grade. They may have started school late (this happens more often for boys), or the state law may require students born after September 1 to enroll the following year.

[4] See *Digest of Education Statistics: 2000*, and *Youth Indicators, 1996*, both at <nces.ed.gov> (Washington, DC, U.S. Department of Education, National Center for Education Statistics).

[5] *Home Computers and Internet Use in the United States: August 2000*, Special Studies Report P23-207 (Washington, U.S. Census Bureau, September 2001).

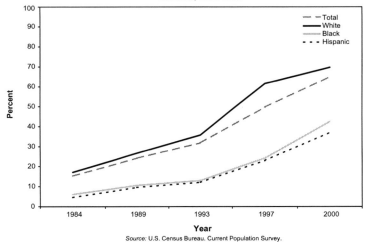

Figure 7-5. Percentage of 3- to 17-Year-Olds with Computer Access at Home, 1984–2000

Source: U.S. Census Bureau. Current Population Survey.

EDUCATIONAL ATTAINMENT AND OUTCOMES

CHANGE AND CONTINUED VARIATION

It was not until the mid-1960s that at least half of the adult population of the United States had completed 4 or more years of high school. The increase in average educational attainment of the U.S. population has continued to improve over the past two decades, with the proportion of young adults (25 to 29 years) who have completed high school increasing from 75 to 86 percent between 1970 and 2000, and the proportion completing 4 or more years of college increasing from about 16 percent to 29 percent.

The proportion of young Black adults who have completed at least high school is almost the same as that of young Whites (93 percent to 87 percent), although the proportion completing college is still considerably lower than that of Whites (18 percent for Blacks, 36 percent for Whites).[6] Young adults of Hispanic origin trail both their White and Black peers, with only 62 percent having graduated

from high school and 9 percent having graduated from college in 2000. On the other hand, Asians and Pacific Islanders have much higher completion rates; 95 percent of the 25 to 29 age group had completed high school in 2000, and 55 percent had completed college.

Overall, 78 percent of the population 25 years of age and over were high school graduates in 2000. This fraction is lower than that for the younger age group discussed above, since about half of the persons at older ages, particularly over the age of 75, are high school graduates. For minorities, the fraction of the population age 25 and over who were high school

graduates was considerably smaller in 2000; for example, only about 40 percent of both Hispanics and Blacks over the age of 65 had graduated from high school. There is considerable variation among states, in part because of these racial and ethnic differences, and in part because of the varied racial composition among states. One of four persons in several southern states—such as Alabama, Arkansas, Kentucky, and Mississippi—was not a high school graduate, while in several states with relatively small minority populations—Utah, Washington, Alaska, Minnesota, Wyoming, Vermont, and Montana—almost 90 percent of the adult population were high school graduates.

In 2000, over one-half of the U.S. population age 25 and over had attended college for at least one course, and about one out of four had a bachelor's degree or higher. A bachelor's degree typically takes 4 years of full-time study beyond the high school level, although there is some variation (in both directions) in this time. Here again, there is considerable variation by state, with more than 30 percent of the population of three different states holding a bachelor's degree or higher, while fewer than 20 percent in nine other states had such a degree. (See Figure 7-6.)

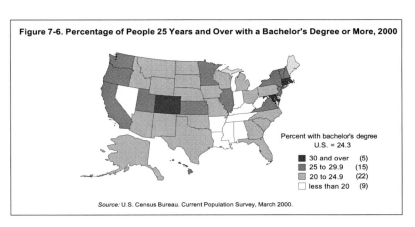

Figure 7-6. Percentage of People 25 Years and Over with a Bachelor's Degree or More, 2000

Percent with bachelor's degree
U.S. = 24.3

- 30 and over (5)
- 25 to 29.9 (15)
- 20 to 24.9 (22)
- less than 20 (9)

Source: U.S. Census Bureau. Current Population Survey, March 2000.

---

6 The figures presented here for Whites and Blacks exclude the Hispanic population.

The economic returns to additional schooling appear to be considerable. As of March 2000, persons (18 years old and over) who had completed high school but no college had average earnings in 1999 of about $23,233, while those with a bachelor's degree could expect earnings of about $53,043, and those individuals with a doctorate had average earnings in 1999 of $87,644. In addition, the average number of months with work activity tends to increase with educational attainment, indicating a greater likelihood of periodic unemployment with lower education.[7]

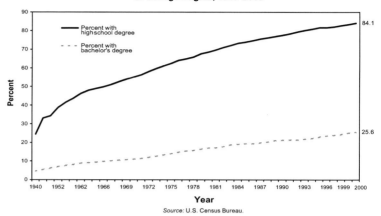

Figure 7-7. Percentage of People 25 Years and Over with a High School Diploma or College Degree, 1940–2000

Source: U.S. Census Bureau.

ADULT LITERACY

One measure of educational outcomes is adult literacy; reading habits are an indication of literacy. A 1999 study reported that about half of all adults 25 and older read regularly, defined as reading a newspaper once a week, at least one magazine regularly, and a book in the past six months. Not surprisingly, the results were positively correlated with educational attainment, ranging from 22 percent of those with less than a high school education to 71 percent for those with a bachelor's degree or higher.[8]

Another outcome correlated with education is personal health.

In a 1997 survey, people with a bachelor's degree or higher were twice as likely as those without a high school diploma or equivalent to report being in excellent or very good health.[9]

TEACHERS: QUANTITY AND QUALITY

An estimated 3.3 million teachers were engaged in elementary and secondary classroom instruction in 1999, 2.9 million of whom were teaching in public schools. The number of teachers increased by 20 percent during the 1990s, a growth level that is slightly higher than the increase in the number of students. Consequently, the student/teacher ratio has declined

slightly, from 16.8 to 16.0 students per teacher in public schools. This figure, however, represents a substantial improvement over the 27.4 ratio of students per teacher in 1955. The ratio for elementary schools (17.4) is higher than that for secondary schools (13.9), because of the greater number of specialized teachers at the high school level.[10]

Research indicates that persons entering the teaching field had lower SAT scores than their non-teaching, college-graduating peers and that those leaving the profession had higher scores than those remaining as teachers. In addition, the scores of those majoring in education were lower than those of graduates who majored in another field. Those who came to teaching without prior preparation, such as student teaching, had higher scores. Finally, private schools appear to attract teachers with higher SAT scores than do public schools.[11]

TEACHER SALARIES

Teacher salaries are one gauge of the public's willingness (or ability) to invest in education. As did the

Table 7-1. Education and Occupation, 1999

(Percent distribution.)

Occupation	Total	Not a high school graduate	High school graduate only	Some college	College graduate or more
Executive, administrative, and managerial	100.0	2.4	19.7	28.8	49.1
Professional specialty	100.0	0.7	5.2	15.7	78.4
Technicians and related support	100.0	1.5	21.5	47.6	29.4
Sales occupations	100.0	5.5	31.9	30.4	32.2
Administrative support, including clerical	100.0	3.6	40.3	40.6	15.5
Service occupations	100.0	20.0	42.8	28.4	8.8
Precision production, craft, and repair (skilled workers)	100.0	17.1	46.5	29.3	7.1
Operators, fabricators, and laborers	100.0	23.2	49.9	21.9	5.0
Farming, forestry, and fishing	100.0	31.8	36.4	21.0	10.8
Armed forces	100.0	0.3	19.5	42.7	37.5

Source: U.S. Bureau of Labor Statistics.

---

[7] See *Educational Attainment in the United States: March 1999*, Current Population Report P20-528 (Washington, U.S. Census Bureau, August 2000), its March 2000 update in P20-528, 2000 Tables 8 and 13, and Historical Table A2, all accessible at <http://www.census.gov/population/www/socdemo/educ-attn.html>.

[8] The *Condition of Education 2001*, (U.S. Department of Education, National Center for Education Statistics), 29.

[9] Ibid, 31.

[10] *Digest of Education Statistics 2000*, (U.S. Department of Education, National Center for Education Statistics), Table 65.

[11] *The Condition of Education 2001*, 69.

salaries of other professions, teacher salaries actually declined (in real terms) during the 1970s, and only returned to their 1972 levels in 1987. In 2000, the average salary for all public school teachers was $41,274. There is little difference between salary levels for elementary teachers and for secondary teachers, although salaries do usually increase with education beyond the bachelor's degree and with seniority. Projections for teacher salaries in the coming decade show little change, with expected increases of only 2 percent (holding inflation constant). In current dollars, representing the actual size of the paychecks taking projected inflation into account, the average salary is expected to rise from about $43,000 in 2001 to $46,600 in 2005.[12]

EXPENDITURES ON EDUCATION

Annual expenditures per pupil are another gauge of the public investment that is devoted to each student's education. Actual current expenditures per pupil, excluding capital budgets, increased from $842 to $6,508 between 1970 and

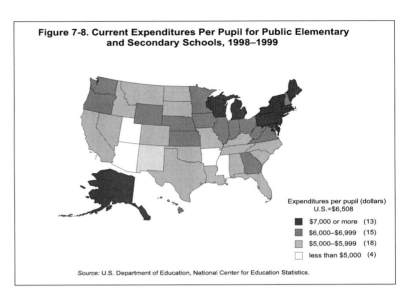

Figure 7-8. Current Expenditures Per Pupil for Public Elementary and Secondary Schools, 1998–1999

Expenditures per pupil (dollars)
U.S.=$6,508

■ $7,000 or more (13)
▨ $6,000–$6,999 (15)
▧ $5,000–$5,999 (18)
□ less than $5,000 (4)

Source: U.S. Department of Education, National Center for Education Statistics.

1999 for elementary and secondary education. Adjusted for inflation, that represents an increase of about 83 percent. However, during the 1990s, there was little change, with per pupil expenditures increasing only about 10 percent in real terms between the 1989–1990 and 1999–2000 school years.

There are wide variations in per pupil expenditures by state. In 1998–1999, New Jersey led the nation with over $10,000 annual current expenditures per student,

followed by New York at $9,300. At the other end of the scale, Utah's figure is only $4,200, followed by Mississippi at $4,600. Nationwide, about 62 percent of the dollars go directly to instruction, with 34 percent spent on support services and 4 percent on other non-instruction activity. These proportions change little with varying levels of overall expenditures.

---

[12] *Digest of Education Statistics 2000*, Table 35.

FOR FURTHER INFORMATION SEE:

Digest of Education Statistics: 2000. National Center for Education Statistics Publication No. 2001-034. Washington, DC: U.S. Department of Education, National Center for Education Statistics.

Dropout Rates in the United States: 1994. National Center for Education Statistics Publication No. 96-863. Washington, DC: U.S. Department of Education, National Center for Education Statistics.

Educational Attainment in the United States. Current Population Reports, Series P-20, No. 536. Washington, DC: U.S. Census Bureau.

Financing the Future: Postsecondary Students, Costs, and Financial Aid: 1993-94. Current Population Reports, Series P-70, No. 60. Washington, DC: U.S. Census Bureau.

School Enrollment–Social and Economic Characteristics of Students. Current Population Reports, Series P-20, No. 533. Washington, DC: U.S. Census Bureau.

The Condition of Education 2001. Washington, DC: U.S. Department of Education, National Center for Education Statistics.

WEB SITES:

National Center for Education Statistics: <www.ed.gov/nces>.

U.S. Census Bureau: <www.census.gov>.

Chapter 8
Crime and Criminal Justice

INTRODUCTION

Defining "crime" is difficult. There are serious questions of conception and measurement. In 1967, The President's Commission on Law Enforcement and Administration of Justice made the following observation: "A skid-row drunk lying in a gutter is a crime. So is the killing of an unfaithful wife. A Cosa Nostra conspiracy to bribe public officials is a crime. So is a strong-arm robbery by a 15-year-old boy. . .These crimes can no more be linked together for purposes of analysis than can measles and schizophrenia, or lung cancer and a broken ankle. . .Thinking of 'crime' as a whole is futile."[1] The irony in the above statement further illustrates the difficulty in defining crime. Since that statement was written in 1967, many jurisdictions have decriminalized public drunkenness, making the commission's first example no longer germane.

Crime does not have only a temporal dimension. It also has a spatial dimension. For example, throughout the early decades of the twentieth century the use of marijuana, cocaine, and opium and its derivatives became illegal in the United States. However, in some countries the use of these substances is not illegal, while in other countries drug use is even more severely punished than it is in the United States. The measurement problem is equally vexing. For example, crimes such as embezzlement or drug possession cannot be identified until the perpetrator is caught. Some others cannot ever be adequately categorized. For example, if, during an inventory, a retail establishment discovers less inventory than expected, is this the result of shoplifting, employee theft, a simple error, or what?

Laying these problems aside, this chapter will address what people understand crime to be, as well as the resulting criminal justice process and the outcomes of that process.

THE GREAT PARADOX

Since 1990, the United States has experienced both a sharply declining crime rate and an exploding prison population. According to the Federal Bureau of Investigation (FBI), serious reported crime in 2000 decreased by 23 percent as compared with 1994. The decrease in the crime rate per 100,000 inhabitants is even more spectacular: 29 percent over the same time period. In contrast, the number of prisoners in federal and state prisons increased from 0.8 million in 1990 to almost 1.4 million in 2000, an increase of about 75 percent. Expenditures for criminal justice activities also increased significantly during this period, with an overall increase of 63 percent between 1990 and 1997.[2]

The explanation for this paradox is demographic. Baby boomers, the largest cohort of the population, were born between 1946 and 1964. In 2002, they are 38 to 54 years old. Following the baby boom, the birth rate dropped sharply; the children born in the late 1960s and 1970s (Generation X, as they are sometimes labeled) comprise a much smaller cohort, in terms of population size, than the baby boomers. As shown later in this chapter, most crimes are committed by people between the ages of 18 and 34. There are now fewer people in this age range, and consequently fewer people to commit crimes. Meanwhile, the nation has been growing at a rapid clip. This demographic pattern leads to the sharp drop in the crime index. However, the convicted criminals among the large baby boomer population occupy today's prisons and jails, and there are a lot of them. Thus, the growth in the corrections population.

Public concern about crime has increased dramatically, notwithstanding the falling crime rate. In a series of surveys conducted by the Gallup Organization, people have been asked what they considered to be the most important problems facing the country. The "crime/violence" category was quite low from 1988 through 1991, began to rise in 1992, and peaked at 52 percent in 1994. It then began to drop, and had returned to the very low level (1 percent) by March 2002. It is important to note, however, that since respondents are asked to name the "most important problem facing this country today," the rate at which crime is mentioned is partly dependent on the importance of other problems to respondents. For example, "the economy" was ranked high in the early 1990s, cropped to a much lower level in the mid-to late-1990s when the U.S. economy was in good shape, and rose again in 2002. "Terrorism" was listed by 22 percent of respondents in 2002, where it had not been an issue of any mention during the 1990s.[3]

---

[1] President's Commission on Law Enforcement and the Administration of Justice, *The Challenge of Crime in a Free Society* (Washington, DC: GPO, 1967).

[2] Bureau of Justice Statistics, *Sourcebook of Criminal Justice Statistics* 2000, p. 3.

[3] Gallup Organization, *The Gallup Report*, several reports between 1988 and 1997. 2000 data obtained from <www.gallup.com/poll/topics>.

CRIME AND VICTIMS

Crime may be defined as "an action or an instance of negligence. . .that is legally prohibited" (*Webster's New Universal Unabridged Dictionary*). There are many kinds of crime, including commercial crime, industrial crime, other white-collar crime, and common crime. While commercial crime, such as the savings and loan scandals of the 1980s or industrial crime involving pollution, may cost society very heavily, commercial and industrial crimes are not subject to simple measurement nor do they come to mind when most people think of crime. In the United States, most people think of crime as those offenses regularly reported by the FBI in its Uniform Crime Reports (UCR).

The set of crimes reported by the UCR is called the Crime Index. The Crime Index is composed of selected offenses used to gauge changes over time in the overall volume and rate of crime reported to law enforcement. The offenses included are the violent crimes of murder and nonnegligent manslaughter, forcible rape, robbery, and aggravated assault, and the property crimes of burglary, larceny-theft, motor vehicle theft, and

arson. For the purposes of this chapter, the set of crimes making up the Crime Index will be referred to as serious crimes. The UCR develops its data by collecting information taken from crimes reported to law enforcement agencies and provided to the FBI by virtually every police agency in the country.

The National Crime Victimization Survey (NCVS), conducted by the Bureau of Justice Statistics, is a survey of a national sample of households in which information about crime victimization is obtained for each household and for each household member 12 years of age and older. Crimes, such as household burglary, motor vehicle theft, and theft in which no victim was present are called property crimes by NCVS, and crimes where the victim is present during the commission of the crime are called personal crimes. While neither of these methods provides a perfect measure of crime, each has its own advantages. For example, because the UCR receives reports from almost all police agencies, it can provide good information on the geographic distribution of crime. Because it is based on a national sample, the NCVS

does not collect data for small geographic areas but it does provide better information on the true incidence of crime since many crimes are not reported to the police. Every effort was made to define criminal events in the same way for both of these surveys. The major differences are that the NCVS does not include murder and nonnegligent manslaughter, since there is no living victim to interview, and that the NCVS includes simple assault in its count of violent crimes, while the UCR does not.

Figure 8-1 shows the number of crimes reported by the FBI via the UCR compared with those reported by the Bureau of Justice Statistics via the NCVS.[4] There are a number of hypotheses explaining the differences, but one thing stands out: where the victim feels that the police are powerless, or that it is not worth the effort to report the crime, the crime will not be reported to the police. That is probably why reports of theft, for example, differ so greatly between the two sources. When the victim feels that there is a chance for recovery by the police or the item is covered by insurance that would require a police report for the insurance claim (motor vehicle theft, for example), the crime is much more likely to be reported. Overall, according to 1999 NCVS data, only 43 percent of violent crimes and 34 percent of property crimes were reported to police, with the highest reporting figures for aggravated assault with an injury, robbery with an injury, and motor vehicle theft, while the lowest reporting levels are for theft with a small monetary value and sexual assaults, including rape.[5]

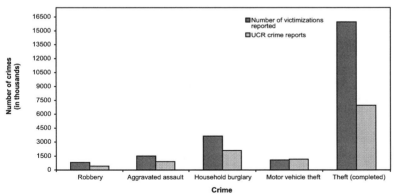

Figure 8-1. Comparison of National Crime Victimization Survey Estimates and Uniform Crime Report Figures, 1999

Source: Bureau of Justice Statistics. *Criminal Victimization in the United States, 1999.*
UCR: Federal Bureau of Investigation. *Crime in the United States, 1999.*

---

[4] It is important to note that the FBI's *Uniform Crime Reports* do not include data for every place in the nation. In 2000, the population included in the reporting communities was about 182 million, or 65 percent of the total population. The distortions that may be caused by the missing data are unknown.

[5] Bureau of Justice Statistics, *Crime Victimization in the United States, 1999*, published January 2001, NCJ184938, Table 91.

Table 8-1. Estimated Rate of Personal Victimization, 1999

(Rate per 1,000 persons 12 years and over, except where noted.)

Characteristic	All personal crimes	Crimes of violence							Personal theft	Property crimes (per 1,000 households)		
		Total	Rape/sexual assault	Robbery	Assault					Household burglary	Motor vehicle theft	Theft
					Total	Aggravated	Simple					
ALL PERSONS	33.7	32.8	1.7	3.6	27.4	6.7	20.8	0.9	34.1	10.0	153.9
Sex											
Male	37.9	37.0	0.4	5.0	31.6	8.7	22.9	0.9	...	...	...
Female	29.7	28.8	3.0	2.3	23.6	4.8	18.8	0.9	...	...	...
Age											
12–15 years	77.5	74.4	4.0	6.7	13.1	4.9	50.6	3.1	...	...	...
16–19 years	78.9	77.4	6.9	8.2	16.8	4.9	45.5	...	...	...	...
20–24 years	69.5	68.5	4.3	7.7	16.7	5.3	39.7	...	...	...	...
25–34 years	37.4	36.3	1.7	4.1	8.3	2.0	22.2	1.2	...	...	...
35–49 years	25.6	25.2	0.8	2.8	4.7	1.7	16.9	...	...	...	...
50–64 years	15.0	14.4	...	1.9	1.8	...	10.5	...	...	...	...
65 years and over	4.4	3.8	...	...	1.1	...	1.9	...	...	...	...
Race											
White	32.7	31.9	1.6	3.1	27.2	6.2	21.1	0.8	31.5	9.0	149.5
Black	42.9	41.6	2.6	7.7	31.3	10.6	20.8	1.3	52.6	16.0	181.2
Other	26.0	24.5	...	...	20.3	5.7	14.6	...	31.2	11.6	163.6
Ethnicity											
Hispanic	35.3	33.8	1.9	5.6	26.3	8.9	17.4	1.5	37.2	17.3	178.0
Non-Hispanic	33.3	32.4	1.7	3.4	27.3	6.4	20.9	0.9	33.7	9.3	151.5
Household Income											
Less than $7,500	59.5	57.5	4.3	8.1	45.1	14.5	30.6	...	67.0	6.2	147.6
$7,500–$14,999	45.6	44.5	1.6	6.9	35.9	10.0	26.0	...	44.2	10.1	145.9
$15,000–$24,999	36.1	35.3	3.2	4.8	27.2	7.2	20.1	...	38.9	11.2	164.9
$25,000–$34,999	39.1	37.9	1.2	3.1	33.7	6.9	26.7	1.2	37.1	10.4	151.7
$35,000–$49,999	30.8	30.3	1.6	3.5	25.3	5.5	19.7	...	30.9	11.7	165.0
$50,000–$74,999	33.7	33.3	1.5	2.2	29.7	7.1	22.6	...	24.1	10.3	179.1
$75,000 or more	24.1	22.9	...	1.8	20.3	4.0	16.3	1.2	23.1	9.7	187.7

Source: Bureau of Justice Statistics. *Criminal Victimization in the United States, 1999.*
. . . = Not available.

VICTIMIZATION

A major purpose of the NCVS is not to measure crime, but to identify and characterize victims of crime. For example, the most likely victim of personal crime, that is, a crime where the victim and the offender are in contact at the time of the criminal event, is male, 16 to 19 years old, Black, and with a household income under $7,500. (See Table 8-1.) High-income households are more likely to be victims of property crime. However, low-income households are still more likely to be victims of burglary, the most invasive of the property crimes. The reason that very low income households (under $7,500) have a lower rate of motor vehicle theft is that these households are less likely to own cars.

CRIME DISTRIBUTION

Crime is not distributed evenly around the country. For example, Figure 8-2 shows that states such as California have violent crime rates well above the average for the country as a whole. A few states such as South Carolina have inexplicably high rates.

ARRESTS

Table 8-2 shows the number of arrests in the United States in 2000 for various offenses, and the incidence rate of arrests compared with the total population. In addition to showing the types of offenses reflected in the Crime Index, the table also shows all of the other offenses for which arrests were made, except for traffic offenses. ("Driving under the influence" is not considered a simple traffic offense and is included on the list of offenses.) The total of drug abuse violations is included here, and is the single largest category of arrests. The figure includes both drug possession and drug trafficking.

Crime is a young person's game. Figure 8-3 shows arrest rate, per 100,000 population, for selected age groups. It is clear that those under the age of 22 are the most likely to commit crimes and to be arrested.

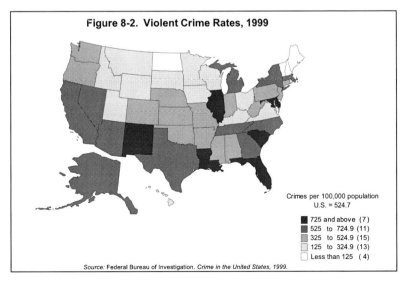

Figure 8-2. Violent Crime Rates, 1999

Crimes per 100,000 population
U.S. = 524.7

- ■ 725 and above (7)
- ▨ 525 to 724.9 (11)
- ▨ 325 to 524.9 (15)
- ☐ 125 to 324.9 (13)
- ☐ Less than 125 (4)

Source: Federal Bureau of Investigation. *Crime in the United States, 1999.*

Table 8-2. Number of Arrests and Arrest Rate by Type of Offense, 2000

(Number, rate of arrests per 100,000 inhabitants.)

Offense charged	Number	Rate
Total [1]	9 123 428	5 010.4
Murder and nonnegligent manslaughter	8 709	4.8
Forcible rape	17 914	9.8
Robbery	72 320	39.7
Aggravated assault	316 630	173.9
Burglary	189 343	104.0
Larceny- theft	782 082	429.5
Motor vehicle theft	98 697	54.2
Arson	10 675	5.9
Violent crime [2]	415 573	228.2
Property crime [3]	1 080 797	593.6
Crime Index total [4]	1 496 370	821.8
Other assaults	858 385	471.4
Forgery and counterfeiting	71 268	39.1
Fraud	213 828	117.4
Embezzlement	12 577	6.9
Stolen property	78 685	43.2
Vandalism	184 500	101.3
Weapons	105 341	57.9
Prostitution and commercialized vice	61 383	33.7
Sex offenses (except forcible rape and prostitution)	61 172	33.6
Drug abuse violations	1 042 334	572.4
Gambling	7 197	4.0
Offenses against the family and children	91 297	50.1
Driving under the influence	926 096	508.6
Liquor laws	435 672	239.3
Drunkenness	423 310	232.5
Disorderly conduct	421 542	231.5
Vagrancy	21 988	12.1
All other offenses (except traffic)	2 411 162	1 324.2
Suspicion	3 704	2.0
Curfew and loitering law violations	105 683	58.0
Runaways	93 638	51.4

Source: U.S. Department of Justice. Federal Bureau of Investigation. *Crime in the United States, 2000.*
[1]Does not include suspicion.
[2]Violent crimes are offenses of murder, forcible rape, robbery, and aggravated assault.
[3]Property crimes are offenses of burglary, larceny-theft, motor vehicle theft, and arson.
[4]Includes arson.

DOES CRIME PAY?

The likelihood that an arrest will be made in a crime varies by the type of offense. Figure 8-4 shows the clearance rates for index crimes in 2000. "To clear" is roughly equivalent to "to solve." Overall, the clearance rates for all of the crimes of violence are higher than for the property crimes. These data demonstrate that most crimes in the United States are unsolved. Although the clearance rate for murder is higher than any other, more than 30 percent of murders still go unsolved. Robbery and the property crimes—burglary, larceny, and motor vehicle theft—show extremely low clearance rates, probably because robbery is generally a stranger-to-stranger crime, and because property crimes are surreptitious and do not involve face-to-face contact between the offender and the victim. This makes them both appear to be less important and less likely to have the offender identified.

CONVICTIONS AND SENTENCES

The criminal justice system in the United States divides the responsibility for judicial processing and corrections between state and local jurisdictions and the federal government. Many offenses are under federal jurisdiction, such as serious crimes that take place on federal property, or are related to national issues only, such as violations of antitrust or customs laws. There are other crimes that have been turned into federal crimes by statute, such as the drug laws. Both states and the federal government have an interest in many of the same offenses. In general, where the state and federal interests are the same, the federal government has the jurisdictional option in individual cases.

As shown in Figure 8-5, sentences imposed in U.S. District Courts vary by the nature of the offense. As expected, the longest sentences are imposed for kidnaping, murder, robbery, and assault. Property offense sentences are much shorter, averaging about 2 years. Drug offenses, however, receive much longer sentences, even for simple possession. Racketeering and extortion are

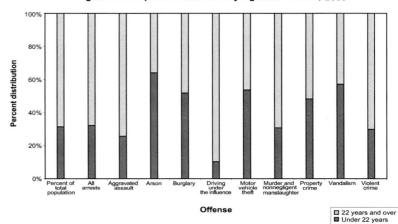

Figure 8-3. Proportion of Arrests by Age and Offense, 2000

Source: Federal Bureau of Investigation. *Crime in the United States, 2000.*

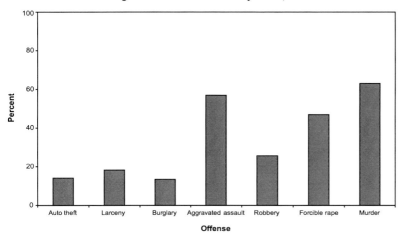

Figure 8-4. Offenses Cleared by Arrest, 2000

Source: Bureau of Justice Statistcs. *Sourcebook of Criminal Justice Statistics, 2000.*

also subject to severe penalties.

Although a significant number of crimes involve the federal system, crime is still primarily a state problem; almost all felony convictions take place in state courts. Sentencing patterns differ considerably between state and federal courts. Overall, an offender is more likely to be sentenced to prison in the federal system—72 percent in federal court versus 68 percent in state court. Average prison sentences in federal courts are also longer than in state courts. The average felony sentence in federal court is 58 months compared with 39 months in state courts.

For violent offenses, the difference is 77 months in state courts and 88 months in the federal system. For drug offenses, the average federal sentence is 75 months versus 31 months in state courts. (See Figure 8-5.)

Most of the offenders convicted in state courts in 1998—83 percent—were male. For violent offenses, the percentage increases to 90 percent. The racial division is 55 percent White and 44 percent Black overall. However, 57 percent of all offenders convicted of murder were Black, and 67 percent of

rape offenders were White. Among persons convicted of robbery, 64 percent were Black. Over two-thirds of convictions were of persons between the ages of 20 and 39.[6]

CORRECTIONS

The corrections system in the United States consists principally of prisons, jails, probation, and parole. Generally, prisons are institutions designed to house convicted felons; they are usually managed by the federal or state governments. Jails are usually locally run (by cities and counties), and are designed to house lesser criminals with sentences of a year or less, persons being held awaiting trial, and others in temporary or short-term situations. In recent years, jails have also been used to house the overflow from an overcrowded prison system.

Parole is the process by which prison inmates are released before their full sentences are completed. The inmate remains under the supervision of the correctional system, usually until his original sentence is completed. Probation, either supervised or unsupervised, generally is a sentence given in lieu of either prison or jail. However, there are occasions, usually at a judge's discretion, in which the offender is given a combination of incarceration and probation.

The number of adults in custody of state or federal prisons or local jails has increased sharply. The number in federal and state prisons more than tripled between 1980 and 2000, while the jail population increased by 238 percent during the same period. These two

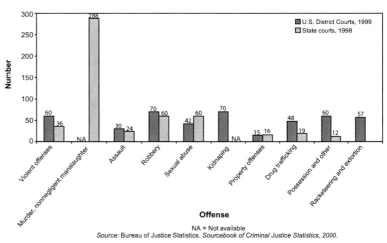

Figure 8-5. Median Months of Incarceration Imposed by U.S. District Courts and State Courts, 1998 and 1999

NA = Not available
Source: Bureau of Justice Statistics. *Sourcebook of Criminal Justice Statistics, 2000.*

6 Bureau of Justice Statistics, *State Court Sentencing of Convicted Felons: 1998*, Statistical Tables, December 2001. NCJ report 190637, located at <www.ojp.usdoj.gov/ bjs/abstract/scsc98st.htm>.

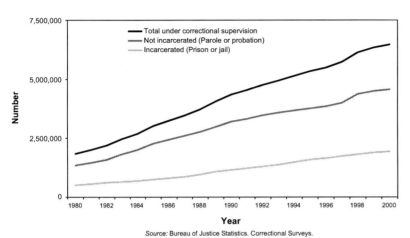

Figure 8-6. Persons Under Correctional Supervision, 1980–2000

Source: Bureau of Justice Statistics. Correctional Surveys.

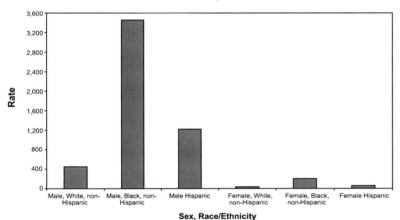

Figure 8-7. Sentenced Prisoners Under State or Federal Jurisdiction Per 100,000 Population, 2000

Source: Bureau of Justice Statistics. *Prisoners in 2000.*

especially in the inner cities. Figure 8-7 shows the incarceration rate per 100,000 by race/ethnicity and sex. In 2000, Black males were more than eight times as likely to be incarcerated as White males; the rate for Hispanic men was about triple that for White men. Incarceration rates for women are much lower, but approximately the same ratios hold.

In 2001, the rising prison population trend began to change. "It appears that the state prison population has reached some stability," said Allen Beck, a statistician with the Bureau of Justice Statistics.[7] The growth rate for 2001, 1.6 percent, was the lowest in three decades. With lower crime rates, steady rates of parole violation, and the movement of the Baby-Buster (or Generation X) cohort through the prime years of criminal activity, the incarcerated prison population could actually decrease in the near future.

EXPENDITURES

Expenditures in all parts of the criminal justice system and at all levels of government have been rising steadily. In 1999, $159.4 billion was expended for criminal justice activities, more than triple the amount spent in 1982 (not corrected for inflation). Corrections accounted for the biggest share of the increase, because of the bourgeoning prison population (and number of facilities) described above. In 1999, the United States spent $571 for every man, woman, and child to maintain the criminal justice system. Of this, $251 went to police protection, another $193 to corrections, and the balance to the legal and judicial functions. Local governments have primary responsibility (and expenditure of

groups, together, are the incarcerated population. (See Figure 8-6.) Another measure is the incarceration rate (the number of incarcerees per 100,000 population); this figure has more than tripled since 1980. A similar increase occurred in the non-incarcerated population, those on probation or parole. Tougher crime-fighting policies and longer sentences have exacerbated the growth. This

growth in the prison population and the commensurate growth in the number of prisons has constituted a new growth industry. Since 1990, the number of jails and prisons has increased significantly, with cities and towns competing for new prisons with their eyes on the number of jobs prisons generate.

The increase in the prison population is having a profound impact on many neighborhoods,

---

[7] Quoted in the *Detroit Free Press*, April 11, 2002.

funds) for police protection, while state governments are responsible for most of the corrections funding. Judicial and legal functions are about evenly divided between state and local, with the federal government spending a smaller amount.[8]

During the 1990s, Congress and many states passed mandatory sentencing and "truth in sentencing" laws that, in effect, increased the amount of time convicted offenders will remain incarcerated, thus decreasing the number of cells available at any given time. The public seems to support the use of mandatory sentences. In a 1995 survey, about 53 percent of the respondents thought mandatory sentences were a good idea, compared with 36 percent who felt judges should decide on sen-

tences. (See Table 8-3.) In a survey of police chiefs on drug offenses conducted by the Police Foundation, only 7 percent of the

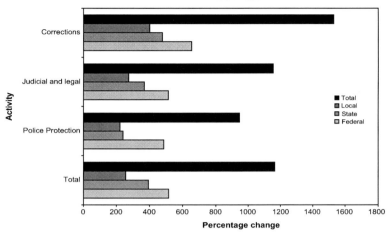

Figure 8-8. Percent Change in Criminal Justice Expenditures Activity, 1982–1999

Source: Bureau of Justice Statistics. *Justice Expenditure and Employment in the United States, 1999.*

nation's police chiefs thought the mandatory sentencing strategy was "very effective" and another 14 percent thought that it was "fairly effective." (See Table 8-4.) In a public survey about proposals to reduce prison overcrowding, 89 percent favored developing programs to keep more nonviolent and first-time offenders working in the community. In the same survey, 63 percent favored allowing prisoners to earn early release through good behavior and participation in educational and work programs, but 31 percent favored raising taxes to build more prisons. (See Table 8-5.)

Conflating the responses to the above-referenced surveys makes it appear that there is a conflict between various American value systems. On the one hand, there is the desire to suppress crime and punish criminals. On the other, there is the desire to be fair to first-time offenders and others who appear to want to work within the system. Although various professionals do not feel that strategies such as mandatory sentences are effective, the public seems to clamor for something to be done. The political establishment appears to be listening, as more

Table 8-3. Survey of Attitudes Toward Mandatory Prison Sentences, by Demographic Characteristic, 1995

Question: "In recent years, some legislators have made imprisonment mandatory for convictions for some types of crimes. Do you think these mandatory sentences are a good idea, or should judges be able to decide who goes to prison and who doesn't?"

(Percent.)

Characteristic	Mandatory sentences are a good idea	Judges should decide	Both	Neither
TOTAL	52.9	36.4	6.0	1.3
Sex				
Male	52.2	38.3	5.8	1.0
Female	53.6	34.5	6.1	1.5
Race				
White	55.0	33.9	6.3	1.1
Black	45.7	48.6	3.8	1.9
Hispanic	43.2	44.6	2.7	2.7
Age				
18 to 29 years	47.7	44.6	5.4	0.5
30 to 39 years	53.4	35.4	9.0	0.4
40 to 59 years	55.3	35.5	2.8	1.9
60 years and older	55.2	28.7	6.9	2.9
Education				
College graduate	52.7	39.8	5.4	1.1
Some college	56.6	31.5	6.6	0.3
High school graduate	53.5	36.0	6.5	1.5
Less than high school graduate	39.6	44.6	5.0	4.0
Income				
Less than $15,000	45.4	43.7	2.5	2.5
$15,000 to $29,999	56.1	33.1	5.9	2.1
$30,000 to $59,999	53.7	35.7	6.1	1.4
$60,000 and over	57.0	37.1	5.9	0.0
Community				
Urban	43.9	43.3	5.1	1.9
Suburban	57.8	33.1	5.3	0.0
Small city	46.3	41.5	6.9	2.1
Rural/small town	56.4	33.1	6.6	1.3
Region				
East	47.5	39.0	8.5	1.7
Midwest	50.0	38.7	6.7	1.3
South	59.7	28.9	5.7	1.1
West	49.6	43.0	3.7	1.2
Politics				
Republican	59.7	31.4	6.1	0.7
Democrat	49.3	39.6	5.7	2.1
Independent/other	51.6	37.6	5.3	1.3

Source: Bureau of Justice Statistics, *Sourcebook of Criminal Justice Statistics 1995.*
Note: The "don't know/refused" category has been omitted; therefore percents may not sum to 100.

---

8 Bureau of Justice Statistics, *Justice Expenditure and Employment in the United States, 1999*, NCJ 191746, February 2002.

and more such laws are being enacted at the state and federal level. Only time will tell if this conflict worsens or tends to resolve itself.

How has all this worked out? A review of sentencing guidelines suggests that the record is mixed. As the new decade and century get underway, several new issues have arisen, including the core principles on which guidelines have been based and their compatibility with a new concept called "restorative justice." [9] This idea promotes reparation rather than retribution, with the community deciding the appropriate punishment for the crime. This, of course, would only apply to the less serious crimes and the non-repeat offenders. Restorative justice is sharply different from previous practices, emphasizing a subjective understanding of the crime and the circumstances surrounding it. Disproportionate sentences for what is objectively the same crime are acceptable. In the current sentencing guidelines atmosphere, the approach is top-down rather than bottom-up. It appears that a hybrid approach needs to be developed.

Table 8-4. Survey of U.S. Police Chiefs' Attitudes Toward the Effectiveness of Mandatory Minimum Sentences for Drug Possession, by Size of Community, 1996

Question: "From your perspective, how effective have mandatory minimum sentences for drug possession been in reducing drug trafficking in your community—very effective, fairly effective, somewhat effective, or not really the answer to the problem in your community?"

(Percent.)

Responses	All police chiefs	Large cities	Medium communities	Small towns
Very effective	7	10	7	6
Fairly effective	14	17	8	14
Only somewhat effective	33	31	37	33
Not really the answer	40	36	40	42
Don't have a mandatory minimum sentencing [1]	4	2	5	4
Not sure	2	4	3	1

Source: Police Foundation and Drug Strategies, *Drugs and Crime Across America: Police Chiefs Speak Out* (Washington, DC: Police Foundation and Drug Strategies, 1996) p.17. Reprinted in *Sourcebook of Criminal Justice Statistics 1996.*
[1]Response volunteered.

Table 8-5. Survey of Attitudes Toward Proposals to Reduce Prison Overcrowding, 1995

Question: "Would you favor or oppose each of the following measures that have been suggested as ways to reduce prison overcrowding?"

(Percent.)

Characteristic	Shortening sentences	Allowing prisoners to earn early release through good behavior and participation in educational and work programs	Developing local programs to keep more nonviolent and first-time offenders active working in the community	Giving the parole board more authority to release offenders early	Increasing taxes to build more prisons
TOTAL	7.5	63.2	89.2	20.3	31.4
Sex					
Male	10.7	70.7	88.0	26.2	34.5
Female	4.4	56.3	90.4	14.8	28.6
Race					
White	6.2	63.1	88.1	17.8	33.9
Black	15.4	69.2	96.2	35.6	21.0
Hispanic	5.5	60.0	91.9	23.0	24.7

Source: Bureau of Justice Statistics, *Sourcebook of Criminal Justice 1995.*

---

[9] Robin L. Lubitz and Thomas W. Ross, "Sentencing and Corrections: Issues for the 21st Century," U.S. Department of Justice, Office of Justice Programs, National Institute of Justice, Papers from the Executive Sessions on Sentencing and Corrections, No. 10, June 2001.

FOR FURTHER INFORMATION SEE:

U.S. Department of Justice, Bureau of Justice Statistics. *The Sourcebook of Criminal Justice Statistics, 2000.*

U.S. Department of Justice, Federal Bureau of Investigation. *Uniform Crime Reports*, 2000.

U.S. Department of Justice, Office of Justice Statistics, Bureau of Justice Programs. *Criminal Victimization in the United States*, 1999.

WEB SITES:

Bureau of Justice Statistics Web site: <http://ojp.usdoj.gov/bjs/>. BJS publishes a series of bulletins which cover a wide variety of topics in criminal justice, and which include annual updates of the types of data presented in this chapter.

Federal Bureau of Investigation Web site: <http://www.fbi.gov>.

Federal Bureau of Prisons Web site: <http://www.bop.gov>.

Inter-University Consortium for Political and Social Research (ICPSR) Web site: <http://www.icpsr.umich.edu/index.html>.

Sourcebook of Criminal Justice Statistics Web site: <http://www.albany.edu/sourcebook>.

Chapter 9
Health

INTRODUCTION

Is the American population more or less healthy today than it was a few decades ago? In terms of life expectancy (see chapter 1), the U.S. population lives longer on average, with life expectancy having increased by 5 years since 1970 to nearly 77 years in 2001. Yet, there are new health concerns today that were virtually nonexistent 25 years ago, such as HIV/AIDS, SARS, and the West Nile virus. There is also emphasis now on risk factors to a healthy life that were only peripheral concerns a few decades ago, such as lowering fat intake, obesity, and smoking.

The U.S. Department of Health and Human Services (HHS) has developed an initiative entitled Healthy People 2010, with the goals of "increasing the span of healthy life for all Americans, decreasing health disparities among Americans, and achieving access to preventive services for all Americans." This initiative has defined "health-related quality of life," reflecting a "personal sense of physical and mental health, and the ability to react to factors in the physical and social environments." This leads to the definition of "Years of Healthy Life," reflecting the "time spent in less than optimal health because of chronic or acute limitations." In these terms, healthy life expectancy has not risen nearly as fast as overall life expectancy, meaning that more time at the end of life is spent in less than good health conditions.

MORTALITY

Death rates for the United States have continued to decline in the past 25 years for the population as a whole, when changes in age composition are taken into account (age-adjusted death rate). The crude death rate in 2001, 849 deaths per 100,000 population, is considerably below the 1970 rate of 945. The infant mortality rate in the United States, 6.9 per 1,000 live births in 2001, was one of the lowest in the world.

Cause of death varies considerably by age. Since about three out of four deaths in the United States each year are to persons over age 65, their causes of death predominate when causes of death are not disaggregated by age. The major causes of death are diseases of the heart, at 29 percent of deaths; malignant neoplasms (various forms of cancer), at 23 percent of deaths; cerebrovascular diseases (stroke), 7 percent; chronic lower respiratory diseases (such as emphysema), 5 percent; and accidents, which cause 4 percent of deaths.

Some causes of death are among the top 10 causes for each age group, including accidents, cancers, diseases of the heart, and cerebrovascular diseases. Others, such as diabetes, HIV infection, or congenital anomalies are significant causes of death primarily for specific age groups.

For any given age group, the top five causes of death account

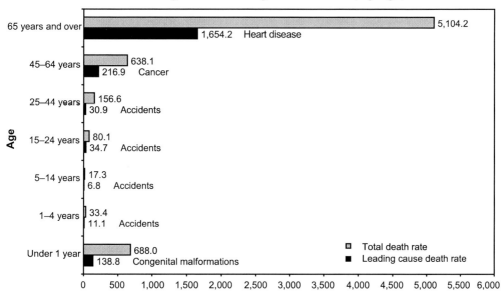

Figure 9-1. Leading Cause of Death, by Age, 2001

Source: National Center for Health Statistics. National Vital Statistics Report.

for the vast majority of deaths, with the 10th most common cause of death typically contributing only about 1 percent of deaths in a group in a given year. Among children under 15, accidents remain the leading cause of death, accounting for about two of every five deaths; motor vehicle accidents predominate for 5-to 14-year-olds, while other types of accidents are more common for younger children. Homicide and suicide are the fourth and fifth most common causes of death for children 5 to 14, with HIV infection ranked 10th. For young adults aged 15 to 24, motor vehicle accidents are still the number one cause of death, followed by homicide and suicide. HIV infection is the fifth most common killer in this age group, while homicide and suicide also rank in the top 10.

Among persons aged 25 to 44, accidents are the leading cause of death, followed by cancer and heart disease, suicide, and HIV infection. In the next oldest group, 45 to 64, the accident death rate remains about the same, but drops to third place as heart disease and cancer increase in frequency with age. Heart disease and cancer continue to be the top two causes for the elderly (65 and over) as well.[1]

DIFFERENCES BETWEEN STATES

As shown in Figure 9-2, there is considerable variation in death rates, even when age-adjusted, among the states. In 2000, 10 states had death rates above 950 per 100,000 population; all are located in the South except West Virginia and Oklahoma. Nine states showed rates below 800; they are located primarily in the Plains states and in the West. The southern states, generally, have larger concentrations of lower-income Black populations. With the exception of California, the states with low death rates also have low minority populations.

The HIV/AIDS epidemic in the United States is measured beginning in 1981. Through 2000, a total of about 807,000 cases had been diagnosed and reported throughout the country, of which 9,000 were children under 13. Of these, 57 percent had died. The epidemic hit its peak in terms of cases diagnosed in 1992–1993 (about 79,000 per year), and 2 years later in terms of deaths (about 50,000 per year). By 2001, the number of new cases dropped to 25,000, and the number of deaths dropped below 9,000. (See Figure 9-3.)

Most of the cases occurring among children under 13 were caused by infection from the mother around the time of birth–perinatal HIV transmission. In 1994, treatment with the drug zidovudine (ZDV) was found to reduce perinatal HIV transmission, leading to a significant decline in the number of

Figure 9-2. Age-Adjusted Death Rates, 2001

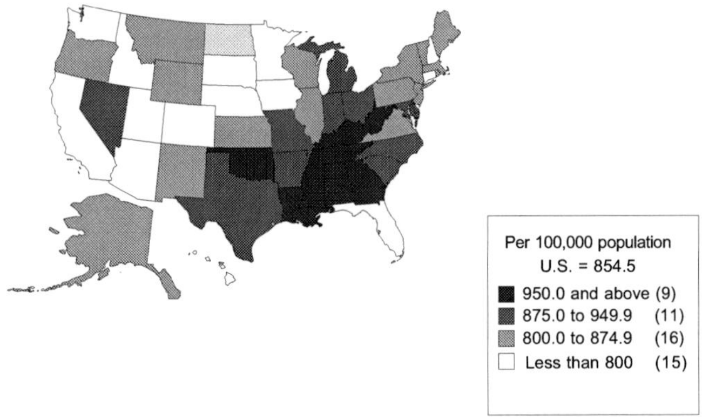

Per 100,000 population
U.S. = 854.5

- 950.0 and above (9)
- 875.0 to 949.9 (11)
- 800.0 to 874.9 (16)
- Less than 800 (15)

Table 9-1. AIDS Cases, by Exposure Category, Race, and Sex, Reported through 2001

(Number, percent distribution.)

Characteristic	Total AIDS cases		Male		Female	
	Number	Percent distribution	Number	Percent distribution	Number	Percent distribution
Total, age 13 years and over	42 983	100.0	31 901	100.0	11 082	100.0
Exposure category						
Men who have sex with men	13 265	30.9	13 265	41.6	NA	NA
Injecting drug use	7 473	17.4	5 261	16.5	2 212	20.0
Men who have sex with men and inject drugs	1 502	3.5	1 502	4.7	NA	NA
Heterosexual contact	6 904	16.1	2 762	8.7	4 142	37.4
Other/risk not reported	13 515	28.1	8 909	25.1	4 606	37.0
Race						
White, non-Hispanic	13 204	30.7	11 164	35.0	2 040	18.4
Black, non-Hispanic	20 918	48.7	13 895	43.6	7 023	63.4
Hispanic	8 183	19.0	6 289	19.7	1 894	17.1
Asian/Pacific Islander	427	1.0	358	1.1	69	0.6
American Indian/Alaska Native	194	0.5	152	0.5	42	0.4

Source: Centers for Disease Control and Prevention. *HIV/AIDS Surveillance Report, 2001*; 13 (No. 2).
NA = Not applicable.

[1] *National Vital Statistics Report*, Vol. 51, No. 5, March 14, 2003. The figures reported are the preliminary data for 2001.

Figure 9-3. AIDS Deaths, Before 1981–2001

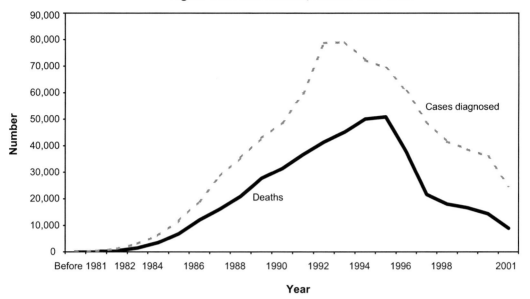

Source: Centers for Disease Control and Prevention. HIV/AIDS Surveillance Report, 2001; 13 (No. 2).

AIDS cases among children. In 2001, only 51 new pediatric cases were diagnosed.

By 2001, there were an estimated half a million people currently living with HIV or AIDS, with approximately 31,000 new HIV infections occurring that year. About 40 percent of the people with HIV develop full-blown AIDS. About 75 percent are men. The proximate cause of the infection in about half of these male cases is homosexual sex. Women are more likely to become exposed to the virus through drug use or heterosexual sex. However, often the actual proximate cause of the infection is not identified. Blacks, both males and females, have a much higher incidence of AIDS cases than do Whites; the rate for Hispanics is in-between these two. In over half of the Hispanics AIDS cases in 2001, the patient was born outside the United States.[2]

ENVIRONMENTAL FACTORS

Changes in the quality of the environment and effects of pollution on health and death rates have been of particular concern over the past 30 years. Concern for illness born of the environment takes an extraordinarily broad sweep—from sick building syndrome (in which building occupants experience acute health problems that appear to be linked to time spent in a particular structure) to exposure to lead (left in the pilings of long-closed mines in Idaho, which sift onto school yards) to public water systems that carry unsafe bacteria levels. Some environmental disease occurs naturally (mosquito-borne malaria), some is man-made.

The fraction of all deaths attributable to environmental causes has decreased dramatically in the United States throughout the last century. Environmental causes were responsible for 40 percent of all deaths at the turn of the twentieth century, but for only 5 percent of deaths in 1970. There is little evidence that the proportion has changed much since 1970.

HEALTHY PEOPLE

The U. S. Department of Health and Human Services has a project which it has labeled Healthy People 2010, an update of the earlier Healthy People 2000 program. There is a set of Leading Health Indicators, which reflect the major health concerns in the nation at the beginning of the twenty-first century. They were selected "on the basis of their ability to motivate action, the availability of data to measure progress, and their importance as public health issues."[3] The leading health indicators are physical activity, overweight and obesity, tobacco use, substance abuse, responsible sexual behavior, mental health, injury and violence, environmental quality, immunization, and access to health care.

An accompanying initiative is Steps to a Healthier US, an initiative established in 2003 to promote creation of health promotion programs, community initiatives, health care and insurance systems that put prevention first, state and federal policies that "invest in the promise of prevention," and cooperation among policy makers, local health agencies, and the public to invest in disease prevention rather than focusing on treating diseases after they arise. The initiative

[2] Centers for Disease Control and Prevention, HIV/AIDS Surveillance Report, Year-end edition, Vol. 13, No. 2. This report includes data reported through December 2001.

[3] Healthy People, at <www.healthypeople.gov/LHI/lhiwhat.htm>.

**Figure 9-4. Chronic Conditions Reported Per 1,000 Persons,
by Sex and Age, 1995**

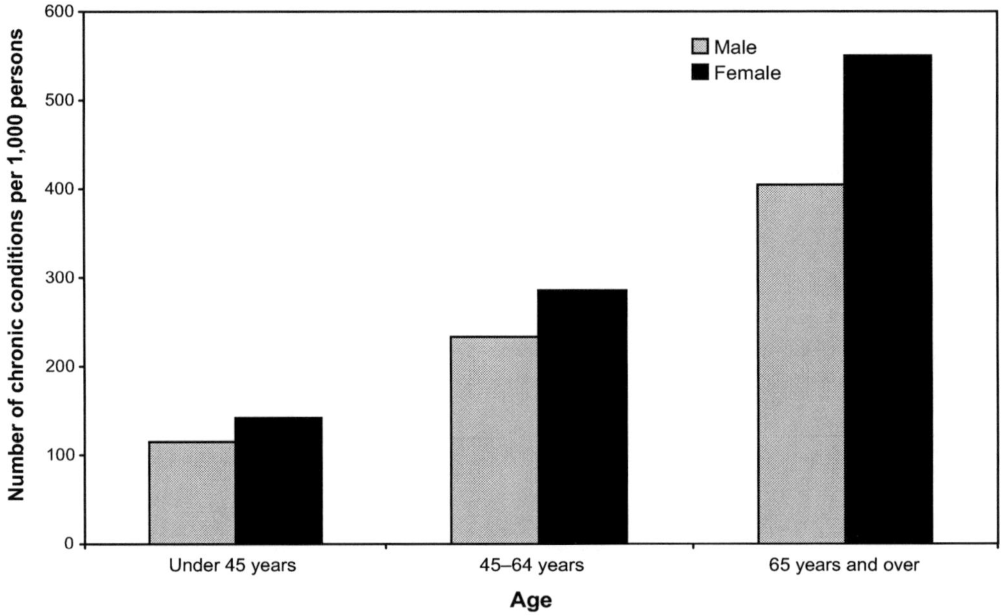

Source: National Center for Health Statistics. *Current Estimates From the National Health Interview Survey, 1995.*

focuses on five disease categories: diabetes, obesity, asthma, heart disease and stroke, and cancer. It also focuses on three lifestyle choices which have significant impacts on health: poor nutrition and physical inactivity, tobacco use, and youth risk-taking.[4]

CHRONIC ILLNESS

Chronic illnesses are those health conditions that have a long duration or frequent recurrence, are associated with age and with causes of death, and tend to occur more frequently with advancing age. The most common conditions, affecting at least 10 percent of the population overall, include arthritis, orthopedic impairments (most often back problems), high blood pressure or hypertension, and chronic sinusitis. Among those 65 and older, arthritis (48 percent), cataracts (17 percent), hearing impairment (30 percent), deformity or orthopedic impairment (16 percent), diabetes (10 percent), heart disease (27 percent), hypertension (36 percent), and chronic sinusitis (12 percent) head the list.

Health experts believe that regular exercise, coupled with healthful diet, can help to prevent some health conditions and ameliorate others. Clearly, not all Americans are listening to this advice. Physical inactivity and poor diet together account for at least 300,000 deaths in the United States each year.

PHYSICAL ACTIVITY

Emphasis on regular physical activity has increased strongly over the past two decades. It is considered important for maintaining a healthy body, enhancing psychological well-being, and preventing premature death. As shown in Table 9-x, participation in leisure-time physical activity is considerably below the recommended level. High-school students are much more likely to be active, with 65 percent engaging in 20 minutes or more of vigorous physical activity at least 3 days a week; however, the target goal for this age group is 85 percent. Adult engagement in moderate physical activity was on the decline in the 1990s, reaching

a low of 20 percent. Several population categories have low rates of physical activity. These include women, people with lower income and lower education, African Americans and Hispanics, and adults in the northeastern and southern states.

OVERWEIGHT AND OBESITY

Overweight is one of the most prevalent and serious health conditions in the United States. If being overweight had no side effect other than to make clothing purchases more difficult, it would be of little more than aesthetic concern. But being overweight is associated with a host of other ailments, including high cholesterol readings, which in turn can lead to high blood pressure, heart disease, and other chronic conditions. As shown in Figure 9-5, the proportion of the adult population (age 20 to 74) that is overweight increased from 47 percent in 1976–1980 to 65 percent in 1999–2000. Men are more likely to be overweight than women, except that black women (78 percent) are overweight more

---

4 Steps to a HealthierUS, at <www.healthierus.gov/steps/steps_brochure.html>.

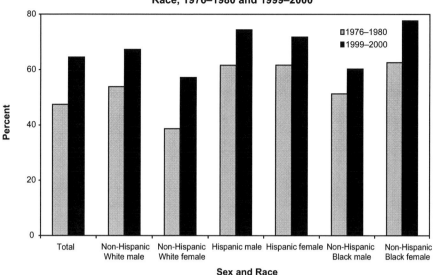

Figure 9-5. Percentage of Population 20–74 Years that is Overweight, by Sex and Race, 1976–1980 and 1999–2000

Source : National Center for Health Statistics. *Health, United States, 2003.*

often than black men (60 percent). The Healthy People 2010 target is that no more than 11 percent of children and adolescents, and 23 percent of adults aged 20 and over, should be overweight or obese.

Despite the increased proportion of the population that is overweight, the percentage of the population that has high serum cholesterol readings has actually declined in the past 30 years, from about 32 percent to 20 percent in the 1988–1994 period. For men, the proportion with high cholesterol readings has declined from about 31 percent to 19 percent; for women, from 37 percent to 21 percent. Similarly, the percentage of the population that suffers from hypertension has declined as well, from about 38 percent of adults (aged 20 and older) in the early 1960s to 24 percent in the early 1990s. Hypertension rates remain higher for men, but the proportion suffering from this disorder has declined for both men and women. All of this decline, for both men and women, has occurred since 1980. The proportion suffering

from this condition actually increased between 1960 and 1980.

What is behind this paradoxical increase in overweight but decrease in cholesterol levels and hypertension? One partial explanation offered is that a large fraction of adults have stopped smoking over this same period. Former smokers have long complained that they gained weight when they stopped smoking. A 1995 study appears to confirm this injustice.[5] Former smokers who had quit in the past 10 years were found to be considerably more likely to have become overweight than their peers who had never smoked. For men, about a fourth and for women about a sixth of the increase in the number of persons who are overweight could be attributed to their stopping smoking.

This theory regarding smoking cessation does not, however, explain the large increase in the occurrence of overweight children and adolescents. In the past 30 years, the percentage of 6 to 17 year olds who are overweight has doubled, with much of this

increase occurring (as in adults) since the late 1970s. About 11 percent of these children are classified as "seriously overweight." Obese children are likely to become obese adults and suffer the health consequences of being overweight, and they are likely to attempt dangerous weight-reducing activities: about 5 percent of youth in a 1995 survey had taken laxatives or vomited to lose or maintain weight during the previous month.[6]

Decreased participation in physical activity with increasing age is part of the problem for children as well as adults. Regular participation in vigorous physical activity was reported by about 7 out of 10 youngsters between 12 and 13 years old, but only about 4 of 10 persons aged 18 to 21. Similarly about 80 percent of 9th graders but only 42 percent of 12th graders were enrolled in a physical education class in 1996.

SUBSTANCE ABUSE: DRUGS, ALCOHOL, AND TOBACCO

Being overweight and lack of exercise

[5] Katherine M. Flegal, et al., "The Influence of Smoking Cessation on the Prevalence of Overweight in the United States," *New England Journal of Medicine 333* (1995), 1165-70.

[6] National Center for Health Statistics, *1999 Youth Risk Behavior Surveillance Survey.*

Table 9-2. Alcohol Use, Selected Years, 1979–1999

(Percent using in past month.)

Characteristic	1979	1985	1990	1995	1998	1999
12 years and over	63	60	53	52	52	52
12–17 years	50	41	33	21	19	19
18–25 years	75	70	63	61	60	60
26–34 years	72	71	64	63	61	62
35 years and over	60	58	50	53	53	53

Source: National Center for Health Statistics. *Health, United States, 2001 with Urban and Rural Health Chartbook.* Hyattsville, Maryland: 2001.

are not the only factors contributing to serious health problems in the United States. Substance abuse—including cigarettes and alcohol as well as illegal substances—persists. Alcohol is the most pervasive, with a fairly constant proportion of the population reporting its use in the past month. In 1999, 52 percent of the population reported using alcohol in the past month, down from 63 percent in 1979. Alcohol usage has declined considerably among teenagers; in 1979, 50 percent of 12-to 17-year olds reporting having a drink in the past month; the comparable figure for 1999 is 19 percent. Similar drops are evident among older persons, although they are not as dramatic. Drinking levels remain quite high among young adults, 18 to 34.

As shown in Table 9-2, certain historical patterns persist. For persons 18 to 25 years of age, alcohol usage remains more prevalent in men than women (70 percent versus 58 percent), and more prevalent in Whites than in Blacks (71 percent versus 40 percent) or Hispanics (53 percent).

Overall, about 52 percent of Americans, age 12 and older, indicate that they had at least one drink over a month's period, according to data collected in the late 1990s. Therefore, 48 percent drink less often, or not at all. In 1999, 15 percent of the population could be characterized as "binge drinkers," those who indicated that they have had five or more drinks on the same occasion in the past month.[7] While possible consequences of alcohol abuse—both

health and societal—are widely known, only recently have groups such as Mothers Against Drunk Driving (MADD) brought to public awareness issues about drinking, such as the consequences of driving while intoxicated. In 1998, about 16,000 persons died in alcohol-related traffic crashes.

After alcohol, the most pervasive drug use is cigarette smoking. Smoking reached a high of about 4,300 cigarettes a year (about 12 per day) per person 18 or older in 1963. The level remained quite high until about 20 years ago, Significant annual declines have brought the figure down to about 2,000 in 2002. The percentage of adults who are current smokers declined from 42 percent in 1965, to 37 percent in 1974, to 23 percent in 2001. This decline is observed among all age groups, among both men and women, and for both Whites and Blacks. Still, almost one out of four Americans smoked cigarettes in 2001. When data on smoking were first collected in 1965, half of adult men and about a third of adult women smoked. Per capita cigarette consumption among adults was still over 2,000 cigarettes per year, less than half the rate in the early 1960s but still very significant. The proportion for both sexes was considerably smaller by 1999, with a reduced sex differential (about 25 percent of men and 21 percent of women smoked in that year). As shown in Table 9-3, not smoking cigarettes, among adults, is highly correlated with education achievement. However, there has been a significant decline at all educational levels. The 2010 target is to cut

Table 9-3. Age-Adjusted Prevalence of Current Cigarette Smoking by Persons 25 Years and Over, 1974 and 1999

(Percent.)

Sex, race, and year	Total	No high school diploma or GED	High school diploma or GED	Some college, no bachelor's degree	Bachelor's degree or higher
All Persons					
1974	36.9	43.7	36.2	35.9	27.2
1999	22.7	32.2	28.0	23.3	11.1
All Males					
1974	42.9	52.3	42.4	41.8	28.3
1999	24.6	36.2	30.4	24.8	11.8
White Males					
1974	41.9	51.5	42.0	41.6	27.8
1999	24.2	36.3	30.5	24.7	11.8
Black Males					
1974	53.4	58.1	50.7	45.3	41.4
1999	29.3	44.0	32.7	24.0	11.0
All Females					
1974	32.0	36.6	32.2	30.1	25.9
1999	20.9	28.2	25.9	21.9	10.4
White Females					
1974	31.7	36.8	31.9	30.4	25.5
1999	21.5	30.0	27.2	22.4	10.5
Black Females					
1974	35.6	36.1	40.9	32.3	36.3
1999	21.6	30.2	22.6	22.6	13.4

Source: National Center for Health Statistics. *Health, United States, 2001 with Urban and Rural Health Chartbook.* Hyattsville, Maryland: 2001.
Note: Totals for each category include unknown education. GED stands for general equivalency exam.

---

[7] National Center for Health Statistics, *Health, United States, 2001 with Urban and Rural Health Chartbook.*

Table 9-4. Use of Selected Substances by High School Seniors and Eighth-Graders, 1980, 1990, and 2000

(Percent using substance in past month, except where noted.)

Substance and grade in school	1980	1990	2000
Cigarettes			
High school seniors	30.5	29.4	31.4
All eighth-graders	. . .	. . .	14.6
Marijuana			
High school seniors	33.7	14.0	21.6
All eighth-graders	. . .	. . .	9.1
Cocaine			
High school seniors	5.2	1.9	2.1
All eighth-graders	. . .	. . .	1.2
Inhalants			
High school seniors	1.4	2.7	2.2
All eighth-graders	. . .	. . .	4.5
MDMA (Ecstasy)			
High school seniors	. . .	. . .	3.6
All eighth-graders	. . .	. . .	1.4
Alcohol			
High school seniors	72.0	. . .	50.0
All eighth-graders	. . .	57.1	22.4
Binge Drinking [1]			
High school seniors	41.2	. . .	30.0
All eighth-graders	. . .	32.2	14.1

Source: National Center for Health Statistics. *Health, United States, 2001 with Urban and Rural Health Chartbook.* Hyattsville, Maryland: 2001.
[1] Five or more alcoholic drinks in a row at least once in the prior 2-week period.
. . . = Not available.

the 1999 level in half, down to 12 percent of all adults.

Perhaps one of the biggest societal changes that has occurred since 1980 had been public attitudes and behavior toward smoking. The U.S. Surgeon General's report of 1964 was the first significant government blast against smoking, linking smoking causally to lung cancer as well as other ailments. Yet prior to 1980, smoking cigarettes, pipes or cigars was still common in most workplaces and in such public accommodations as restaurants and airplanes. After 1980, amid mounting evidence of the health effects of smoking, effects of secondhand smoke in the workplace, and the legal right and obligation of employers to protect their workers, smoking in the workplace began to be severely limited, first restricted by employers to particular locations, then banned entirely from the interior of buildings. By the end of 1994, 48 states and the District of Columbia had laws restricting smoking in public places. In addition, most states restrict smoking in government workplaces, and 23 have extended those limitations to private sector workplaces[8].

While alcohol remains as the primary substance abuse problem, as measured by admissions for treatment, illicit drug use has been a serious concern for several decades. After alcohol, heroin use causes the most such admissions, followed by cocaine and marijuana/hashish. Other substance abuse includes stimulants, sedatives and tranquilizers, hallucinogens, PCP, and inhalants. Over the 1994–1999 period, cocaine declined as a proportion of all admissions, while heroin increased by about 10 percent. There has been increasing availability of "high purity heroin," which can be inhaled instead of being injected.[9]

Substance abuse among teenagers has long been of special concern. As shown in Table 9-4, this remains a serious issue, but there has been improvement over the past 20 years for all the reported categories except for cigarettes.

Still, recent data show that half of high school seniors drink alcoholic beverages, with three in 10 engaging in binge drinking. Marijuana use remains high as well.

CONTRACEPTIVE USE, ABORTION, AND SEXUALLY TRANSMITTED DISEASES

CONTRACEPTIVE USE

The U.S. Government was first involved in family planning services in the 1960s, as part of the war on poverty declared by President Johnson in 1964. The first funding was earmarked to provide family planning services to women receiving public assistance. In 1970, Title X of the Public Health Service Act created a comprehensive federal program to provide family planning services (but prohibited abortion as a family planning method); these services were available to anyone in need. Additional public support for family planning has come from Medicaid, the social services block grant, and state contributions.

As described by the Alan Guttmacher Institute, family planning services have been plagued by political controversy since their inception. Conservatives have claimed that the availability of confidential contraceptive services encourages sexual activity among teenagers and that the family planning clinics promote abortion. Supporters point to the success of the family planning services network, whose 6.5 million clients annually represent one-quarter of women receiving these types of services. The network services go primarily to poor or low-income women, the majority of whom are White, and to women under age 30. In addition to advice on contraceptive methods, the clinics provide

---

[8] See National Center for Health Statistics, and the American Lung Association's Web site <www.lungusa.org>.
[9] Substance Abuse and Mental Health Services Administration (SAMHSA), data from the TEDS and DASIS reporting system, at <www.drugabusestatistics.samhsa.gov>. The TEDS data set also provides many state-level tabulations.

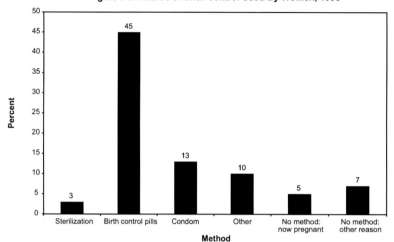

Figure 9-6. Method of Birth Control Used By Women, 1995

Source: National Center for Health Statistics. *Health, United States, 2001.*

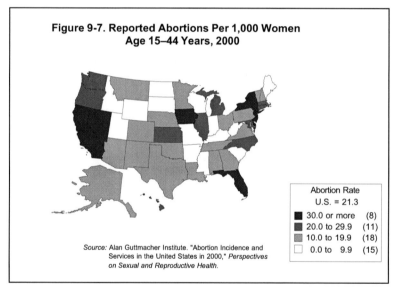

Figure 9-7. Reported Abortions Per 1,000 Women Age 15–44 Years, 2000

Abortion Rate
U.S. = 21.3
■ 30.0 or more (8)
▨ 20.0 to 29.9 (11)
▨ 10.0 to 19.9 (18)
□ 0.0 to 9.9 (15)

Source: Alan Guttmacher Institute. "Abortion Incidence and Services in the United States in 2000," *Perspectives on Sexual and Reproductive Health.*

ing below the poverty level. A 1994 study showed that almost half of all women of childbearing age have had at least one unintended pregnancy, with the figure rising as high as 60 percent among women in their thirties.[11]

Nearly 9 of 10 sexually active women in the 15- to 44-year-old age group, women who are not pregnant and do not wish to become so, report using some contraceptive method. The most commonly used method, is oral contraceptives- the "Pill", reported as being used by half of all women who use some birth control method. The second most common method is the recently developed injection, which provides protection for several weeks or months. Third is the condom. All other methods are used comparatively rarely. (See Figure 9-6.)

ABORTION TRENDS

Abortion was legalized in the United States by the Supreme Court in the 1972 Roe v. Wade decision. In recent years, the actual number of induced abortions has tended to decline, as has the ratio of abortions to live births, after initial increases in the late 1970s. Between 1975 (when such data were first collected) and 1979, the number of abortions increased from about 1 million to 1.5 million, and the ratio of abortions to live births increased from 331 to 420 per 1,000 live births. From 1979 to 1993, the actual number of abortions was relatively stable, despite a large increase in the number of women of childbearing age (from 52 to 59 million) during this period. The number of abortions peaked in 1990 at 1.6 million, and then declined to about 1.3 million in 2000.

A better way of measuring, however, is to look at the abortion rate. Two methods of calculating the rate are available: abortions per 1,000 women of childbearing

Pap smears, pelvic examinations, testing and treatment for gynecologic infections, and testing for HIV and other sexually transmitted diseases (STDs). This work has been carried out in an atmosphere of severely reduced funding: inflation adjusted, the funding level in 2000 was 60 percent lower than 20 years earlier.[10]

As indicated in a previous chapter (Chapter 2, Households and Families), average family size in the United States has decreased considerably over the past several

decades, with the unplanned pregnancy rate decreasing as well. A major contributor to the decrease in the number of children born to American women has been the increased use of and improvements in contraceptives. However, almost half of all pregnancies still are unintended, and half of the unintended pregnancies end in abortion. These unintended pregnancies occur most often among the young (over 75 percent of those in women under age 20), the unmarried, and among women liv-

---

[10] The Alan Guttmacher Institute, "Fulfilling the Promise: Public Policy and U.S. Family Planning Clinics, at <http://www.agi-usa.org/sections/prev.html>.

[11] Stanley K. Henshaw, "Unintended Pregnancy in the United States," *Family Planning Perspectives,* vol. 30, no. 1.

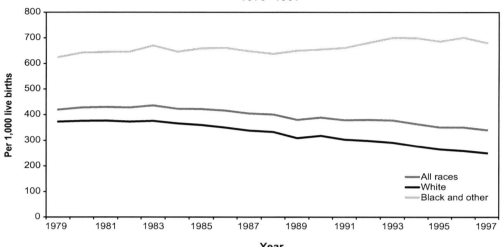

Figure 9-8. Abortion Ratio Per 1,000 Live Births, by Race, 1979–1997

Source: U.S. Census Bureau. *Statistical Abstract, 2001.*

age and abortions per 1,000 live births in the same year. By either measure, the rates have dropped steadily from their peak in 1981. Figure 9.7 shows the 2000 state by state abortion rates based on the first measure. The rate is very low in South Dakota, West Virginia, Idaho, Utah, and Wyoming (under 10). It is very high, over 40, in New York, California, Hawaii, and Nevada.

SEXUALLY TRANSMITTED DISEASES

Sexually transmitted diseases (STDs) have increased as a public health problem in the United States over the past two decades. Despite the fact that the number of cases per 100,000 for syphilis and gonorrhea declined throughout the 1990s, chlamydia was on the rise. Five STDs are among the 10 most frequently treated infections, including chlamydia, gonorrhea, AIDS, syphilis and hepatitis B. Women are more likely than men to become infected with an STD.

The most commonly reported STD (and, for that matter, any type of infection) in the United States is Chlamydia trachomatis. While this condition is usually asymptomatic,

it often leads to pelvic inflammatory disease (PID), a major cause of infertility, ectopic pregnancy, and chronic pelvic pain in women. Chlamydial infection also facilitates the transmission of AIDS and can be passed from mother to child during delivery. The rate of chlamydial infection has been increasing steadily since first reported in 1984, partly because diagnostic tests and reporting have improved. Chlamydia affects many more women than men, and the rate for women has been increasing at a faster pace. It is primarily a disease infecting young people between the ages of 15 and 29.

Rates for older STDs–gonorrhea and syphilis–have been decreasing over time, and the disease is almost non-existent in northern New England and the northern Rocky Mountain region. The syphilis rate has dropped so much—almost 90 percent in the 1990s alone—that the Centers for Disease Control (CDC), a unit of the Department of Health and Human Services, has developed a National Plan to Eliminate Syphilis from the United States. Geographically, the highest rates are found primarily in the states of

the deep South. Several other STDs are tracked by the public health system, but their incidence is quite low. Genital herpes falls in this category.[12]

Compared with older adults, teenagers and young adults are at higher risk of acquiring STDs, because they are more likely to have multiple partners and more likely to engage in sex without appropriate protection. In addition, they are less likely to seek treatment because of confidentiality concerns, transportation, and ability to pay. Between 1970 and 1990, there was a steady rise in the proportion of teenage women who indicated they had ever had sexual intercourse. This rise contributes to the increase in the spread of STDs. In 1995, however, that proportion dropped for the first time, as did the proportion reported for men. In addition, the proportion of teens reporting use of contraception in general and condoms in particular has increased dramatically, from about 18 percent using condoms in 1970 to 54 percent in 1995. Aside from abstinence, the use of condoms is the most effective means of minimizing the risk of sexually transmitted diseases. The increased use of birth control at

---

[12] See "Sexually Transmitted Disease Surveillance 2000," Division of STD Prevention, U.S. Department of Health and Human Services, Public Health Service, Centers for Disease Control and Prevention, <http://www.cdc.gov/std/stats>.

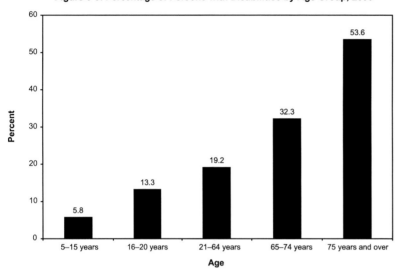

Figure 9-9. Percentage of Persons with Disabilities by Age Group, 2000

Source: U.S. Census Bureau. Census 2000.

first intercourse is often cited as the reason that the teenage birth rate has begun to decline.

Another problem among adolescents is the common practice of oral sex. While non-coital sex avoids the risk of pregnancy and some of the emotional problems associated with intercourse, it still carries a significant risk of transmitting STDs. Research has shown that teen-agers are likely to engage in oral sex at younger ages than beginning intercourse.[13]

DISABILITY

DEFINING AND GAUGING DISABILITY

The term "disability" has many connotations; it can be defined very broadly or very narrowly. The proportion of the population that has a disability varies considerably, depending on the definition. A relatively narrow definition, that employed or formerly employed persons are considered to be disabled if they are "unable to engage in substantial gainful activity," is used by the U.S. government in the Social Security Disability program. A considerably broader definition is used in the far-reaching Americans with Disabilities Act of 1990 (ADA), which defines disability as a "physical or mental impairment that substantially limits one or more of the major life activities."

Early surveys relating to disability concentrated on the presence of a physical, mental, or other health condition that limited the kind or amount of work a person could do. In recent surveys to determine the extent of disability, the ADA definition is typically operationalized by asking questions relating to (a) "limitations in functional activities" (for example seeing, hearing, using stairs, lifting, and carrying); (b) "activities of daily living" (ADLs), such as washing, eating, and dressing; and (c) "instrumental activities of daily living (IADLs), such as difficulty going outside the home or in keeping track of money or bills. ADA assessment also includes questions relating to ability to work and, for children, limitations in their ability to do school work and other

usual activities.

In the 2000 Census, respondents were asked about several categories of disability: sensory, physical, mental, self-care. In addition, adults 16 and over were asked about disability related to going outside the home, and persons of work age (16 to 64) were asked about disabilities which prevent them from holding a job. People could report that they were disabled in none, one, or more than one of these categories.

The likelihood of having some type of disability increases with age; in 2000, about 6 percent of children between 5 and 15 years of age had a disability, compared with 14 percent of adults 21 to 64 years and 54 percent of persons 75 years old and over. Because disability is correlated with advancing age, persons 65 years and over composed 28 percent of all persons reporting a disability. Among children, boys tended to have higher disability rates than girls, while for adults, the rates by sex were similar. Among older adults, women tended to have slightly higher disability rates, primarily because there are more women in the very oldest age groups.

TYPES OF DISABILITY AND EFFECTS ON LIVELIHOOD

The first type of disability is sensory. This category includes eyesight and hearing disorders. One in seven older Americans (14 percent) reports blindness, deafness, or a severe hearing or vision impairment. Physical disability refers to "a condition that substantially limits one or more basic physical activities such as walking, climbing stairs, reaching, lifting, or carrying."[14] This is the most common disability, reported by 29 percent of senior citizens and about 6 percent of working-age adults. Mental disability is defined as a problem with learning, remembering

[13] Lisa Remez, "Oral Sex Among Adolescents: Is It Sex or Is It Abstinence?", *Family Planning Perspectives*, vol. 32, No. 6, November/December 2000.

[14] Bureau of the Census, 2000 Census Questionnaire, Question 16b. The questionnaire itself is the best reference for each of the six individual disability categories discussed here.

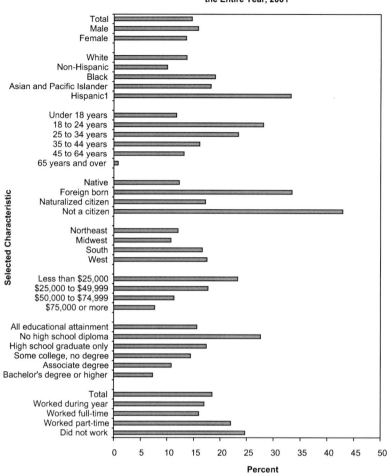

Figure 9-10. Percentage of Persons Without Health Insurance for the Entire Year, 2001

Percent

Selected Characteristic

1May be of any race.
Source: U.S. Census Bureau. Current Population Survey.

or concentrating. It is the most common disability among children age 5 to 15, at 5 percent of the total. About 11 percent of seniors are affected by this problem.

Self-care disability refers to bathing, dressing, or getting around inside the home. It is a relative uncommon problem, experienced by only 1 percent of children and adults, and 10 percent of seniors. Going outside the home was asked in reference to shopping or visiting a doctor's office. Six percent of adults reported this category of disability; the figure for senior citizens rises to 25 percent. Finally, working-age adults were asked if they had a disability which caused difficult in working at a job or business; 12 percent responded

"yes" in the Employment category. There is some evidence, however, that people who have trouble finding work may report a disability, such as "back trouble" to explain their lack of looking; this category is likely to rise during economic downturns.

HEALTH INSURANCE COVERAGE

WHO IS NOT COVERED

Unlike some countries, the United States does not have a national health insurance program that covers everyone regardless of age or income. Thus, for many people in the United States, the greatest

impediment to a healthy life is lack of adequate health insurance. Lack of health insurance coverage can delay or prevent treatment for a specific ailment as well as impede access to information or preventive services.

In 2001, about 15 percent of the U.S. population (41.2 million people) had no health insurance at any time during that year. In addition, some other people were covered by health insurance only part of the year. This often results when people are unemployed for a short time, have a change in employment, or do not pay their insurance premiums. The uninsured numbers for 2001 were higher than those for 2000, because of the worsening economy (and consequently loss of employer-sponsored health insurance), and because of continuing high immigration.

Men were somewhat more likely than women to be uninsured in 2001, perhaps because they are less likely to be covered by Medicaid as a result of receiving public assistance. Young adults (18 to 34) were more likely to lack insurance than other age groups. Hispanics were considerably more likely than Blacks or non-Hispanic Whites to lack insurance, with a non-coverage rate of 33 percent. Migrant farm workers are usually not covered. Immigrant non-citizens were more than twice as likely as natives to lack insurance, with almost two-thirds of non-citizens with poverty-level income lacking health insurance in 2001. (See Figure 9-10.)

SOURCES OF COVERAGE

There are three main government health insurance programs: one to provide coverage for the elderly (that is, persons 65 years old and older) regardless of income level (Medicare), one to provide coverage for low-income Americans (Medicaid), and a third group of programs that provide care for the military and veterans. Together, these programs provide health insurance coverage to about one-

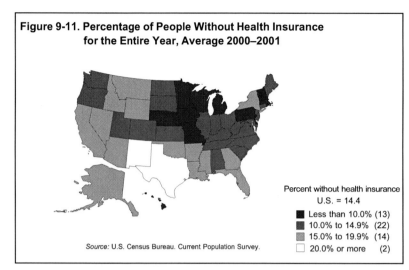

Figure 9-11. Percentage of People Without Health Insurance for the Entire Year, Average 2000–2001

Percent without health insurance
U.S. = 14.4

- Less than 10.0% (13)
- 10.0% to 14.9% (22)
- 15.0% to 19.9% (14)
- 20.0% or more (2)

Source: U.S. Census Bureau. Current Population Survey.

fourth of the U.S. population, with Medicare covering 14 percent, Medicaid about 11 percent, and military health insurance covering about 3 percent. Some people may have coverage from more than one of these sources.

The vast majority of the insured, representing some 241 million people or 71 percent of the total population, have private health insurance of one sort or another. Since there are gaps in the insurance coverage of government-sponsored programs, some persons who have Medicare coverage, for example, also have private health insurance. In about 9 out of 10 cases, the private health insur-

ance is obtained through employment. Persons with unstable employment or with part-time work were considerably more likely than full-time workers to be uninsured or to have periods when they were uninsured. Such persons may not be eligible immediately for a government program like Medicaid, because their income was too high (or has recently been too high), but they may not feel that they can afford to continue private insurance coverage.

Working for small companies also tends to be associated with a greater likelihood of being uninsured. Many small employers do not offer an employee health insur-

ance plan. In 2001, among workers age 18 to 64, only 31 percent of those working for small companies (less than 25 employees) received employment-based health insurance. Once the company has 100 or more employees, however, two-thirds of the workers are covered, with the figure reaching 70 percent for those working for companies with 1,000 or more employees.[15]

In the United States coverage varies considerably between health plans. Some plans only cover catastrophic illnesses and may have large copayment amounts that must be paid by the insured individual, while other plans cover virtually everything from prescriptions to long-term hospital care. In addition, while a plan may "cover" virtually all health conditions, health insurance plans have caps that limit the amount the health-care provider will be paid for a particular service, which may be considerably less than the actual charge. In some cases, the insured individual is responsible for any amount above the charge allowed by the insurance company; in some instances the health-care provider will accept the insurance company's allowed charges as full payment.

[15] U.S. Census Bureau, *Health Insurance Coverage: 2001*, Current Population Report P60-220, September 2002. Additional information on the relationship between employment and health insurance is included in Chapter 4.

FOR FURTHER INFORMATION:

Centers for Disease Control and Prevention, HIV/AIDS Surveillance Report, 2000, U.S. Department of Health and Human Services, Atlanta, GA.

Donovan, Patricia. "Confronting a Hidden Epidemic: The Institute of Medicine's Report on Sexually Transmitted Diseases." Family Planning Perspectives 29, No. 2 (March/April 1997).

National Center for Health Statistics. Health, United States, 2002, U.S. Department of Health and Human Services, Hyattsville, MD.

WEB SITES:

Alan Guttmacher Institute: <www.agi-usa.org>.

Centers for Disease Control: <www.cdc.gov>.

National Center for Health Statistics: <www.cdc.gov/nchs>.

National Clearinghouse for Alcohol and Drug Information: <www.health.org>.

Substance Abuse and Mental Health Services Administration: <www.samhsa.gov>.

U.S. Census Bureau (for health insurance data and data on disabilities): <www.census.gov>.

Chapter 10
Leisure, Volunteerism, and Religiosity

TRENDS IN LEISURE TIME

What do Americans do with their nonworking, or in the case of children, nonschool hours? While most nonwork time is spent in commuting and the everyday tasks of daily living, Americans average about 40 hours a week that could be spent on leisure activities. Such activities can take a variety of forms, from watching television to participating in an athletic pursuit, from volunteer work to singing in the church choir.

According to data from time-use studies, Americans used to spend a large portion of their free time in civic activities such as working for a political party, attending religious services, participating in church or synagogue activities, or in joining such organizations as parent-teacher associations and labor unions. Membership in civic groups has declined in the past two decades, as has time spent socializing, visiting, and attending church, according to data from the General Social Survey and the Gallup Poll. What has increased considerably is time spent watching television. Americans on average spend between two and three hours a day watching television, or approximately 40 percent of their free time. One author feels the two—declining civic association and watching television—are causally related.[1]

There is a large gap between Americans' perception of how much time they have for leisure, and the actual amount of time they have, according to a recent study, with the perception considerably short of reality.[2] Time-diary data indicate on average that both men and women were spending less time at paid work in 1995 than they did in 1965, and that free time had increased for both, whether or not they were employed. However, women still spend more time than men on family care, and somewhat less time at paid work.

TYPES OF LEISURE ACTIVITIES

Not only does the amount of leisure time vary throughout the life cycle, but the favorite free time activities of Americans vary by age. (See Figure 10-2.) For example, the most popular sports activity of Americans 65 years and over is exercise walking, in which about 46 percent participated. For children between 7 and 11, bicycle riding and swimming were the most popular sports activities, with about half of the children participating in one or both. Teenagers, age 12 to 17, are also into bike riding and swimming, but the percentage participating is smaller. For young adults (18 to 24 years), exercise walking, exercising with stationary bicycles or steppers, and swimming head the list, along with sports such as billiards and bowling. Similar numbers of both men and women enjoyed cross-country skiing and volleyball. The participants in other sports were

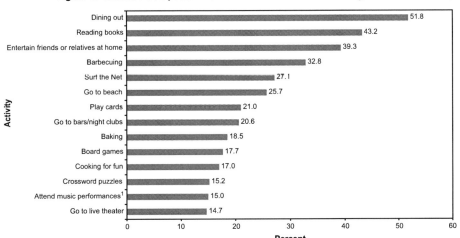

Figure 10-1. Adult Participation in Selected Leisure Activities During the Last 12 Months, 2001

Source: U.S. Census Bureau. *Statistical Abstract, 2002.* Table 1223.
[1]Excluding country and rock.

---

[1] Robert D. Putnam, "The Strange Disappearance of Civic America," *The American Prospect* (Winter 1966).
[2] John P. Robinson and Geoffrey Godbey, *Time for Life: The Surprising Ways Americans Use Their Time* (University Park: Pennsylvania State University Press, 1997).

predominantly of one sex or the other. While aerobics is primarily an activity of women, men predominated in the "ball" games (football, baseball, and basketball), as well as golf and hunting. Looking at income, higher income persons are more likely to be involved in sports such as swimming, bicycle riding, and golf, which usually require an expenditure of personal funds in order to participate.

Looking at all types of leisure activities, the one enjoyed by more people than any other is eating out, followed by entertaining friends or relatives at home. These activities are enjoyed by nearly half the U.S. population at least once during a 12-month period, with most engaging in them at least two or three times a month. (See Figure 10-1.) The other activities high on the list are also quite passive: reading books, barbecuing, playing cards, and going to the beach.

One specific category of leisure activities is the arts: participating in or attending music, dance, or theatric performances, or visiting museums, historic parks, and arts/craft fairs. Of these types of activities, art/craft fairs are the most popular, with a 48 percent participation rate in 1999.[3] Historic parks and art museums are next on the list. Generally, adults of all ages participate equally in these types of activities, except that persons 75 years old and over show lower rates. Education, however, makes a big difference. For all types of arts activities, participation increases significantly as the amount of education increases.

Looking at spectator attendance at sporting events, baseball remains the top attractor, with about one person in six (16 percent) saying they attended one or

Table 10-1. Percentage of Adults Meeting Recommended Standard for Physical Activity, 2000

(Percent.)

Characteristic	Percent who meet recommended activity [1]	Percent with insufficient activity [2]	Percent who are physically inactive [3]
TOTAL	26.2	46.2	27.6
Sex			
Male	27.1	47.5	25.3
Female	25.5	44.8	29.7
Race and ethnicity			
White, non-Hispanic	27.5	48.3	24.2
Black, non-Hispanic	21.9	43.3	34.8
Hispanic	21.1	37.9	41.0
Other	27.3	42.9	29.8
Men			
18–29 years	26.9	54.6	18.5
30–44 years	23.7	52.2	24.2
45–64 years	26.0	45.5	28.5
65–74 years	33.7	38.7	27.6
75 years and over	35.9	29.2	34.9
Women			
18–29 years	25.4	49.3	25.3
30–44 years	24.7	47.1	28.2
45–64 years	25.7	44.9	29.4
65–74 years	24.6	40.9	34.4
75 years and over	28.4	27.8	43.8
Education			
Less than 12 years	14.5	36.2	49.3
12 years	21.9	44.7	33.4
Some college	28.3	48.2	23.5
College graduate	34.2	50.0	15.8
Houshold income			
Less than $10,000	18.9	36.7	44.5
$10,000–$19,999	18.9	40.2	40.9
$20,000–$34,999	23.3	44.3	32.4
$35,000–$49,999	27.8	47.8	24.5
$50,000 or more	33.5	50.3	16.3

Source: U.S. Census Bureau. Statistical Abstract of the United States, 2002. Table 191.
[1]Recommended activity is physical activity at least five times/week x 30 minutes/time or vigorous physical activity for 20 minutes at a time at least three times/week.
[2]Persons whose reported physical activity does not meet recommended level.
[3]Persons with no reported physical activity.

more games in the course of a year. Next is high school sports, at 10 percent, followed by college football at 7 percent. These data show clearly that sports events, both professional and school-based, are attractive to only a minority of the population.[4]

Physical activity has become increasingly important, as people are educated to its benefits to good health. However, in 2000 only about one-quarter of all adults reported engaging in physical activity at the recommended levels. Women are slightly less likely to achieve this goal than are men. Age appears to make little difference, except that men are somewhat more active after the age of 65, perhaps because retirement makes the time available.

However, engaging in such activity is highly correlated both with education and with income. (See Table 10-1.)

What else do people do with their time? Some other activities—which some people might think would more appropriately be classified as work—are nevertheless reported as leisure activities by large portions of the U.S. population. For example, 66 percent of adults 18 years and over indicated home improvement and repair as a leisure activity in 2001. Charity work remains important, engaged in by nearly half the adult population. Three-quarters indicate participation in exercise programs, 45 percent play sports (while 41 percent attend sports events, many of which are not organized), and 40

---

[3] U.S. Census Bureau, Statistical Abstract of the United States, 2002. Table 1216.
[4] U.S. Census Bureau, Statistical Abstract of the United States, 2002. Table 1224.

Figure 10-2. Percentage Participating in Activities by Age, 2000

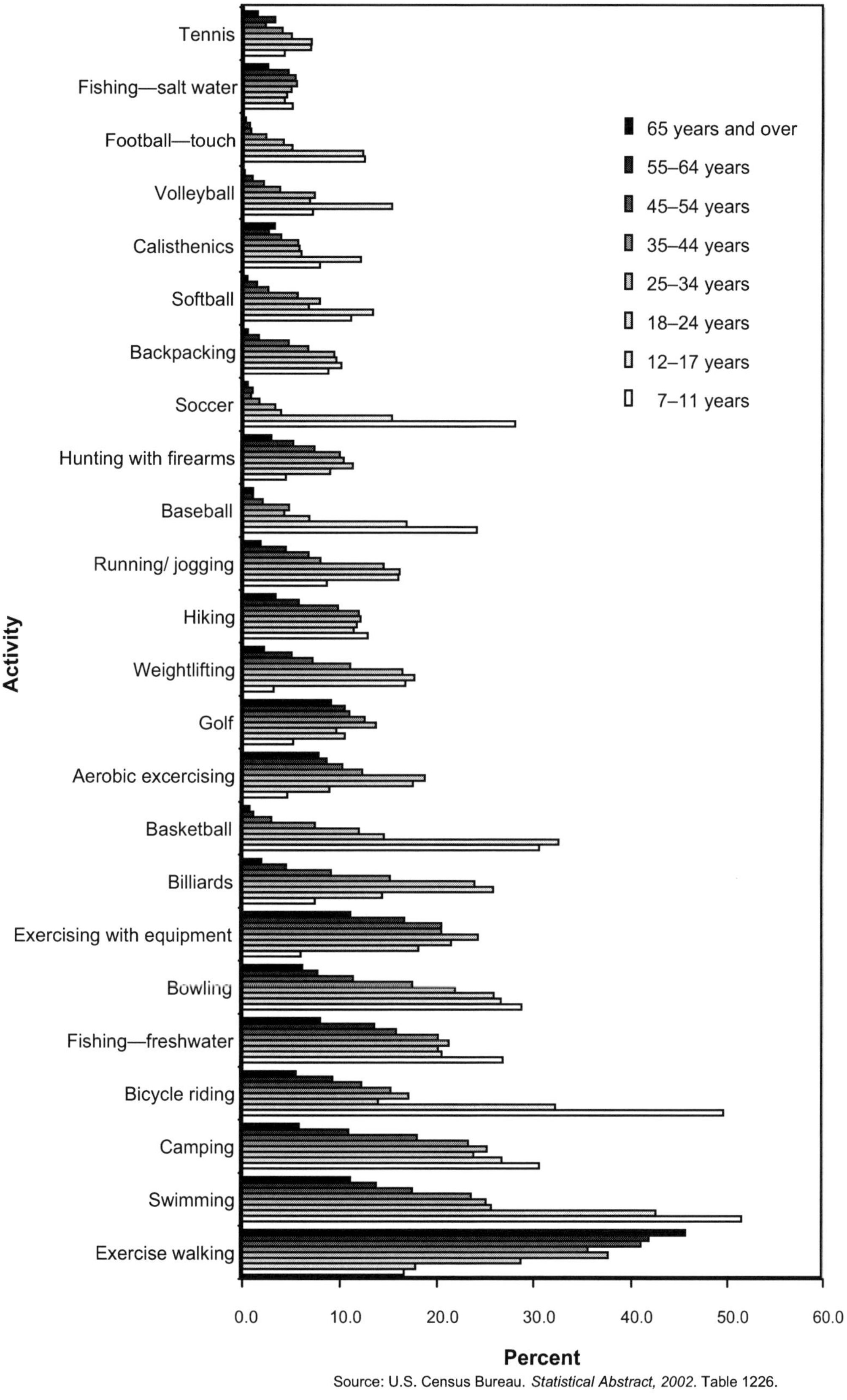

Source: U.S. Census Bureau. *Statistical Abstract, 2002*. Table 1226.

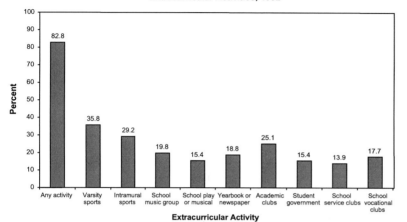

Figure 10-3. Percentage of High School Seniors Participating in Extracurricular Activities, 1992

Source: National Center for Education Statistics. *The Condition of Education, 1995.*

percent spend time on computer hobbies. Two-thirds say that they attend movies. As with activities in the arts, participation increases with education and with income; clearly, it costs money to engage in most leisure activities. Again, there are few differences by age except for the 75 and over group, although, as we would expect, playing sports does decrease with age, as do spectator activities such as movies, sporting events, and amusement parks. In fact, attending movies—possibly the most common "date" event—is reported by 88 percent of persons 18 to 24 years old.

Public high schools in the United States typically have a core of extracurricular activities for students to participate in after school hours. Virtually all seniors in public high schools reported the availability of extracurricular activities at their school in the 1992 National Education Longitudinal Study conducted by the U.S. Department of Education. Included are such activities as sports; theater; band; clubs such as photography, math, or astronomy; and service clubs. Four out of five seniors reported participating in some activity, with about

42 percent participating in a sport, and about one of four participating in a performing arts club or an academic club. About 15 percent of students participated in student government, and about 15 percent in a service club.

Students who participated in extracurricular activities were found to have higher school attendance than nonparticipants, to perform better on standardized math and reading tests, and to aspire to higher education at a higher rate than nonparticipants. There is some evidence to suggest that a sense of attachment to school that is fostered by participation in extracurricular activities decreases the likelihood of school failure and dropping out.[5]

With specific reference to organized physical activity at the high school level, slightly more than half of all students were enrolled in physical education classes in 2001. As we might expect, boys were more likely to be enrolled than girls, and participation levels decreased as the students moved from ninth to twelfth grade. However, 55 percent were involved in a school sports team (61 percent of boys; 50 percent of

girls), and the dropoff with age was considerably smaller in this category. These data may reflect the fact that, in many schools, physical education is not a mandatory requirement after the 9th or 10th grade.[6]

EXPENDITURES ON LEISURE

Expenditures per consumer unit (usually a household) on entertainment and reading by Americans almost doubled, from $1,311 in 1985 to $2,009 in 2000, the latter averaging about 5 percent of average household total expenditures. This includes expenditures on fees and admissions, television and sound equipment, play and sports equipment, and reading. Three and four person households spent the highest proportion (11 percent); the figure for households with five or more persons is only 5 percent. Looking at the data another way, total recreation expenditures rose from $285 billion in 1990 to $574 billion in 2000, and increased from 7.4 percent to 8.5 percent of all personal consumption expenditures.[7] The largest dollar category, at both points in time, was spending on video and audio products, computer equipment, and musical instruments. Computer equipment spending, specifically, including peripherals such as printers and software, almost quadrupled, rising from $9 billion in 1990 to $34 billion in 2000.

These figures on consumer spending for leisure do not include spending on travel (or lodging) and thus underestimate the real expenditures on leisure. Pleasure travel increased from 645 million "person trips" in 1994 to 690 million in 2001. While the number of pleasure trips increased in the 1990s, the average length of pleasure trips, both in terms of nights per trip and miles traveled, appears to have remained relatively stable.[8]

[5] National Center for Education Statistics, *Extracurricular Participation and Student Engagement*, Report No. 95-74 (Washington, DC: U.S. Department of Education, June 1995).

[6] U.S. Census Bureau, *Statistical Abstract of the United States, 2002*. Table 1227. Youth Risk Behavior Surveillance–United States, 2001.

[7] U.S. Census Bureau, *Statistical Abstract of the United States, 2002*. Tables 1212 and 1213.

[8] U.S. Census Bureau, *Statistical Abstract of the United States, 2002*. Table 1237. Travel Industry Association of America.

VOLUNTEERISM AND GIVING

HOW MANY VOLUNTEERS?

Some persons feel guilty about spending time in leisure activities because of the historic emphasis in American society on success in the world of work. Since the image of having a strong work ethic is so highly prized in the United States, taking part in (or having time to take part in) leisure activity is equated with sloth by some people. "The ancient Athenian ideal of leisure, the absence of the necessity of being occupied, is not only rarely realized but most Americans regard contemplation as simply a waste of time—being busy has become a primary indicator of importance."[9]

Some people spend their free time not on themselves but on others through voluntary activities, some through formal organizations, others through informal assistance (for example providing childcare for a neighbor or relative). Such activities can take a wide range of forms, from volunteering to fight fires with the local fire station to assisting teachers at the local elementary school by cut-

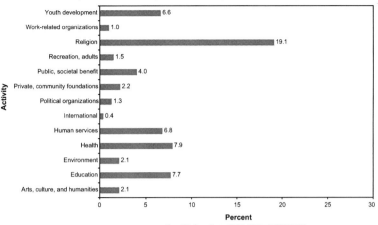

Figure 10-4. Percentage of Adults Doing Volunteer Work by Type of Activity, 2001

Source U.S. Census Bureau. *Statistical Abstract, 2001.* Table 558.

ting out paper circles that will symbolize planets in the next lesson on astronomy. Volunteerism can foster a sense of doing something worthwhile with one's leisure time and of actually helping others.

The extent of help that volunteers bring to their activities has recently become the subject of some debate. There is at times an inherent conflict between paid staff and volunteers, for example, because the "chain of command" is blurred. And some people feel that the amount of time offered by volunteers does more harm than good (for example, the Big

Brothers program needs long-term volunteers rather than just an hour here or there). Nonetheless, Americans spend an estimated 15.5 billion hours annually in volunteer work.

According to the Independent Sector, 44 percent of adults (21 and older) volunteered with a formal organization in 2001, averaging 3.6 hours per week each. Volunteers are more likely to belong to religious organizations (76 percent), compared to those who do not (58 percent), and women volunteer at a somewhat higher rate than men.[10] The likelihood of volunteering increases both with income and with education; of course, these two characteristics are correlated with each other. However, the average number of volunteer hours remains relatively constant, regardless of other characteristics. Informal activities and religious activities command the greatest volunteer efforts, followed by educational and human services activities.

The types of activities in which people volunteer are shown in Figure 10-4. Religious activities lead the list, followed by education, human services, and youth development—these latter three being quite interrelated.

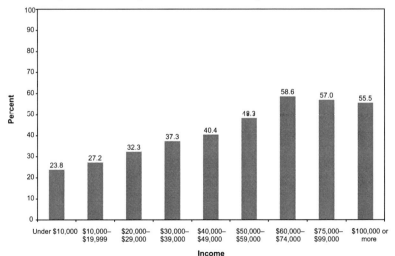

Figure 10-5. Percentage of Adults who Volunteer by Household Income, 2001

Source: U.S. Census Bureau. *Statistical Abstract, 2001* Table 558.

---

[9] Geoffrey Godbey, "The Problem of Free Time—It's Not What You Think," University of Waterloo, Department of Recreation and Leisure Studies, Academy of Leisure Sciences Web site at <http://www.geog.ualberta.ca/als/alswp8.html>.

[10] Independent Sector, "Giving & Volunteering in the United States, 2001," and *Statistical Abstract of the United States, 2001.* Table 565.

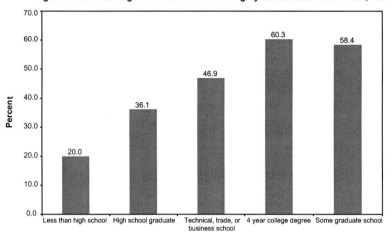

Figure 10-6. Percentage of Persons Volunteering by Educational Attainment, 2001

Source: U.S. Census Bureau. *Statistical Abstract, 2001*. Table 558.

GOVERNMENT INVOLVEMENT IN VOLUNTEERISM

Government encouragement of volunteer efforts expanded in the 1990s amid continued discussion about whether or not charitable organizations have sufficient resources to pick up social services when government support for such services is diminished. In the 1960s, the federal government initiated two volunteer programs—one with an international focus (the Peace Corps) and one with a domestic view (Volunteers in Service to America, or VISTA). About 165,000 Peace Corps volunteers have served in 135 countries since 1961, typically spending 2 years in a country requesting assistance. They have provided a wide variety of assistance, from water, sanitation, and health programs to teaching English and helping launch small businesses. In 2001, there were about 7,000 Peace Corps volunteers serving in over 70 countries throughout the world. VISTA volunteers, who typically served for a year, have numbered about 100,000 since 1960. Both VISTA and Peace Corps volunteers were paid a small stipend on which to live during their serv-

ice tour. VISTA volunteers were placed with community-based agencies involved in fighting poverty both in urban and rural settings in the United States. In 1994, VISTA became part of the AmeriCorps national service program.

In addition to VISTA, the largest program of AmeriCorps is the National Civilian Community Corps (NCCC), which was modeled after the Civilian Conservation Corps (CCC). The CCC put thousands of people to work in the United States during the Great Depression in the 1930s. NCCC service is restricted to 18- to 24-year-olds, who work in teams and focus on environmental improvements, although programs are also involved in public safety, education, and disaster relief. In exchange for a year of service (during which time volunteers receive a living allowance and health insurance coverage), volunteers receive an education voucher worth $4,725 for help in paying for their own education. In 1997, there were approximately 25,000 AmeriCorps members serving in over 400 programs across the United States.

Americorps is a component of the Corporation for National

Table 10-2. Percentage of Students in Grades 6–12 Participating in Community Service, 1999

(Percent.)

Characteristic	Percent
TOTAL	52
Grade Level	
6–8	48
9–10	50
11–12	61
Sex	
Male	47
Female	57
Race	
White	56
Black	48
Hispanic	38
Other	54
Language Spoken Most At Home By Student	
English	53
Other	35
Parents' Education	
Less than high school	37
High school diploma or equivalent	46
Some college, including vocational/technical	50
Bachelor's degree	62
Professional/graduate degree	64
School Type	
Public	50
Private	
Religious	71
Nonsectarian	68
Enrollment	
Less than 300	56
300–599	48
600–999	52
1,000 or more	54
School Practice	
Requires and arranges service	60
Requires service only	35
Arranges service only	54
Neither requires nor arranges service	29

Source: U.S. Department of Education. National Center for Education Statistics. *Youth Service-Learning and Community Service Among 6th- Through 12th-Grade Students in the United States: 1996 and 1999* (NCES 2000–028), 2000.

Service, which also includes Senior Corps and Learn and Serve. The National Senior Service Corps helps persons 55 and over find volunteer activities, with three programs that receive federal funds: the Grandparents Program (which provides support to children with special needs), the Senior Companions Program (which helps frail elderly people live independently), and the Retired and Senior Volunteers Program (which provides a wide range of community service). Learn and Serve is a program for students. Service-Learning, as it is often called, is a method whereby students learn and develop through active participation in thoughtfully organized service that is conducted in and meets the needs of communities. It is coordinated with an elementary school, secondary school, institution of higher education, or community service program and the community. The programs help foster civic responsibility, are integrated into and enhance the academic curriculum of the students, or the education components of the community service program in which the participants are enrolled, and provide structured time for students or participants to reflect on the service experience.[11]

As of this writing in 2003, funding for these government volunteer programs is under a severe threat. Whether or not one or all of them survive is a question for the near future.

School districts in the United States are attempting to increase community service participation of students, some requiring a minimum number of hours of community service to graduate from high school, while others attempt to encourage participation without requiring students to do so. A recent survey revealed that 52 percent of students in grades 6

through 12 were involved in community service in 1999. Over half of these students participated in service-based learning as well. Teen-aged volunteerism often occurs because the school arranges the program in which the students participate. This type of activity is more likely to occur in private (religious or non-sectarian) schools than in public schools, and happens more often among children whose parents have a college degree or more.[12]

GIVING

Charitable giving complements volunteerism, representing the gift of money as opposed to time. Many people, of course, do both. Almost all (88 percent) households in the United States reported contributing to charity in 2000; their average annual contribution was $1,620 or 3.2 percent of their total income. Giving was even higher among households which include people

who volunteer as well, with an average contribution of nearly $2,300. Overall, 42 percent of households both volunteer and give, 46 percent report contributing only, 2 percent volunteer only, and 10 percent do neither. Factors which influence giving include being asked for gifts, having been involved with giving and volunteering as youths, views of the household's economic outlook, and participation in religious services.[13] (See Table 10-3 and Figure 10-7.)

Religious organizations are the most likely to receive charitable gifts and have the highest average contribution. Other types of organizations which receive gifts from at least 20 percent of all households include education, health, human services (including United Way), and youth development programs.

As in many other areas of American life, the Internet is becoming important for volunteering and for giving. According to

Table 10-3. Charity Contributions, Selected Years, 1991–2000

(Dollars, percent.)

Characteristic	All contributing households		Contributors and volunteers	
	Average amount (dollars)	Percent of household income	Average amount (dollars)	Percent of household income
1991	899	2.2	1 155	2.6
1995	1 017	2.2	1 279	2.6
1998	1 075	2.1	1 339	2.5
2000, TOTAL	1 623	3.2	2 295	4.0
Age				
18 to 24 years	958	2.3	1 635	3.1
25 to 34 years	1 002	2.3	1 411	3.1
35 to 44 years	1 831	2.8	2 471	3.5
45 to 54 years	1 818	2.9	2 632	3.8
55 to 64 years	1 888	3.3	2 626	4.3
65 to 74 years	1 798	4.5	2 307	5.5
75 years and over	1 628	5.1	2 498	6.5
Race/Ethnicity				
White	1 693	3.2	2 359	4.0
Black	1 488	3.3	2 300	4.3
Hispanic [1]	1 276	2.5	2 285	3.6
Household Income				
Under $10,000	296	5.5	382	6.7
$10,000–$ 19,999	465	3.3	624	4.4
$20,000–$ 29,999	916	3.9	1 299	5.5
$30,000–$ 39,999	1 036	3.1	1 408	4.2
$40,000–$ 49,999	1 147	2.7	1 638	3.8
$50,000–$ 59,999	1 566	3.0	1 989	3.8
$60,000–$ 74,999	1 935	3.0	2 483	3.8
$75,000–$ 99,999	2 119	2.6	2 530	3.1
Itemizers [2]	3 976	2.7	4 894	3.3
Itemizers	2 288	3.6	2 903	4.3
Claimed charitable deduction	2 733	4.0	3 262	4.6
Didn't claim charitable deduction	868	2.4	1 207	2.9
Nonitemizers	954	2.7	1 464	3.6

Source: U.S. Census Bureau. *Statistical Abstract of the United States, 2001.* Table 552.
[1] May be of any race.
[2] Persons who itemized their deductions on their 2000 federal tax returns.

---

[11] See <http://www.learnandserve.org/about/service_learning.html> and <http://www.seniorcorps.org/>.
[12] National Center for Education Statistics, "The Condition of Education," discussion on learner outcomes, at <nces.ed.gov/programs/coe>.
[13] Independent Sector, "Giving and Volunteering in the United States: 2001", available at <www.IndependentSector.org>. Also see U.S. Census Bureau, *Statistical Abstract of the United States, 2002.* Tables 552 and 553.

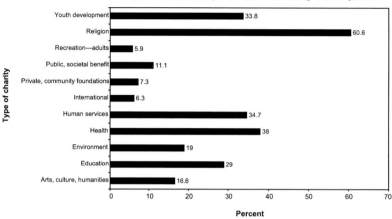

Figure 10-7. Percentage of Households Giving to Charity, 2001

Source: U.S. Census Bureau. *Statistical Abstract, 2001.* Table 553.

years, is a significant growth in the proportion of the population reporting their religion to be other than Christianity or Judaism. In 2002, one American in eight identified with another specific religion, such as Greek Orthodox, Mormon, Buddhism, or Hinduism. This is one effect of the substantial Asian immigration to the United States over the two decades. Still, over half the population identifies as Protestant, and another one-quarter as Catholic. The proportion reporting no religion has also increased in recent decades. (See Figure 10-8.) Among Protestants, Baptists are the leading denomination with about one-third of the total, followed by Methodists. About half of all Christians describe themselves as "born-again" or "evangelical," according to a recent Gallup poll.

The Gallup Organization reports on a composite Index of Leading Religious Indicators, which includes measures such as belief in God, having a religious preference, being a member of a church, attending church weekly, and the respondents' views of the role of religion in their lives. In the 1950s, the Index score peaked at 746 (of a possible 1000). It declined slowly over the years, with a low point of 650 in 1988, but increased during the 1990s and was measured at 671 in 2001. Its top components are belief in God (95 percent) and stating a religious preference (92 percent). The lowest component is church attendance in the past week (41 percent). About 58 percent indicate that religion is very important in their lives.

The proportion of people who neither belong to a church (or synagogue), nor attend services which are not holiday or life-cycle related, has been growing over time, from 41 percent in 1978 to 47 percent in

VolunteerMatch, a non-profit service that lists volunteer opportunities from almost 20,000 organizations nationwide, in 27 different categories, the events of September 11, 2001 prompted a significant increase in people seeking such opportunities on the Web. Referrals, which actually match a volunteer with an opportunity, are up as well.[14] The Independent Sector notes that volunteering and charitable giving via the Internet are increasing, with about one in eight of the households who have Internet access using this route. This trend is expected to continue.

Charitable giving is also linked to the giver's level of confidence in the charity seeking the gift. A 1999 survey showed that youth development and recreation services and human service organizations ranked highest in givers' views; more than two-thirds of respondents reported that they had high confidence in these two types of organizations. Educational organizations also rank high, along with religious institutions. Organizations at the other end of the scale include political parties, lobbying organizations, the

Congress and the federal government in general. Confidence and giving levels are also linked to well-known events. For example, overall public confidence in religious organizations waned in the light of several well-publicized scandals in the late 1980s. Finally, donors are more likely to have confidence in local charities than in national organizations.[15]

Giving is also inevitably tied to the state of the economy. When asked about their giving levels during "tough times," respondents to an Independent Sector survey stated that they would reduce their giving by amounts ranging from $130, or 23 percent, for the poorest households, to at least $1,300, or 33 percent, in the wealthiest households. The greatest decline is projected in households earning between $25,000 and $50,000 per year, where giving would decline by 45 percent (from $1,300 to $710).[16]

RELIGIOSITY

RELIGIOUS IDENTIFICATION

The most important trend in religious identification, in recent

[14] *The Detroit News*, article of April 1, 2002.

[15] Independent Sector, "Taking the Pulse of Americans' Attitudes Toward Charities," at <www.IndependentSector.org>.

[16] Independent Sector, "Giving in Tough Times," at <www.IndependentSector.org>.

2001. The Gallup Organization labels people in this category the "unchurched." Many of these people, however, have been or will be "churched" at some point in their lives. Affiliation with religious institutions tends to be highest among families with children, and lowest among young people and people who are single.

Among people who do belong to congregations, about one-quarter are actively engaged with the institution; they are more spiritually committed and devote more time and money to these organizations than members who are not engaged. About half the members are minimally engaged, and one in five is actively disengaged, with most attending services rarely.

A higher proportion of the elderly attend church regularly relative to other age groups (39 percent of those over age 65 compared with 26 percent of young adults, for example). Women tend to attend religious services more regularly than do men, with about a third of women and one-quarter of men in the United States reporting weekly attendance. (See Figure 10-13.) Blacks report weekly attendance more frequently than do Whites (40 percent versus 29 percent). Weekly attendance is considerably more likely among residents of the Southern (38 percent) and the Eastern United States (34 percent) than among the Midwest (26 percent) or the Western United States, where only 19 percent report weekly church attendance. There is not much difference by

educational attainment between weekly churchgoers and those who do not attend church weekly (27 percent with a college degree and 33 percent with no college degree), but there is significant difference by political affiliation. Republicans are considerably more likely to be weekly churchgoers (44 percent) than either Democrats or independents (25 percent and 22 percent, respectively).

RELIGION AND POLITICS

The U.S. Constitution states that Congress cannot make any laws specifying the establishment of a state religion and that Americans are free to worship as they see fit. While politics may not shape religion in America, religious affiliation does influence political values. The

general tendency is that the more devout a person is the more politically conservative he or she is, not only on matters such as abortion, homosexuality, and family, but also on national security and environmental issues. While the fundamentalist classification cuts across denominations, Baptists make up the largest share of "born-again" or evangelical Christians.

Views on the level of religion's influence on American life are subject to real time events. Polls showed that, in the wake of the September 11, 2001 attacks, the proportion of Americans believing this influence was on the rise increased substantially. By March 2002, however, the proportion was back to where it had been before September 11. About half of Americans believe that the United States has special protection from God; this view is held by 71 percent of evangelical white Christians, but by only 40 percent among mainline Protestants and Catholics. Almost all white evangelicals believe that America's strength is based on religious faith;

Figure 10-8. Percent Distribution of Population by Religion, 2002

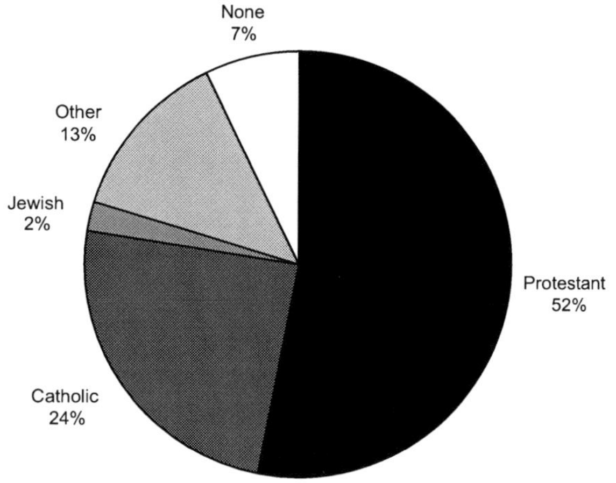

None 7%

Other 13%

Jewish 2%

Protestant 52%

Catholic 24%

Source: The Gallup Organization, Inc.

Table 10-4. Historic Trends in American Religious Preferences, Selected Years, 1952–2002

(Percent.)

Year	Protestant	Catholic	Jewish	Other	None
1952	67	25	4	1	2
1962	70	23	3	2	2
1972	63	26	2	4	5
1982	57	29	2	4	9
1992	56	26	2	7	7
2002	52	24	2	13	7

Source: The Gallup Organization, Inc.

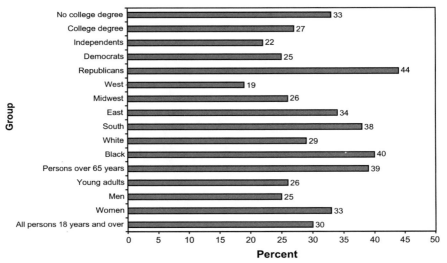

Figure 10-9. Percentage of Selected Groups That Attend Religious Services at Least Once a Week, 1997

Source: The Gallup Organization, Inc.

in contrast, only 20 percent of people identifying themselves as secular hold this view.[17]

A July 2003 study by the Pew Center shows that a 62 percent majority of Americans think that President Bush "strikes the right balance" in his frequent mentions of his religious faith, and 58 percent believe the President's reliance on religion in policy-making is OK. However, many Americans "express a general discomfort when exposed to actual religious statements by various politicians." However, 58 percent say that religion does not affect their voting decisions.[18]

[17] The Pew Research Center for the People and the Press, "Americans Struggle with Religion's Role at Home and Abroad," <www.people-press.org/reports>, April 2002.
[18] Pew Research Center, "Religion and Politics: Contention and Consensus," at <www.people-press.org.>, July 2003.

FOR FURTHER INFORMATION SEE:

The Gallup Poll Monthly. Princeton: The Gallup Poll (various issues).

WEB SITES:

Corporation for National Service: <http://www.cns.gov>.

Peace Corps: <http://www.peacecorps.gov>.

Pew Research Center: <http://www.people-press.org>.

The Independent Sector: <http://www.IndependentSector.org>.

U.S. Census Bureau, Statistical Abstract: <www.census.gov/statab/www/>.

Chapter 11
Voting

ELIGIBILITY TO VOTE

Until 1920, the right to vote to elect the president, Congress, and local officials was restricted to a minority of the adult population in the United States; women did not have the right to vote. Indeed, prior to 1900 the voting franchise was generally limited to White males. Early in the nation's history, some of the states (especially in New England) required religious tests, and others required ownership of property in order to be eligible to vote. Since eligibility was determined by each state, the removal of these requirements was uneven, although they had largely disappeared by the time of the Civil War.

In the aftermath of that war, Congress enacted constitutional amendments to elevate the status of former slaves to full citizenship, which included the right to vote—15th Amendment to the U.S. Constitution, enacted in 1870. The greatest expansion of the electorate was the inclusion of females, beginning in 1869 when Wyoming Territory gave women the vote. By the time the 19th Amendment was added to the Constitution in 1920, 15 states had granted women full suffrage. That amendment extended eligibility to all women, regardless of residence.

After the Civil War, Black citizens' attempts to register and vote were often frustrated by devices such as poll taxes and literacy tests, especially in the South. The literacy test was especially susceptible to manipulation by unsympathetic electoral officials. Efforts to overturn discrimination against Black citizens who tried to exercise their right to vote culminated in the 24th Amendment to the U.S. Constitution in 1964. That amendment prohibited the payment of poll taxes as a requirement for voting in federal elections. The Voting Rights Act of 1965 and subsequent amendments abolished literacy tests as a prerequisite for voting and reduced the residence requirement for voting in presidential elections to 30 days.

In 1971, the 26th Amendment lowered the voting age for all persons from 21 to 18 years. Now, any person who is 18 years of age or older, who is a citizen of the United States, who meets local residence requirements, and who is not a convicted felon or mentally incompetent, is eligible to vote in federal elections.

REGISTRATION

In most jurisdictions in the United States, a registration process is required before becoming eligible to vote.[1] In most cases, the voter must register at least 30 days prior to the election. Once registered, a person stays on the election rolls as long as he or she lives at the same address and meets the state requirement for frequency of voting (usually at least once every 4 years). Some states have permanent registration, regardless of voting turnout.

Barriers to registration have been substantially removed since World War II. Through a combination of constitutional amendments, acts of Congress, and Supreme Court decisions, registration has been greatly simplified. For example, residence requirements were once as much as 2 years in some states, while the maximum residence requirement for federal elections is now 30 days.

The National Voter Registration Act of 1993 is the most recent attempt to expand the core of registered voters. In the Federal Election Commission's (FEC) 2001–2002 report to Congress on the impact of the act, the FEC noted that there were about 148 million people registered to vote in the 2002 election, representing about 70 percent of the voting-age population.[2] This is a decline from the level reported in 1999 (74 percent), and is likely due, at least in part, to the increasing proportion of the voting age

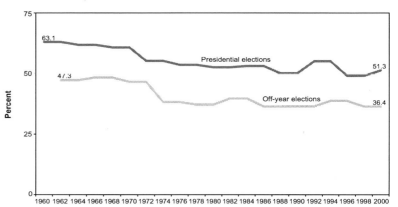

Figure 11-1. Voter Turnout in National Elections, 1960–2000

Source: Federal Election Commission.

---

[1] North Dakota does not have a registration requirement. Wisconsin, and some communities in other states, permit election day registration.

[2] Federal Election Commission, "The Impact of the National Voter Registration Act of 1993 on the Administrations of Elections for Federal Office 2001–2002," located at <www.fec.gov/pages/nvrareport2002/nvrareport2002.pdf>.

population which is composed of new immigrants who are not citizens.

The largest number of registration applications processed during the 2001–2002 period (42 percent) were those generated by state motor vehicle departments, under the so-called "motor voter" provisions of the act whereby voter registration is simultaneously completed while applying for a driver's license. Mail registration accounted for an additional 28 percent of new registrants, and is increasing because of the increasing availability of voter registration forms on the Internet and elsewhere. Public Assistance Offices and State designated sites accounted for 3 percent each, while the remaining 24 percent were from a wide variety of other sources.

TURNOUT IN NATIONAL ELECTIONS

A higher proportion of eligible voters who participate in national elections is considered by some as a measure of the health of the body politic, but this is an oversimplification, since "more is better" is not necessarily indicative of a healthy democratic society. Nazi Germany routinely proclaimed

Table 11-1. Voter Turnout, 2000

(Percent of voting age population which voted in 2000 election.)

State	Percent
Highest States	
Minnesota	68.8
Maine	67.3
Alaska	66.4
Wisconsin	66.1
Vermont	64.0
Lowest States	
Hawaii	40.5
Arizona	42.3
Texas	43.1
Nevada	43.8
Georgia	43.8

Source: Federal Election Commission.

voter turnouts approaching unanimity in the various referenda they conducted. Some countries attempt to guarantee high turnouts by making voting compulsory, fining nonvoters who do not provide a valid excuse. However, there is no evidence that these devices promote more beneficial results. On the other hand, an unusually low turnout in a national election would indicate a level of apathy that would be considered unhealthy in a democratic society.

Since the vote was extended to a majority of the population, the highest turnout in an election in the United States occurred in the presidential election of 1960, when 63 percent of those eligible participated. (See Figure 11-1.) This contrasts with a 49 percent turnout in

1996, a post-World War II low.

In an election when voters choose a president, there is an approximately 5 percentage point drop-off in votes for members of the House of Representatives; that is, about 1 in 20 people who cast votes for a presidential candidate do not do so for Congress or in other races on the ballot. Elections for president occur every 4 years (the most recent one in 2000), while elections for Congress and many state and local offices occur every two years. Elections in non-presidential years exhibit substantially lower voting participation, by 13 to 17 percentage points. This discrepancy results from lower voter interest in these elections due to the absence of the contest for president, plus situations where incumbents are unopposed or where longtime incumbents are perceived to be invulnerable.[3]

Voting participation differs substantially among the 50 states. For example, in 2000, Minnesota achieved the highest turnout at 68 percent, and Hawaii was last with 41 percent. States below the national average were disproportionately located in the South. (See Figure 11-2.) The below-average turnouts for California, New York, and the southwestern states can be attributed to their sizable populations of non-citizens. The very high turnout states are located in the upper Midwest and west, and

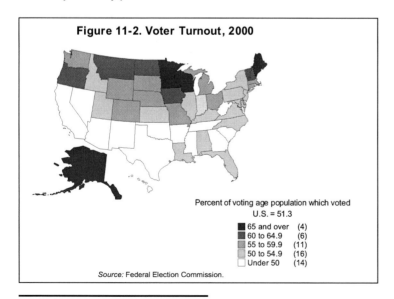

Figure 11-2. Voter Turnout, 2000

Percent of voting age population which voted
U.S. = 51.3

- ■ 65 and over   (4)
- ▨ 60 to 64.9   (6)
- ▨ 55 to 59.9   (11)
- ▨ 50 to 54.9   (16)
- ☐ Under 50   (14)

Source: Federal Election Commission.

---

[3] Survey data, such as the data discussed here which come from the Census Bureau's *Current Population Survey*, tend to overestimate voting participation relative to administrative tallies of votes cast. The reason for this is that many people do not vote but will report on a survey that they did vote in a particular election. For further discussion, see U.S. Census Bureau, *Voting and Registration in the Election of November 2000*, Current Population Report P20-542, February 2002.

are states both with low immigration levels and lower levels of poverty population.

Numerous studies have demonstrated that participation in elections varies by population groups. Turnout increases with age, with the youngest of the potentially eligible voters (those under age 25) having the lowest turnout. Persons 65 to 74 years old voted at twice the rate of those in the age 18 to 24 category in 2000. (See Figure 11-3.) Educational level and income are also strong predictors of turnout. Those with college degrees or more education and those with high incomes vote at levels that are up to 40 percentage points higher than persons at the opposite ends of the scale.

Members of minority groups have traditionally exhibited low electoral participation, although the gap between Blacks and Whites has narrowed since the 1960s as formal and informal barriers to registration and voting have been removed. (See Figure 11-4.) These data, calculated using the citizen voting age population as a base, show Hispanics behind Blacks but by a much smaller margin than if the figures were calculated using the total voting age population.

Identification with the two major political parties in the United

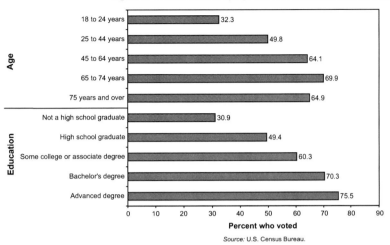

Figure 11-3. Voter Turnout by Age and Educational Attainment, 2000

Source: U.S. Census Bureau.

States (Democratic and Republican) has remained relatively constant for the past 50 years, with variations closely tied to the party holding the White House. (See Figure 11-5.) The proportion reporting themselves to be "independent" or "apolitical" has grown over the years. It was only 9 percent in 1952, rose to a high of 16 percent in 1974, and settled back to 13 percent in 1998 and 2000. About one-quarter of voters currently identify themselves weakly with one party or the other, while 31 percent are strong partisans. Among both Republicans and

Democrats, the proportion saying they are an "independent [party]" has grown, at the expense of stronger identification with either party. Democrats still lead Republicans in overall identification patterns, but the margin has been shrinking over time.[4]

Looking at party identification by selected demographic and economic characteristics (see Table 11-2), there is remarkably little change over time in the proportion of various group populations who identify as Republican. In 2000, men were more likely than women to fall in this category. College graduates, high income persons, and professionals have always had higher Republican identification than their opposites: non-high school graduates, low income persons, and blue collar workers. However, more blue collar workers, and more union members, have identified as Republican in recent years than in the past. Again, the impact of the presidential winner is apparent, especially in 1964 when Barry Goldwater was heavily defeated by Lyndon Johnson. For most of the groups shown, Republican identification was at its low point that year.

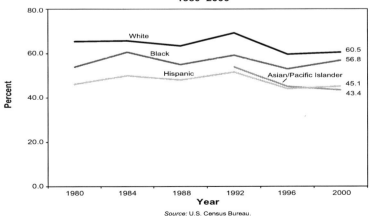

Figure 11-4. Voter Turnout in Presidential Elections by Race, 1980–2000

Source: U.S. Census Bureau.

---

[4] See tables available from the Center for Political Studies, Institute for Social Research, University of Michigan, at <www.umich.edu/~nes/>. This organization originated the concept of "leaning" toward a particular party identification.

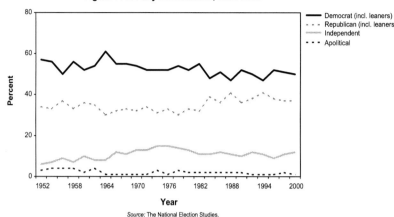

Figure 11-5. Party Identification, 1952–2000

Legend:
- Democrat (incl. leaners)
- Republican (incl. leaners)
- Independent
- Apolitical

Source: The National Election Studies.

PAYING FOR POLITICAL CAMPAIGNS

U.S. political campaigns have become increasingly expensive over the years, even taking inflation into account. (See Figure 11-6.) In the 1999–2000 election cycle (January 1, 1999, through December 31, 2000), the official party committees (including national, state, and local) raised $741 million in "hard money"[5] for use in federal campaigns. When non-federal funds are included (funds raised by the national party organizations for use in gubernatorial and other state level campaigns), the total spent exceeded $1.2 billion.

The Republicans were more successful than the Democrats, raising $466 million and spending $420 million; comparable figures for the Democratic party were $275 million and $266 million. The Republican total of funds raised represented a 12 percent increase over the previous presidential election cycle, whereas the Democrats raised 24 percent above previous levels. For both parties, the great majority of these hard money funds came from individual contri-

butions, with a minority of the funds coming from political action committees (PACs) and from the candidates themselves, in the form of either loans or gifts.

Contributions of nonfederal funds have also increased substantially in recent years. This money (popularly referred to as "soft money") is used to support the candidacy of state and local aspirants for office and to pay for the generic expenses associated with issue advocacy and party-

building (get-out-the-vote drives), activities that benefit both federal and nonfederal candidates. There has been recent controversy over the fact that these funds have increasingly been diverted to advertising for the benefit of party candidates, especially presidential nominees. In so doing, these activities appear to violate the intent of campaign finance laws that banned contributions to presidential nominees who accept public funding. This led to new legislation in 2002 which will change the ways in which these contributions may be made.

Under the law in effect for the 2000 campaign, individuals could contribute up to $1,000 to a candidate's compliance fund, which helps to pay legal and accounting expenses incurred in conjunction with the campaign finance law. Independent expenditures, either for or against a specific presidential candidate, also do not count as a contribution within the meaning of the law as long as they are not made "with the cooperation or prior consent of, or in consultation with or at the request or suggestion of,

Table 11-2. Percent of Voters Identifying as Republican or Democrat, Selected Years, 1952–2000

(Percent.)

Characteristic	1952	1964	1976	1988	2000
Republican					
Males	33	30	33	45	40
Females	35	30	33	38	34
Whites	36	33	37	48	42
Blacks	17	8	6	12	7
Not a high school graduate	28	20	24	21	30
College graduate or more	53	46	48	52	48
Very low income	29	24	26	30	22
Very high income	59	48	68	77	54
Professionals	42	43	42	48	44
Blue collar workers	27	21	24	33	31
Union households	28	17	25	33	37
Non-union households	36	34	36	43	38
Democrat					
Males	58	61	50	43	46
Females	56	61	52	50	53
Whites	56	59	47	39	44
Blacks	63	82	85	80	83
Not a high school graduate	59	70	62	56	58
College graduate or more	44	48	40	42	44
Very low income	57	65	60	55	62
Very high income	28	44	23	19	36
Professionals	51	49	44	43	46
Blue collar workers	66	70	58	51	55
Union households	66	77	62	55	61
Non-union households	54	56	49	45	48

Source: The National Election Studies. *The NES Guide to Public Opinion and Electoral Behavior.*

---

[5] The term "hard money" means funds raised directly for candidates for federal office, in accordance with the requirements of campaign finance laws.

Figure 11-6. Amounts Raised for Federal Campaigns, 1979–2000

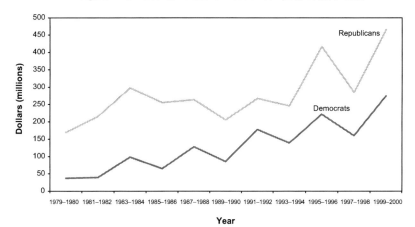

Source: Federal Election Commission.

taxpayer, on their income tax returns. Originally $1, the voluntary checkoff amount is now $3. The checkoff neither increases the amount of taxes owed nor decreases any refund due.

Funding is available to any presidential candidate seeking nomination by a political party. The candidate must show broad-based public support, defined as raising at least $5,000 in each of at least 20 states in contributions of $250 per person or less. Candidates must also agree to limit primary election campaign spending to $10 million[8], limit spending in individual states according to an established formula, and limit spending from personal funds to $50,000.[9] In the general election, Republican and Democratic nominees are eligible for a public grant of $20 million, but must agree to limit their spending to this amount plus, if desired, $50,000 in personal funds.

There are also provisions for minor party candidates to receive such funding based on the party's performance in the preceding presidential election. In addition, each major party may receive $4 million to finance its nominating convention. If violations of the law are

any candidate or authorized committee or agent of a candidate."[6]

The law also provides for the expenditure of funds by national party committees on behalf of their presidential nominees. These are called "coordinated party expenditures" and are limited by a formula that authorized the expenditure of approximately $12 million by each party in 1996. As the name implies, these funds are expended in consultation with the presidential nominee, but the funds are not transferred to the candidate or the campaign committee. Coordinated party expenditures may also be made for the benefit of other candidates for federal office.

In addition to the political parties, individual candidates for the House and Senate in 2000 raised a total of $1.05 billion and spent $1 billion, representing increases of about 35 percent over the 1997–1998 cycle. (See Figure 11-7.)

Political Action Committees (PACs) continue to represent a significant portion of political funds raised. PAC contributions to all federal candidates for the 1999–2000 election cycle were $245 million, up 19 percent from 1997–1998. Democrats received $117 million of these funds,

Republicans $128 million, and candidates from other parties less than $1 million. Incumbents are the primary beneficiaries of PAC money.[7]

Paying for political campaigns out of public funds was first proposed by President Theodore Roosevelt in his 1907 State of the Union message. However, legislation to finance presidential election campaigns with tax dollars was not enacted until 1971, with the first funds dispersed for the 1996 election. The funds are authorized through an option, offered to each

Figure 11-7. Contribution to Candidates for the U.S. Senate and House of Representatives, 1988–2000

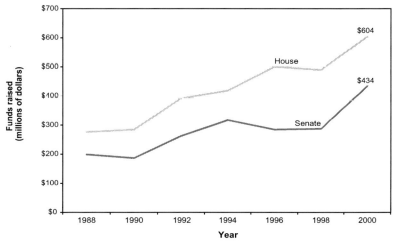

Source: Federal Election Commission.

[6] Federal Election Commission, *Campaign Guide for Political Party Committees*, August 1996.

[7] Federal Election Commission, "FEC Reports on Congressional Financial Activity for 2000", press release dated May 15, 2001.

[8] All figures cited here are subject to cost of living adjustments (COLA), and thus are higher for recent and future elections.

[9] Federal Election Commission, *Public Funding of Presidential Elections*, August 1996.

discovered during an audit, the candidates and convention committees must repay the public funds to the U.S. Treasury.

During the primary campaigns for the 2000 presidential election, candidates received a total of $57.7 million in matching funds. The largest amounts went to Democrat Albert Gore ($15.3 million), Republican John McCain (14.5 million), and Democrat William Bradley ($12.5 million). Republican George W. Bush declined matching funds but raised $91.3 million in private contributions, far more than the total of private and matching funds available to any other candidate.

For Further Information See:

Brace, Kimball W., et al. *The Election Data Book*: 1992. Lanham, MD: Bernan Press, 1993.

The United States Government Manual:1997/98. National Archives and Records Administration, Office of the Federal Register, 1997.

U.S. Census Bureau. *Statistical Abstract of the United States: 2002*. 122nd edition. Washington, DC: U.S. Census Bureau, 2003.

Voting and Registration in the Election of November 2000. Current Population Reports P20-542. Washington, DC: U.S. Census Bureau. Earlier election data are in P20 series reports and at <www.census.gov/population/www/socdemo/voting.html>.

Web Sites:

Federal Election Commission Web site: <http://www.fec.gov>.

National Election Studies at the University of Michigan Web site: <http://www.umich.edu/~nes>.

U.S. Census Bureau Web site: <http://www.census.gov>.

Chapter 12
Government

INTRODUCTION

This chapter brings some perspective, context, and background to discussions about government and government spending in the United States. Looking at American government through the prism of these statistics, this chapter will address such questions as:

- Compared with other countries, is government a large or small part of the U. S. economy?

- How many governments are there in the United States?

- Just how big is government compared to the private sector?

- What are the sources of government revenues overall? Do the sources differ much for the federal, state and local governments? Do they differ much from area to area?

- On what does government spend its money? How much does government spending vary for different areas?

- Has the emphasis of government activity changed much over the past several decades?

GOVERNMENT AND THE ECONOMY: AN INTERNATIONAL COMPARISON

The classic conservative-liberal discussions in the United States have often been framed around the issues of whether the government is too big, is too intrusive, is a drag on the economy, or whether government needs to do more for care of neglected people, as well as other societal concerns such as labor/management issues or education funding. Compared with other countries, just how big is our government—federal, state, and local—relative to the economy?[1]

One measure of the size of a country's government relative to the size of its economy is a comparison of taxes relative to gross domestic product (GDP).[2] This is a fair measure because taxes are, by far, the single largest governmental revenue. Relative to other industrialized countries, the United States was ranked 27th out of 30 OECD[3] countries in 2000, a position that has varied very little since 1980. To some, this low rank is positive because they see taxes as a drag on the economy—the higher the ranking, the less money for business investment. Others also see this in positive terms, but with an entirely different slant—the United States has a much greater taxing capacity than it is using. This "extra" capacity might be available to help reduce social problems, maintain or extend infrastructure, or make important government investments in the future for activities such as education. However it is interpreted, the fact is that compared with these other industrialized countries, the United States is a "low tax" nation.

GOVERNMENT AND THE ECONOMY: A STATE COMPARISON

Just as we can observe the varying economic role of government within nations, we can see the same thing within our own states. Each state can be visualized as if it were an individual entity with the economic attributes of a separate nation, so that its economic growth can be gauged by the measures similar to those used for a nation's GDP. This measure is known as gross state product (GSP). Some states (California, for example) have such large economies that they would be among the world's top 10 if they were countries.

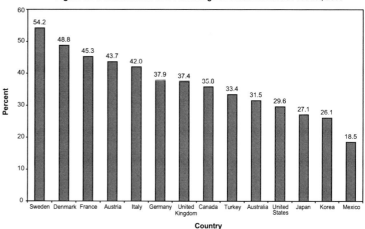

Figure 12-1. Tax Revenue as a Percentage of Gross Domestic Product, 2000

Sweden 54.2, Denmark 48.8, France 45.3, Austria 43.7, Italy 42.0, Germany 37.9, United Kingdom 37.4, Canada 35.0, Turkey 33.4, Australia 31.5, United States 29.6, Japan 27.1, Korea 26.1, Mexico 18.5

Country

---

[1] It is important to be cautious in comparing government activity among different countries. First, the definition of government can vary considerably. Some countries are highly socialistic, where almost everything is government; others are free-market where government is minimal. Second, it is very difficult to determine the defining line between national and subnational government activity.

[2] Gross domestic product (GDP) is quantitative economic measure of a country's economy. In this instance, taxes become the measure of the size of government. Although the resulting comparison requires some caution in interpretation, it is a reasonable measure of the impact of government on an economy.

[3] OECD is the "Organisation for Economic Co-operation and Development," headquartered in Paris. OECD members include Canada, Mexico, and the United States, Australia, Japan, Korea, New Zealand, and 23 European nations. See <www.oecd.org> for more information.

Table 12-1. State Government as a Percentage of Gross State Product, 2001

(Percent.)

State	Percent
Highest states	
Hawaii	21.5
Alaska	19.5
New Mexico	18.1
Virginia	17.7
Maryland	17.6
Lowest states	
New Jersey	9.8
Massachusetts	9.0
Connecticut	9.0
Delaware	8.5
New Hampshire	8.1

Source: Bureau of Economic Analysis.

GSP, a statistic produced by the Bureau of Economic Analysis, is the state equivalent of the national-level GDP. The role of government in a state's economy can be measured by looking at the percentage of the GSP that can be attributed to government. The range for 2002, excluding the District of Columbia, is from 7.7 percent in New Hampshire to 21.4 percent in Hawaii. There are some geographic patterns among the 2002 rankings. For example, three of the six New England states are among the bottom five, while the high ranking of Alaska and Hawaii shows their dependence on federal government activities.

Government has composed a decreasing share of most states' economies since 1977, when GSP was first measured. At the national level, the percentage of GSP represented by government has dropped from 13.5 percent in 1977 to 12.0 percent in 2002. The picture for the future depends largely on the degree to which states continue programs which were formerly conducted at the federal level but have now devolved to the states. Welfare is a prime example of this type of program.

THE STRUCTURE OF GOVERNMENT

Just as government has a different economic impact in each state, the structure of government takes on a very different cast when you look in different parts of the country. Though people sometimes perceive that government has a cer-

tain uniformity, in reality it is a series of 50 variations. The role of counties varies widely. In about half the states, the county governments share responsibilities with sub-county governments and special districts. In New England, counties are very weak; in fact, in Connecticut and Rhode Island, county governments do not exist at all. In those two states, the primary local governments are cities and towns.

In about 20 states, however, there are no county subdivisions; counties carry out most of the governmental functions (other than school districts) in territory which is not incorporated. Maryland and Virginia have no sub-county governments at all; when a city incorporates it is no longer part of its old county and instead becomes a county-equivalent.

Even the federal government—ostensibly the same wherever one travels—has different looks in various parts of the country. For example, the federal government owns a considerable portion of the land in some states and very little in others. Of all the land area in the United States, more than one-quarter—a rather surprising 28.8 percent —belongs to the federal government. This national percentage was 33.9 percent in 1960. Between the mid-1970s and mid-1980s the percentage fell,

reaching the current level in the late 1980s. Although it might seem that the federal portion would be highest in the District of Columbia (23.2 percent), all the 13 states in the Western region, except Hawaii, exceed that figure, some by a considerable amount. In five of those West and Pacific area states, more than half of the land is federally owned, led by Nevada at 83 percent. (See Figure 12-2.)

Within other regions there is considerable variation in how much land belongs to the federal government. The nine Northeast states range from 0.5 percent (Connecticut) to 13.2 percent (New Hampshire). In the 12 Midwest states, the range is from 1.3 percent in Kansas to 11.2 percent in Michigan. The percentage of land ownership and the type of land owned (national forests, military bases, grazing lands, national parks, and the like) give the federal government a very different presence among the states. These differences might influence feelings about taxes, specific laws, or media treatment that likely translate into very different social, political, and economic views by the citizens of the federal government. Whether these thoughts are extended to governments as a whole is unknown. Yet the public does have opinions about which levels of government they like and

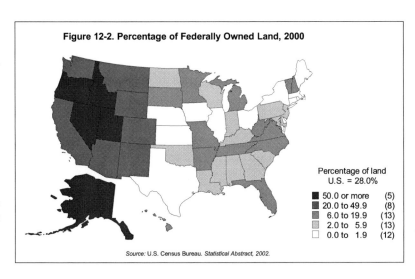

Figure 12-2. Percentage of Federally Owned Land, 2000

Percentage of land
U.S. = 28.0%

■	50.0 or more	(5)
▨	20.0 to 49.9	(8)
▥	6.0 to 19.9	(13)
▢	2.0 to 5.9	(13)
□	0.0 to 1.9	(12)

Source: U.S. Census Bureau. *Statistical Abstract, 2002.*

various facets of government that please or displease them.

VARIATIONS IN THE STRUCTURE OF STATE AND LOCAL GOVERNMENTS

The immediacy and importance of local government today make it difficult to remember that local governments are not mentioned in our U.S. Constitution. The Tenth Amendment divides all powers between just two governmental levels, a central federal government and the states. Each state constitution sets the rules for dividing power between the state governments and their subordinate governments. Local governments are, to quote a renowned Iowa judge and local government legal commentator, John F. Dillon, "creatures of the state."[4] Using their legal authority, the states have developed a tapestry of state and local government structures that are showcases for our federal system as laboratories of government. The richness and diversity of the state and local governing institutions are the result of the different mixes of geography, history, and economic factors.

The first thing one notices about governments is just how many of them there are—about 87,500 in 1997. The largest number was in Illinois (6,836) and the smallest, excluding the District of Columbia, in Hawaii (19). The number of governments correlates roughly with population—that is, more people, more governments—with Illinois (6,836), Pennsylvania (5,159), Texas (4,792), and California (4,393) in the top four spots and Ohio (3,524) and New York (3,299) coming in seventh and eighth and Michigan (2,776) in twelfth position. However, Kansas

Table 12-2. Rank of States by Number of Internal Governments and Population, 1997

(Number, rank.)

State	Governments		Population		Difference in government/ population rank
	Number	Rank	Number (thousands)	Rank	
Illinois	6 836	1	12 012	6	5
Pennsylvania	5 071	2	12 016	5	3
Texas	4 701	3	19 355	2	1
California	4 608	4	32 218	1	3
Kansas	3 951	5	2 616	32	27
Ohio	3 598	6	11 212	7	1
Minnesota	3 502	7	4 688	20	13
Missouri	3 417	8	5 407	16	8
New York	3 414	9	18 143	3	6
Indiana	3 199	10	5 872	14	4
Wisconsin	3 060	11	5 200	18	7
Nebraska	2 895	12	1 656	38	26

Source: U.S. Census Bureau. "Government Organization, 1997," *1997 Census of Governments*.

and Nebraska—with fairly low rankings in population—appear among the top dozen states in terms of numbers of governments. (See Table 12-2.)

The governing systems that exist today have both historical roots and modern origins. For example, townships in Midwestern states have a direct link to the Federal Northwest Territory Ordinance of 1787, which mandated the creation of townships.[5] The continuing growth in special district governments in California over the past two decades is attributed by some to the passage of Proposition 13 in 1978.

The sheer number of governments is only one measure of the differences that exist in governing styles among the states. First, there is the division of duties—which services are provided and how they are financed—that the state governments decide. From public welfare, to public elementary and secondary education, to highways, to sewerage treatment, there are significant differences in approaches.

Some state governments take on certain governmental functions themselves, based on financial, administrative, political, geograph-

ic, or historical criteria. In Hawaii, for example, all public elementary and secondary education is a state activity. Though states fund a significant portion of elementary and secondary education, the administration in all other states is generally carried out by local governments. Streets and highways in Virginia are largely a state government activity; in most other states the responsibility is more evenly divided. In Maryland, elementary and secondary school construction is a state activity, but the operation of schools is a local government responsibility.

The states have developed two categories of subordinate governments to provide local services, general purpose and special purpose. General purpose governments usually perform a variety of services for their citizens—public safety and health, various types of public works, social services, and the like. Usually the general purpose governments carry designations such as counties, municipalities, villages and towns or townships.[6] Townships and other subcounty unincorporated governments exist in only 20 states, and are active governments in only 12. In the six New England states,

---

[4] John F. Dillon, *Commentaries on the Law of Municipal Corporations* (Boston: Little, Brown and Co., 1911).

[5] The Federal General Revenue Sharing Program was a direct distribution of federal funds to state and local governments. It began in the early 1970s and continued for about 15 years. This may have been a factor in the maintenance of very small general purpose governments, such as townships. However, townships in the Midwest have been around for two centuries, and show little inclination to dissolve. On the contrary, at least in Michigan, township government has grown larger and stronger, and as population size increases these communities tend to retain the township form of government rather than incorporate as cities.

[6] There is wide variety in the naming conventions for local governments. The Midwestern township is called a "town" in Wisconsin. County-equivalent governments are called "parishes" in Louisiana and "boroughs" in Alaska. In New Jersey, however, boroughs are municipal corporations. For an excellent description of these patterns, state by state, see *A Guide to State and Local Census Geography*, a joint venture of the Census Bureau and the Association of Public Data Users, 1990 CPH-I-18, June 1993.

most government functions are carried out through towns. In the Middle Atlantic states of New York, New Jersey, and Pennsylvania, and in the upper Midwest states of Michigan, Minnesota, and Wisconsin, townships are active governments providing a range of the same types of services as provided by cities. In the other eight states, township governments have few or no governmental functions, with the appropriate services being provided by the counties instead.

Special purpose governments are created to provide either a single service or a very limited number of services to a population or an area. The most common special purpose government is a school district; the 1997 Census of Governments enumerated about 15,000. There is a wide variety of other types of special districts. Some are very large and well known—the Port Authority of New York and New Jersey, for example. By and large, however, special districts are neither a well-known nor well-understood facet of local government.

While the number of some types of governments have changed considerably over the past few decades, some have changed little. Among general purpose governments, only the count of municipalities shows much change, up 15 percent from 1952 to 1997. The reason for growth here is due, in part, to the fact that municipalities are designed to

serve populations; as populations grow, the number of municipalities generally does also.[7] In contrast, counties and townships, which have a geographic base, have not changed much.

The special purpose governments—special districts and school districts—present a considerable contrast to the general purpose governments. The number of school districts decreased by 80 percent from 1951 to 1997. This largely reflects the consolidation of relatively small schools with multi-grade classrooms into larger school districts to provide a more balanced and cost-effective educational system, and to provide for high school education within each district. In some states, primarily in the Midwest, the results of this process were quite dramatic. Nebraska, for example, went from 6,392 districts in 1951 to 681 in 1997. (See Table 12-3.)

Special districts show the opposite trend from school districts, up 1000 percent from 1952 to 1997. The states that used special districts the most in 1952 (Illinois and California) remain the primary users of this form of government today. Other states with more than 1,000 special districts include Colorado, Indiana, Kansas, Missouri, Nebraska, New York, Pennsylvania, Texas, and Washington. On the other hand, many states have less than 300 such districts. The reasons for the differences are rooted in individual state politics, economies, and his-

tories. The influence of Proposition 13 in California was cited above. New York, by way of contrast, limits the activity of this type of government to fire districts (which account for about 90 percent of the New York special district total), health districts, and a few miscellaneous activities. Nevertheless, special districts are where government structure is showing the most dynamic adaptability.

COMPARING PUBLIC AND PRIVATE SECTORS OF THE ECONOMY

Talk of "big" government in the United States is often directed at the size and influence of the federal government. The place of state and local governments in these discussions seems to be absent or minimized. There is another way to look at the relative size of these governments, however, that does provide a good perspective on the size of government below the federal level.

The Fortune 500 is a popular and widely used listing of the biggest and most important corporations in the United States. Ranking U.S. state governments against this list based on their general revenues demonstrates their size relative to the largest businesses in the United States. (See Table 12-4.) That California ranks number 1, New York number 3, and Texas number 7 might not be surprising. However, the 6 smallest state governments in terms of general revenue fall below the smallest of the Fortune 500 companies. And, these are just the state governments. If local governments were included, in California alone five county governments (Los Angeles, Orange, San Bernardino, Santa Clara, and San Diego), two cities (Los Angeles and San Francisco), one school district (Los Angeles Unified), and one special

Table 12-3. Local Governments by Type of Government, Selected Years, 1952–1997

(Number.)

Year	Total	County	Municipal	Township	Special district	School district
1952	102 392	3 052	16 807	17 202	12 340	67 355
1962	91 237	3 043	17 997	17 144	18 323	34 678
1972	78 269	3 044	18 517	16 991	23 885	15 781
1982	81 831	3 041	19 076	16 734	28 078	14 851
1987	83 237	3 042	19 200	16 691	29 532	14 721
1992	84 955	3 043	19 279	16 656	31 555	14 422
1997	87 453	3 043	19 372	16 629	34 683	13 726

Source: U.S. Census Bureau. "Government Organization, 1997," *1997 Census of Governments*.

---

[7] Municipalities also grow in size, if not in number, through annexation. The procedures that permit existing municipalities to annex adjacent areas varies for each state. The level of difficulty in annexation procedures likely has an effect on the development of new municipalities. In addition, often there is a difference in statutory taxing authority between townships and cities. A desire to keep taxes low is a factor in discouraging township incorporation into cities.

Table 12-4. Rank of U.S. State Governments in Combined Ranking with Fortune 500 Corporations, 1999

(Rank. Corporations based on sales, state governments based on general revenue.)

State	Combined rank of states with Fortune 500 corporations
California	5
New York	9
Texas	13
Florida	23
Pennsylvania	24
Michigan	32
Illinois	35
Ohio	40
New Jersey	47
Massachusetts	60
North Carolina	66
Georgia	82
Virginia	85
Washington	91
Wisconsin	101
Minnesota	103
Indiana	113
Maryland	124
Missouri	128
Connecticut	134
Tennessee	138
Louisiana	139
Kentucky	149
Alabama	160
Arizona	161
South Carolina	170
Oregon	174
Colorado	177
Oklahoma	206
Iowa	214
Mississippi	221
Arkansas	243
Kansas	268
New Mexico	279
Utah	283
West Virginia	298
Alaska	325
Hawaii	333
Nebraska	360
Nevada	364
Maine	372
Delaware	435
Rhode Island	443
Idaho	463
Montana	(1)
New Hampshire	(1)
Vermont	(1)
North Dakota	(1)
Wyoming	(1)
South Dakota	(1)

Source: U.S. Census Bureau. *Fortune Magazine.*
[1] General revenue is exceeded by sales of all Fortune 500 corporations.

district (Los Angeles County Transportation Commission) would each rank higher than South Dakota.

This comparison of government with the private sector holds in many different areas. In the obscure, but financially important, field of retirement or pension systems, for example, the very largest system in terms of assets is a state retirement system—the California Public Employee Retirement System—with assets

about 25 percent greater than General Motors. State and local government public employee retirement systems occupy 7 of the top 10 spots in this ranking of pension/retirement systems and 28 of the top 50.[8]

A regional ranking of almost any financial activity, such as revenues, expenditures, indebtedness, assets, employment, or payroll, no matter the location, would yield similar results. State and major local governments would rank as, or among, the leaders in most categories. State and local governments are significant "businesses" and economic forces almost no matter how measured.

As one of the authors of the state governments /Fortune 500 ranking: "This ranking dramatizes that the governors are the chief executive officers of some of the largest human enterprises in the country. If you want to get a good sense of the significance of a governor's managerial responsibilities, just look at corporations that are similar in size to his or her state."[9]

Though the responsibilities might be similar, there is a significant disparity in the financial compensation of public and private chief executive officers (CEOs). While the compensation of private sector executives of Fortune 500 companies extends into the hundreds of thousands or millions of dollars, the highest governor's salary is $179,000 (New York) and the lowest $65,000 (Nebraska). There are 21 states in which the governor's salary is less than $100,000.[10] It is also relevant, perhaps, to point out that the annual salary of the most important and powerful chief executive in the world, the president of the United States, is $400,000.

THE MONEY THAT FUNDS GOVERNMENT

Taxes are the largest and most vis-

ible source of government funding. There are also four other important sources: fees or charges for specific services, "contributions" for social insurance and other retirement programs, intergovernmental revenue, and miscellaneous items such as fines, interest earnings, sales of property, and lottery revenue.

The mix among these components is very different depending on the level of government. Figure 12-3 shows the differences. Most of the federal government's income comes from income taxes (individual and corporate) and from the social insurance taxes which support the Social Security and Medicare programs. Looking at the states, sales taxes are a very important source of revenue; aggregated nationwide, they are almost equal to income taxes on individuals and corporations. The states also have a great variety of revenue sources, including gasoline taxes, license fees, taxes on insurance premiums, and so forth. As with the federal government, states collect retirement system contributions for their own employees (often including teachers). Both local and state governments receive a significant proportion of their revenue from the federal government. Local governments depend on property and on income taxes, but rely heavily on intergovernmental revenue and other forms of general revenue as well.

Federal revenues have increased rapidly over the past several decades. As shown in Figure 12-4, the federal budget level was at just about 100 billion in 1962. It passed 200 billion in the early 1970s, 500 billion around 1980, and 1,000 billion (or 1 trillion) in 1990. For almost all of this time, expenditures exceeded revenue, thus adding to the federal debt. This trend was not reversed until 1998, but appears headed

8 "The 1,000 Largest Pension Systems," *Pensions and Investments* (20 January 1997).
9 Press release, "Duke Study Ranks Governments in Comparison with the Fortune 500" (January 1993).
10 The Council of State Governments, *Book of the States*, Table 4.3. Salary figures accurate as of March 2002.

Figure 12-3. Revenues by Major Source

Federal government, 2001

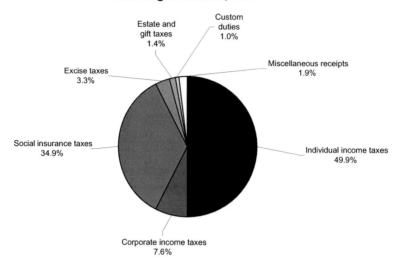

State government, 1998–1999

Local government, 1998–1999

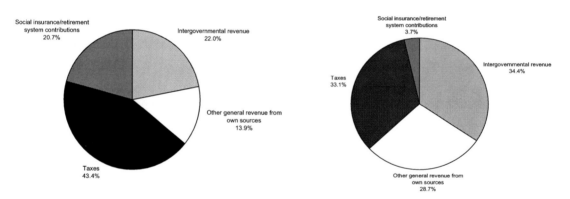

Source: Federal government: Congressional Budget Office.
The Budget and Economic Outlook: Fiscal Years 2003–2012.
State and local government: U.S. Census Bureau, Government Division.

back toward the negative in 2002.

School systems derive revenue from local property taxes, from the state government, and from the federal government. The proportions vary by state. (See Table 12-5.) In Hawaii, public education is essentially state-funded; the schools are an arm of the state government. Michigan revised its tax structure for education in 1994, making individual school districts less dependent on local property taxes and more dependent on state sources.

TAXES

The contribution of taxes to overall government revenue was demonstrated earlier. But what types of taxes? Without delving into the arguments of progressivity or the effect on economic development, it is useful to look at the variations that exist in the American tax system.

When social insurance premiums are excluded, income taxes—personal and corporate—account for seven out of every eight federal tax dollars. Individual income taxes

alone provide nearly three-fourths of federal tax revenue. That is why discussions about reforming the federal government tax system start and end with individual income taxes. Other specific taxes such as the estate tax and the gift tax account for very small proportions of federal revenue, although they often take on a much bigger role in the political context.

State and local governments have an entirely different tax mix than the federal government. For local governments, the property

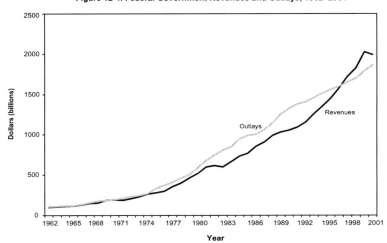

Figure 12-4. Federal Government Revenues and Outlays, 1962–2001

Source: Congressional Budget Office. *The Budget and Economic Outlook: Fiscal Years 2003–2012.*

Table 12-5. Percentage of Elementary-Secondary Education Revenue Funded by Federal, State, and Local Government Sources, 1998–1999

(Percent.)

State	Total (percent)	Percent from federal sources	Percent from local sources	Percent from state sources	Rank by state funded
Hawaii	100.0	9.8	2.3	87.9	1
Vermont	100.0	5.9	18.0	76.0	2
Arkansas	100.0	8.8	15.8	75.4	3
New Mexico	100.0	13.4	13.6	73.0	4
Delaware	100.0	6.3	27.8	65.9	5
North Carolina	100.0	6.6	27.8	65.6	6
Washington	100.0	6.7	28.4	64.9	7
Michigan	100.0	6.9	28.2	64.8	8
Nevada	100.0	4.4	32.1	63.5	9
Kansas	100.0	6.0	31.9	62.1	10
West Virginia	100.0	8.6	29.5	61.9	11
Idaho	100.0	6.9	31.3	61.8	12
Kentucky	100.0	9.1	29.2	61.8	12
Alabama	100.0	8.8	29.6	61.6	14
Utah	100.0	7.2	31.7	61.1	15
Alaska	100.0	15.1	25.4	59.5	16
California	100.0	8.9	32.4	58.7	17
Minnesota	100.0	4.8	37.7	57.5	18
Oklahoma	100.0	8.8	34.1	57.1	19
Oregon	100.0	7.0	36.1	56.9	20
Wisconsin	100.0	4.4	40.7	54.9	21
Mississippi	100.0	13.4	32.2	54.4	22
Wyoming	100.0	7.4	40.2	52.4	23
South Carolina	100.0	7.9	39.8	52.3	24
Indiana	100.0	4.7	43.8	51.4	25
Florida	100.0	7.4	41.6	51.0	26
Louisiana	100.0	11.5	37.5	51.0	26
Iowa	100.0	5.3	43.9	50.8	28
Georgia	100.0	6.5	43.9	49.6	29
United States Average	100.0	6.9	43.6	49.5	
Missouri	100.0	6.5	45.6	47.9	30
Tennessee	100.0	8.3	44.7	47.0	31
Maine	100.0	5.4	49.5	45.1	32
Arizona	100.0	9.8	45.4	44.8	33
Montana	100.0	11.0	44.3	44.7	34
Massachusetts	100.0	5.0	52.1	42.9	35
Virginia	100.0	5.1	52.3	42.7	36
Colorado	100.0	5.0	52.4	42.6	37
Rhode Island	100.0	5.8	52.2	42.1	38
Ohio	100.0	5.5	52.5	42.0	39
New York	100.0	6.0	52.1	41.9	40
Texas	100.0	8.3	50.2	41.5	41
New Jersey	100.0	3.7	55.8	40.5	42
North Dakota	100.0	12.7	47.8	39.5	43
Maryland	100.0	5.4	55.3	39.2	44
Connecticut	100.0	3.9	57.5	38.6	45
Pennsylvania	100.0	5.9	55.8	38.3	46
Nebraska	100.0	7.0	55.7	37.3	47
South Dakota	100.0	10.3	53.7	36.0	48
Illinois	100.0	6.9	57.2	35.9	49
New Hampshire	100.0	4.0	87.1	8.9	50
District of Columbia	100.0	16.2	83.8	0.0	51

Source: U.S. Census Bureau. "Public Elementary-Secondary Education Finances: 1998–1999."

tax is, without question, the dominant levy, though not as preeminent as it once was. From 1950 through 1970, property taxes composed about 85 percent of all local government taxes. From 1970 through 1980 the percentage drifted down to about 75 percent of the total, where it has remained. Though property tax restriction movements of the late 1970s, such as Proposition 13 in California and Proposition Two and a Half in Massachusetts, provided additional impetus, the trend had already been firmly established earlier in that decade.

There were three interrelated movements taking place in the 1970s which contributed to the reduced role of property taxes. The property tax restriction movement has already been mentioned. The second was property tax relief programs, some of which replaced property taxes with intergovernmental revenue from the states. The third was the diversification of local revenues, as state legislatures allowed local governments to impose other taxes, especially sales taxes. The states, though they allowed local governments more use of other taxes, still kept a tight rein because, in many instances, those same taxes were primary state tax producers, such as general sales taxes.

State governments rely on two pillars for taxes, general sales taxes and individual income taxes, which accounted for 32 percent and 37 percent, respectively, of all state government taxes in fiscal year 2001. States supplement these with a variety of other levies, such as specific sales taxes (motor fuel, alcohol, tobacco, and utilities, for example), license taxes, death and gift taxes, severance taxes, and other imposts. These state government totals provide some good general comparisons in relationship to what is happening in federal and local government taxes.

Table 12-6. Percent Distribution of Local Taxes, Selected Years, 1950–1999

(Percent.)

Tax	1950	1960	1970	1980	1990	1999
Total Taxes	100.0	100.0	100.0	100.0	100.0	100.0
Property tax	88.2	87.4	84.9	75.9	74.5	72.3
Nonproperty tax	11.8	12.6	15.1	24.1	25.5	27.7
General sales tax	...	4.8	5.0	9.4	10.7	11.5
Motor fuels tax	...	0.2	0.1	0.1	0.3	0.3
Individual income tax	0.8	1.4	4.2	5.8	4.8	5.2
Other taxes	11.0	6.2	5.8	8.7	9.7	10.7

Source: U.S. Census Bureau.
. . . = Not available.

HOW ONEROUS IS THE TAX BURDEN RELATIVE TO PERSONAL INCOME?

While states obviously choose different paths for obtaining tax revenues, the question arises whether there are measures of what the states do collect compared with what they have the capacity to collect. This is especially important in arguments about equity. That is, measured against their ability to raise revenue, what efforts are states making in supplying services to citizens. Are "poor" states putting relatively less, the same, or more resources toward supplying services than "rich" states?[11]

One method for calculating this is simply the amount of taxation per resident of the state (per capita). Table 12-8 presents a ranking of the states for the taxes per capita in 2001. The overall distribution of the states is remarkable. The tax burden in Connecticut, at $3,092, is 57 percent higher than the United States average of $1,968 and 139 percent higher than South Dakota. There is no particular geographic or size

What these national totals hide, however, is some of the differences found among the state tax systems. Table 12.7 provides some examples showing some of the wide variations in state tax systems. Alaska, which has built its tax system largely around its oil and gas reserves, levies neither an individual income nor a general sales tax. Delaware is the U.S. home of many large corporations, drawn there by business-friendly corporation laws. It has taken advantage of this significant corporate presence by levying corporate license taxes, and this has given it sufficient leeway so that, while Delaware does impose an individ-

ual income tax, it does not have a general sales tax. Pennsylvania has what most economists would say is a balanced tax system, with a fairly even reliance on its two major sources. Texas does not impose an individual income tax. Until recently, Texas obtained a significant percentage of its total from severance taxes, but has made a successful effort to move away from these taxes because they had become an unreliable revenue source. Washington emphasizes the use of the general sales tax, with no income tax. Right next door in Oregon, just the reverse is true.

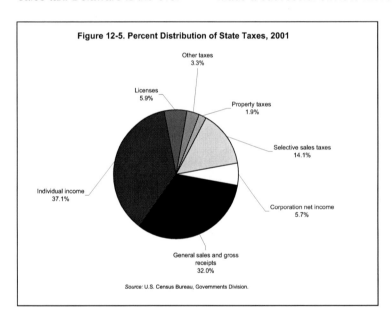

Figure 12-5. Percent Distribution of State Taxes, 2001

- Other taxes 3.3%
- Licenses 5.9%
- Property taxes 1.9%
- Selective sales taxes 14.1%
- Corporation net income 5.7%
- General sales and gross receipts 32.0%
- Individual income 37.1%

Source: U.S. Census Bureau, Governments Division.

Table 12-7. Top Three Tax Sources for Selected States, 2001

(Percent.)

State and tax source	Percent
Alaska	
1. Severance	54.1
2. Corporate net income	28.0
3. Motor fuel sales	2.6
Delaware	
1. Individual income	33.1
2. Corporate license	27.6
3. Corporate net income	9.5
Pennsylvania	
1. General sales	32.1
2. Individual income	31.7
3. Corporate net income	6.2
Texas	
1. General sales	50.0
2. Motor fuel sales	9.4
3. Severance	6.9
Washington	
1. General sales	63.6
2. Property taxes	11.0
3. Motor fuel sales	5.8

Source: U.S. Census Bureau.

---

[11] The U.S. Advisory Commission on Intergovernmental Relations (ACIR), which no longer exists, made an effort to focus attention on this issue starting in the early 1980s. The earlier ACIR work on this subject extends back to the 1960s. Starting in 1982, the commission issued a series of reports entitled "Measuring State Fiscal Capacity," in which it developed alternatives to the tax/personal income measure. A report issued in 1986, U.S. Advisory Commission on Intergovernmental Relations, *Measuring State Fiscal Capacity: Alternative Methods and Their Uses*, Report M-150 (Washington, DC, September 1986) provides a good discussion of six potential fiscal capacity measures: per capita personal income, gross state product, total taxable resources, export-adjusted income, the representative tax system, and the representative revenue system. The last ACIR study on this subject was for 1991, "State Revenue Capacity and Effort" (Washington, DC, September 1993). A forthcoming analysis from the Federal Reserve Bank of Boston will update the ACIR study to 1994.

Table 12-8. States Ranked by Per Capita Taxes, 2001

(Dollars.)

State and rank	Taxes per capita	Percent difference from U.S. average
United States	1 968	
1. Connecticut	3 092	57.2
2. Hawaii	2 865	45.6
3. Delaware	2 731	38.8
4. Minnesota	2 722	38.3
5. Massachusetts	2 700	37.2
6. California	2 622	33.3
7. Vermont	2 533	28.7
8. New York	2 359	19.9
9. Wyoming	2 274	15.6
10. New Jersey	2 269	15.3
11. Alaska	2 250	14.4
12. Michigan	2 228	13.3
13. New Mexico	2 188	11.2
14. Wisconsin	2 179	10.7
15. Rhode Island	2 118	7.7
16. Washington	2 117	7.6
17. Maine	2 074	5.4
18. Maryland	2 007	2.0
19. North Dakota	1 940	-1.4
20. Idaho	1 936	-1.6
21. Kentucky	1 931	-1.9
22. North Carolina	1 909	-3.0
23. West Virginia	1 900	-3.5
24. Illinois	1 855	-5.7
25. Kansas	1 853	-5.8
26. Pennsylvania	1 836	-6.7
27. Oklahoma	1 833	-6.8
28. Arkansas	1 824	-7.3
29. Nevada	1 820	-7.5
30. Utah	1 791	-9.0
31. Nebraska	1 768	-10.2
32. Iowa	1 765	-10.3
33. Virginia	1 745	-11.3
34. Ohio	1 725	-12.3
35. Georgia	1 714	-12.9
36. Colorado	1 713	-12.9
37. Oregon	1 697	-13.8
38. Indiana	1 669	-15.2
39. Mississippi	1 662	-15.5
40. Montana	1 654	-15.9
41. Louisiana	1 611	-18.1
42. Arizona	1 593	-19.0
43. Missouri	1 570	-20.2
44. Florida	1 521	-22.7
45. South Carolina	1 513	-23.1
46. Alabama	1 426	-27.5
47. New Hampshire	1 410	-28.3
48. Texas	1 380	-29.9
49. Tennessee	1 363	-30.7
50. South Dakota	1 292	-34.3

Source: U.S. Census Bureau.

of state pattern to the distribution. There are more "lower-taxing" states than "higher taxing."

WHERE DOES THE MONEY GO?

In Table 12-9, we can see the distribution of money, by major categories, at the federal level. As discussed above, the total amount of federal expenditures has risen dramatically, more than tripling between 1980 and 2001. During that same period, spending on national defense rose at a much smaller rate, dropping from 22 percent of the overall budget to 16 percent. Spending on human resources programs quadrupled, growing from 53 percent of the budget to 65 percent. This category includes medicare and social security disbursements, which are entitlements; these budget lines now account for 58 percent of the total expenditures in the human resources category.

The other very large component of federal expenditures is interest on the national debt. This figure has dropped since 1995, when serious efforts to balance the budget were put into place by Congress. All of this federal budget information pre-dates two important events and actions: the major income-tax reduction plan passed

by Congress in 2001, and the change in national priorities as a result of the September 11, 2001 attack on the nation. We may see very different income and expenditure priorities in budgets for 2002 and following years.

Table 12-10 focuses on expenditures by state and local governments. The first and greatest expenditure at this level is on education, including operation both of the elementary and secondary school systems and support for the public institutions of higher education in the states. Three of every 10 state/local dollars go to education. The second greatest expenditure is for public welfare, consuming about 13 percent of state/local budgets. Capital outlay is also a significant budget item. The remaining expenditure categories cover a wide range of functions, including transportation needs (primarily road construction), hospitals, government administration, and disbursement of insurance trust income, such as unemployment compensation.

An issue of significant concern around the country is the proportion of federal government expenditures that come back to each state. These data are reported annually in the Census Bureau's Consolidated Federal Funds Report. The state which receives

Table 12-9. Federal Budget Outlays—Defense, Human and Physical Resources, and Net Interest Payments, Selected Years, 1980–2000

(Dollars in billions. For fiscal year ending in year shown. Minus sign (-) indicates offsets.)

Outlays	1980	1985	1990	1995	2000
Federal Outlays, Total	590.9	946.4	1 253.2	1 515.8	1 788.8
National defense	134.0	252.7	299.3	272.1	294.5
Human resources	313.4	471.8	619.3	923.8	1 115.3
Education, training, employment, and social services	31.8	29.3	38.8	54.3	59.2
Health	23.2	33.5	57.7	115.4	154.5
Medicare	32.1	65.8	98.1	159.9	197.1
Income security	86.6	128.2	147.1	220.5	247.9
Social security	118.5	188.6	248.6	335.8	409.4
Veterans benefits and services	21.2	26.3	29.1	37.9	47.1
Physical resources	66.0	56.8	126.0	59.1	84.7
Energy	10.2	5.6	3.3	4.9	-1.1
Natural resources and environment	13.9	13.4	17.1	21.9	25.0
Commerce and housing credit	9.4	4.3	67.6	-17.8	3.2
Transportation	21.3	25.8	29.5	39.4	46.9
Community and regional development	11.3	7.7	8.5	10.7	10.6
Net interest	52.5	129.5	184.4	232.2	223.2
International affairs	12.7	16.2	13.8	16.4	17.2
Agriculture	8.8	25.6	12.0	9.8	36.6
Administration of justice	4.6	6.3	10.0	16.2	27.8
General government	13.0	11.6	10.6	14.0	13.5
Undistributed offsetting receipts	-19.9	-32.7	-36.6	-44.5	-42.6

Source: U.S. Census Bureau. *Statistical Abstract, 2001.*

Table 12-10. State and Local Expenditures by Function, 1998–1999

(Dollars, percent.)

Expenditure	Amount in dollars	Percent
Total Expenditures	1 622 102 644	100.0
Capital outlay	176 610 417	10.9
Education	483 259 476	29.8
Libraries	6 840 982	0.4
Social services and income maintenance		
Public welfare	215 189 660	13.3
Hospitals	71 733 493	4.4
Health	47 627 722	2.9
Transportation	93 017 969	5.7
Public safety	53 366 526	3.3
Natural resources, parks and recreation	41 649 048	2.6
Housing and community develoment	25 233 673	1.6
Sewers and solid waste management	43 046 839	2.7
Government administration	76 699 233	4.7
Interest on general debt	67 293 670	4.1
Utility expenditure	104 851 065	6.5
Insurance trust expenditure	115 172 181	7.1
Other	84 600 523	5.2

Source: U.S. Census Bureau. Government Finances, 1998–1999.

Table 12-11. Federal and State and Local Government Employment and Payroll, 2001

(Ranked by leading number of employees. Number, dollars in millions.)

Function	Full-time employees	Annual payroll (millions of dollars)
Total Federal Government	2 411 630	136 438
1. Postal service	666 976	37 284
2. National defense/international relations	662 093	30 509
3. Natural resources	175 111	10 060
4. Hospitals	131 949	7 834
5. Financial administration	125 853	6 784
Total State and Local Governments	15 378 924	591 149
1. Elementary and secondary education	6 144 086	221 138
2. Higher education	1 769 877	73 867
3. Hospitals	922 320	34 125
4. Police	884 671	41 078
5. Corrections	700 734	26 541

Source: U.S. Census Bureau.

the most funds, in total dollars, is California, followed closely by Virginia. The state that receives the most money per capita is Alaska (see Figure 12-6), at more than $10,000 per person per year. Virginia ranks high because the Pentagon is located there. As a result, the state receives credit for Defense Department spending there and receives, by far, the highest per capita expenditure for defense.

At the low end of the scale, expenditures hover around $5,000 per capita in a dozen states. Nevada is the lowest, followed by Wisconsin and Minnesota, while Michigan ranks sixth from the bottom. Clearly, the upper Midwest is a loser on this scale of measurement.

PUBLIC EMPLOYMENT

In 2001, the federal government employed about 2.7 million people, and another 15.4 million worked for state and local governments. (See Table 12-11.) At the federal level, the single largest "employer" is the Postal Service, followed by the Defense Department. Health and hospitals also have large numbers of employees, as does natural resources, which includes all of the National Park Service rangers. At the state/local level, and paralleling the expenditures data we reviewed earlier, education is far and away the largest employment category. Correction, or operation of jail and prisoners, is also large, along with health and hospitals. Hospitals have higher employment relative to other measures because they have workers around the clock.

Table 12-12 shows some characteristics of federal workers and how they have changed over the past decade. The average age and average length of service is rising; that is, the federal workforce is aging. We note that the proportion of workers with at least a bachelor's degree has increased steadily over this period of time. Minority employment has increased slightly. The number of employees with veterans' preferences has decreased, as veterans are passing out of the labor force.

Table 12-12. Federal Employment Trends, Selected Years, 1990–1999

(Percent, except where noted.)

Year	1990	1992	1993	1994	1995	1996	1997	1998	1999
Average age (years) of full-time employees	42.3	43.0	43.8	44.1	44.3	44.8	45.2	45.6	46.3
Average length of service (years)	13.4	14.1	14.9	15.2	15.5	15.9	16.3	16.6	17.1
Retirement Eligible									
Civil Service Retirement System	8.0	10.0	10.0	10.0	10.0	11.0	12.0	13.0	16.6
Federal Employees Retirement System	3.0	3.0	4.0	5.0	5.0	6.0	7.0	8.0	. . .
Bachelor's degree or higher	35.0	36.0	37.0	38.0	39.0	39.0	40.0	40.0	40.5
Race And National Origin									
Total minorities	27.4	27.9	28.2	28.5	28.9	29.1	29.4	29.7	30.4
Black	16.7	16.7	16.7	16.7	16.8	16.7	16.7	16.7	17.1
Hispanic	5.4	5.5	5.6	5.7	5.9	6.1	6.2	6.4	6.6
Disabled	7.0	7.0	7.0	7.0	7.0	7.0	7.0	7.0	7.1
Veterans' preference	30.0	28.0	27.0	27.0	26.0	26.0	25.0	25.0	24.2
Vietnam Era veterans	17.0	16.0	16.0	17.0	17.0	17.0	15.0	14.0	13.7
Retired military	4.9	4.4	4.3	4.3	4.2	4.3	4.2	3.9	3.9

Source: U.S. Census Bureau. Statistical Abstract, 2001.
. . . = Not available.

Figure 12-6. Federal Government Expenditure Per Capita Amounts by State by Major Agency, Fiscal Year 2001

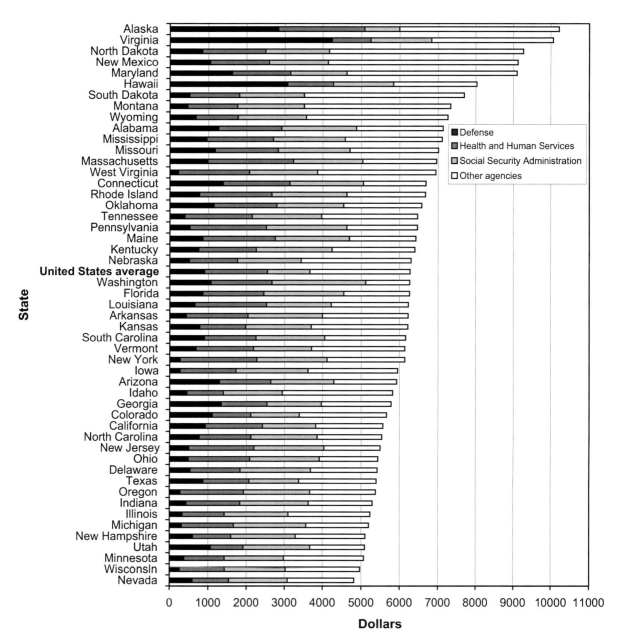

Source: U.S. Census Bureau. Consolidated Federal Funds Report for Fiscal Year 2001.

FOR FURTHER INFORMATION SEE:

Book of the States 2001. Lexington, KY: Council of State Governments.

John F. Kennedy School of Government. *The Federal Budget and the States 1995.* Cambridge: Harvard University Press.

National Association of State Budget Officers. *State Expenditure Report and Fiscal Survey of the States.* (various years).

National Conference of State Legislatures. *State Tax Actions and State Budget Actions.* (various years).

Nelson A. Rockefeller Institute of Government, Center for the Study of the States. *State Fiscal Brief, State Revenue Report, and State Employment.* August 1997.

U.S. Advisory Commission on Intergovernmental Relations. *Significant Features of Fiscal Federalism.* (various years).

U.S. Bureau of the Census. *Statistical Abstract of the United States: 2002.*

WEB SITES:

Congressional Budget Office: <www.cbo.gov>.

Council of State Governments: <www.csg.org>.

Governing Magazine: <www.governing.com>.

National Conference of State Legislatures: <www.ncsl.org>.

U.S. Bureau of Economic Analysis: <www.bea.gov>.

U.S. Census Bureau: <www.census.gov>.

Index